# Using

# Microsoft® Money for Windows® 95

# Using

# Microsoft® Money for Windows® 95

Faithe Wempen

# Using Microsoft Money for Windows® 95

Library of Congress Catalog No.: 95-71433

ISBN: 0-7897-0606-7

98  97  96      6  5  4  3  2  1

Interpretation of the printing code: the rightmost double-digit number is the year of the book's printing; the rightmost single-digit number, the number of the book's printing. For example, a printing code of 96-1 shows that the first printing of the book occurred in 1996.

Screen reproductions in this book were created using Collage Plus from Inner Media, Inc., Hollis, NH.

Composed in *ITC Century*, *ITC Highlander*, and *MCPdigital* by Que Corporation.

# Credits

**President**
Roland Elgey

**Vice President and Publisher**
Marie Butler-Knight

**Associate Publisher**
Don Roche Jr.

**Editorial Services Director**
Elizabeth Keaffaber

**Managing Editor**
Michael Cunningham

**Director of Marketing**
Lynn E. Zingraf

**Senior Series Editor**
Chris Nelson

**Acquisitions Editor**
Deborah Abshier

**Product Director**
Lorna Jane Gentry

**Assistant Product Marketing Manager**
Kim Margolius

**Technical Editor**
Nanci Jacobs

**Acquisitions Coordinator**
Tracy M. Williams

**Operations Coordinator**
Patty Brooks

**Editorial Assistant**
Carmen Phelps

**Book Designer**
Ruth Harvey

**Cover Designer**
Nathan Clement

**Production Team**
Steve Adams
Becky Beheler
Brian Buschkill
Jason Carr
Joan Evan
Bryan Flores
DiMonique Ford
Trey Frank
Amy Gornik
Jason Hand
John Hulse
Daryl Kessler
Clint Lahnen
Bob LaRoche
Michelle Lee
Julie Quinn
Kaylene Riemen
Laura Robbins
Bobbi Satterfield
Craig Small
Jody York
Kelly Warner
Todd Wente

**Indexer**
Carol Sheehan

# Acknowledgments

Thanks to everyone at Que for their help during this project: Debbie, Lorna, Michael, and especially the Production team!

# Dedication

*To Margaret...*

# About the Author

**Faithe Wempen** left the corporate world awhile back to become a freelance writer and editor, and has been deliriously happy ever since. She has a M.A. in English from Purdue University, and got interested in computers by accident—through a temp job working on an IBM mainframe back in the '80s. Now a self-described computer geek, her most prized possession is her Gateway P90 computer, and her favorite activities are surfing the Internet and convincing strangers at parties that they need to buy home computers. She lives in Indianapolis with Margaret (an engineer and ex-rugby player) and their two shetland sheepdogs, Sheldon and Ashley.

# We'd like to hear from you!

As part of our continuing effort to produce books of the highest possible quality, Que would like to hear your comments. To stay competitive, we *really* want you, as a computer book reader and user, to let us know what you like or dislike most about this book or other Que products.

You can mail comments, ideas, or suggestions for improving future editions to the address below, or send us a fax at (317) 581-4663. For the online inclined, Macmillan Computer Publishing has a forum on CompuServe (type **GO QUEBOOKS** at any prompt) through which our staff and authors are available for questions and comments. The address of our Internet site is **http://www.mcp.com** (World Wide Web).

In addition to exploring our forum, please feel free to contact me personally to discuss your opinions of this book: I'm **74404,3307** on CompuServe, and I'm **lgentry@que.mcp.com** on the Internet.

Thanks in advance—your comments will help us to continue publishing the best books available on computer topics in today's market.

Lorna Jane Gentry
Product Development Specialist
Que Corporation
201 W. 103rd Street
Indianapolis, Indiana 46290
USA

# Contents at a Glance

# Table of Contents

## Part II: Making Money Work for You

### 3 Money In, Money Out: Entering Transactions

### 4 Making Changes to Transactions

## Part III: Routine Money Maintenance

## 11 The Big Picture: Reports and Charts

## 12 Online Banking and Bill Paying

## Part VI: Are You Ready for the Real World?

### 13 Planning for the Future with the Planning Wizards

## FYI

# Introduction

Congratulations on choosing Microsoft Money 4.0 for Windows 95 to handle your finances! You've made a smart decision.

Because Money is so inexpensive and easy to use, you might at first view it as a beginners program with limited features. And you'd be right about one thing—Money is easy for beginners to learn and use. But in this book, you'll discover just how versatile and sophisticated Money can be when it comes to organizing your finances. Money not only keeps your checkbook balanced, but it can organize your debts, help you pay your bills online, print your checks, track your investments, and much more.

Money is built for people like you, who have messy, complicated, real-world finances. Whether you're a single person at an hourly job, the head of a growing household, or even a small business entrepreneur, I think you'll find that Money is one of the best values in the financial software arena.

 **TIP** **Microsoft Money 4.0 is a Windows 95 program. That means you** need to be using Windows 95 as your operating system in order to use the product. If you are using Windows 3.1 instead, you'll want to get Microsoft Money 3.0.

# What can MS Money do for me?

My retired father is the ultimate do-it-yourself man. When he first started using computers, he created a huge, complicated spreadsheet to keep track of his many investments and bank accounts. Of course, it turned out a lot like his workshop area—everything's there, but darned if anyone can find it.

Then for his birthday, I gave him a copy of MS Money. He read the documentation, played with it a little bit, and then announced that the software just wasn't as powerful as his homemade spreadsheet, that he would stick with his own system.

A few weeks passed, and I noticed he had started keeping his checking account in Money. He said it was easier to reconcile the bank statement with

Money than it was by hand on his spreadsheet. Then a few months later, I saw that his investment portfolio had crept into Money as well. He had found that Money could knock out monthly net worth reports for him with a few keystrokes, and he was loving the fact that he could get stock quotes online! He's a die-hard Money enthusiast now, and only uses his old spreadsheet to keep track of his address book.

Like my father, you'll discover that Microsoft Money can do some pretty amazing things for you, with hardly any effort at all on your part. For example, with Money, you can:

- **Keep track of your muddled checking account**. Math errors can kill you on a paper register, but Money never makes math mistakes. Your checkbook will always balance—that is, if you remember to enter the transactions into Money. Money can print checks for you, too.

- **Look for ways to cut your costs**. Money lets you break down each transaction by category and classification, so you can figure out exactly where your money is going. For instance, you could create a classification called Telephone, and every time you write a check to the phone company, that transaction would be classified as such. Then at the end of the year, you can be appalled to note that you spent over $1,000.00 on long-distance calls, and you can vow to do better in the future.

- **Organize your debts.** Money can remind you of upcoming payments, and store information about your payees, so you'll always know when your debts are due. Money can even keep track of the addresses you should mail your payments to!

- **Track your assets.** If you're fortunate enough to have a variety of assets, such as savings accounts, Certificates of Deposit, stocks, CDs, and mutual funds, Money can keep track of them for you. It'll create reports and charts that can show you (or someone you're trying to impress) what you're worth at any given time.

- **Help you plan and budget.** Whether it's your dream vacation you're planning, or your retirement you're pondering, Money can help. Its budgeting feature can help you figure out where your money is coming from, where it is going, and how much of it you'll have left after a certain time.

- **Let you know how much money to set aside for taxes**. If you're self-employed, or you earn lots of interest or dividend income, you may end up owing a lot of money in taxes at the end of the year. How much? Hard to say. Will you have enough money saved up to pay? Who knows. That is, unless you let Money step in and track your tax-deductible expenses and your taxable income.

# What makes this book different?

Most user manuals that come with your software are hefty and solemn and boring. They're about as engaging as the average auto repair manual, and they dump *every detail* about the program onto your plate, including the obscure settings that only a propeller-head would care about. Some people find these books invaluable, but personally, I can't make it past the first chapter—by the time I hit page 22 or so, I'm snoozing.

But *Using Microsoft Money for Windows 95* isn't your average computer book. It's organized and written with real people in mind—people who have absolutely no desire to memorize every single command and feature of the software. This book will show you the fastest and easiest ways to set up accounts, enter transactions, balance your accounts, and plan for the future. I'll explain any terms that you may not have encountered before, and stick with you through the tricky parts. In this book, we'll look at tax planning, budgets, and even small-business accounting with Money. There'll be no wasted time, and no technobabble.

# How to use this book

If you have the time and energy, you can read this book from cover to cover. The chapters are arranged in a logical order that parallels most people's experience with Money, from setting up accounts to experimenting with advanced features.

If you're new to Money, start at the beginning of the book and work your way through—Parts I and II will be especially helpful. If you've used Money before, or are just one of those intrepid types who like to head out on their own, you may want to skip to the more advanced chapters toward the end.

When you start a new chapter, check out the list of topics at the beginning—they provide a concise list of what I'll be trying to cover in that chapter. From there, you can either read straight through the chapter, or jump immediately to the topic on which you need help.

# How the book is organized

This book is broken down into five parts, each with a specific theme:

## Part I, Introducing Microsoft Money

This part is for first-time users. You'll learn your way around the program, and you'll set up your accounts.

## Part II, Everyday Money Operations

The chapters in this part teach you the routine chores that we all face—tracking income and expenses, printing checks, and making payments.

## Part III, Routine Money Maintenance

This part helps you keep your financial records well-organized. You'll learn how to reconcile an account, manage your account files, track investments, and create reports. Part III also covers Money's online banking features.

## Part IV, Are You Ready for the Real World?

In this section, you'll tackle some of Money's most powerful features, like planning and budgeting. Be ready for the future by setting up special tax categories and planning what accounts and classifications you need.

## Part V, FYI

These chapters are chock-full of reference material you might need. Here, you'll find step-by-step instructions for installing Money, and you'll find out how to customize how Money works to suit your preferences. Finally, you'll learn how to protect your Money account files from snoops and disasters.

# Special book elements

This book has a number of special elements and conventions to help you find information quickly—or skip topics you don't want to read right now.

 **TIP**    **Tips either point out information often overlooked in the** documentation, or help you use your software more efficiently, like a shortcut. Some tips help you solve or avoid problems.

 *CAUTION*    **Cautions alert you to potentially dangerous consequences of a** procedure or practice, especially if it could result in serious or even disastrous results, such as losing your data.

 **Q&A**    *What are Q&A notes?*

Cast in the form of questions and answers, these notes provide you with advice on ways to avoid or solve common problems.

 *Plain English, please!*

These notes explain the meanings of technical terms or unavoidable computer jargon.

Throughout this book, we'll use a comma to separate the parts of a pull-down menu command. For example, to start a new file in Money, you'll choose File, New. That means, "Pull down the File menu, and choose New from the list." (The underscore indicates hot keys that you can press to perform a specific task rather than using your mouse.)

If you see two keys separated by a plus sign, such as Ctrl+X, that means to press and hold the first key, press the second key, then release both keys.

## Sidebars are interesting nuggets of information

Sidebars provide interesting, nonessential reading, side-alley trips you can take when you're not at the computer or when you just want some relief from "doing stuff." Here you may find more technical details, funny stories, personal anecdotes, or interesting background information.

# Part I: Introducing Microsoft Money

# 1

# Getting Acquainted with MS Money

● **In this chapter:**

● Getting up and running with Money

● It's a pretty screen, but what does it mean?

● Calling for Help

● How do I shut this thing off?

*Shake hands with Money—soon to be your best friend in*
*financial record-keeping . . . . . . . . . . . . . . . . . . . . . . .* ⊳

**M**eeting new people has always seemed a bit awkward to me, even though I'm usually eager to get to know the folks, and I'm interested in what I'll be learning from them. But there are these inane social rituals we all have to follow! You shake hands, and get this goofy frozen smile on your face, and say "Nice to meet you." Then you make some small talk, still with the same goofy smile, then shake hands again and say "Nice to have met you." I tell ya, it's stuff like that which drove me out of the business world and into a job as a freelance writer!

There's a similar awkwardness the first time you fire up a new computer program, only the goofy look on your face is probably a grimace rather than a grin. What do all the pictures mean? What does this button over here do? How do you get out of here? Even in a program as friendly and simple as Money, you might feel that way at first.

But don't fear. Money has a friendly face and warm handshake that will soon put you at ease. Stick with me through this "getting to know you" chapter, and before long Money will seem like your old friend.

# Starting up the program for the first time

Money starts up like any other Windows 95 program. (It's considerate that way.) When you installed it (see Appendix A), Microsoft Money was placed on the Programs menu off the Start button. Figure 1.1 shows where the program is located on your desktop. To get there, just click the Start button to open the Start menu, then move your mouse pointer to Programs to open the Programs menu. Now, move your mouse pointer to Microsoft Money and click.

Easy enough, eh?

If you find yourself using Microsoft Money a lot, you may want to create a shortcut on your desktop for it. A desktop shortcut is just what it sounds like: a quick-access path to an original program file. When you put a program shortcut on your desktop, a double-click on its icon and you're in the program.

**Fig. 1.1**
To start the program, select it from the Start button's menu system.

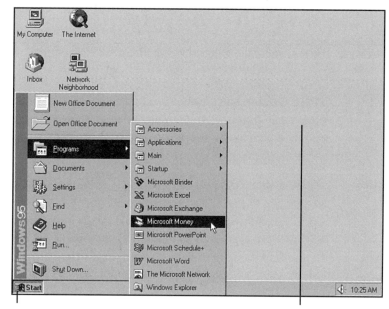

The Start button is your gateway to Money.

For even quicker access, put a Money shortcut here on the desktop.

There are lots of ways to create a shortcut, but here's one of the easiest:

**1** Right-click the Start button, and select Open from the menu that appears.

**2** Double-click on the Programs icon. You'll see a window with several programs and folders in it, including one for Microsoft Money.

**3** Right-click the Microsoft Money icon, and select Create Shortcut from the menu that appears. A second icon for Microsoft Money appears in the folder, labeled Microsoft Money (2).

**4** Drag the new icon onto your desktop.

You can start Microsoft Money from now on by double-clicking that icon, and you don't have to bother with the Start button.

**TIP** **Who needs that (2) next to the name Microsoft Money on the** shortcut? You can change the name by clicking once on the icon, then pressing F2 and typing a new name. Get creative—change it to something like My Great Fortune. It's OK to dream, isn't it?

# A tour through Money-land

By starting the program, we've made eye contact with Money. Now it's time to introduce ourselves and do the "Nice to meet you" ritual.

When you first meet Money, it doesn't leave much time for small talk. A quick handshake from the welcoming dialog box, then Money tells you that you should create a new **account** right away, by giving you the New Account Wizard opening dialog box (see fig. 1.2).

It's true—you do need to create a new account before you can use the majority of Money's features, so it's a good idea to make that one of your first priorities. But what's the hurry? Let's take a look around first. We're going to talk about new accounts in Chapter 2, and you'll get enough information there to make an intelligent decision about the kind of account you want to set up. For now, just click Cancel to tell Money "Thanks, but not now."

**Fig. 1.2**
The first thing Money asks you to do is set up a new account. Click Cancel, since we're not ready to do this yet.

## 66 *Plain English, please!*

An **account** in Money corresponds to an account at your bank or other financial institution. You'll probably have several accounts, and you can work with all of them at once, since Money keeps them all in a single account file. If you like, you can create a separate account file for another person's accounts, or for your business accounts, to keep them completely separate from your personal ones. You'll learn that in Chapter 9. 99

After you cancel the new account setup, the New Account Wizard goes away, and you're left with a good view of the entire Money screen, like the one in Figure 1.3.

**Fig. 1.3**
At last you're looking Money full in the face.

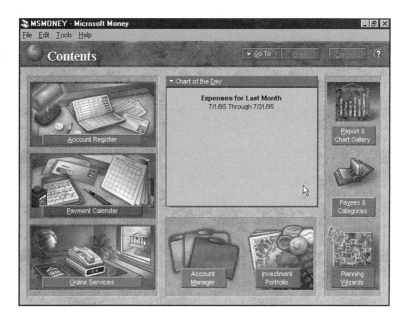

# Checking out the parts of the Contents screen

Microsoft Money, as you can tell right away, does not look like most other Windows programs. Sure, it has a menu bar and some window controls, but some other things are happening, too.

The Contents screen shown here is your home base. It's like a lobby, from which you can access all the other "doors" that lead to various areas of the program.

*This main screen is called the Contents screen.*

*These buttons remain on-screen no matter which area you're working in. Click the Go To button to open a menu of the areas available on the Contents screen, then choose from the menu to move to a different area. Click the Back button to return to an area you previously worked in. Click the Contents button to return immediately to this Contents screen.*

*The menu bar is just what you would expect. Click on a menu name to open the menu, then click on a menu command.*

*Each of these buttons represents an area of Money. Click any button to move to that area.*

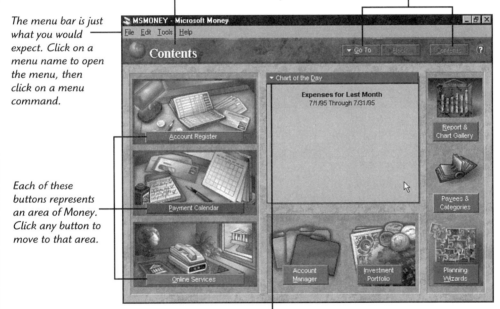

*Every day, Money shows a different chart that analyzes your finances. There's nothing here now because we haven't created any accounts or transactions yet. Click on the Chart of the Day arrow to choose a different chart.*

# How do I select one of the Money features to use?

As you can see, there are lots of program areas at your disposal—Account Register, Payment Calendar, and so on. Don't worry about which ones you should use now, or how to do it—that's the subject of the rest of the book! For now, let's focus in on what I will mean later when I say "select the Account Register" or "go to Account Manager."

 *Plain English, please!*

> Money has many work areas (also referred to in this book as "features" or just "areas"), each one handling a certain aspect of your finances. For instance, there's one for your Account Register, one for Pay Online, and one for your Investment Portfolio.

Select, choose, go to—they're all the same thing, and I'll be using those terms interchangeably. To select a feature, you can do either of the following:

- Click on its button on the Contents screen. (If you aren't at the Contents screen, click the Contents button first to go there.)

- From any screen, click the Go To button, then click on your choice from the drop-down list.

For instance, Figure 1.4 shows the screen you'll see if you click on the Report and Chart Gallery button or select Report and Chart Gallery from the Go To drop-down menu. Notice that the Back and Contents buttons are both available. You can return to the Contents screen by clicking either of them.

 **Q&A** *Why are there two buttons, Back and Contents, that both do the same thing?*

> Actually, they don't usually do the same thing. Contents always takes you back to the Contents screen, no matter what else you've been doing. Back takes you to the previous screen you were working with. In fact, it will step you back, one by one, through all the previous screens you've worked with in a given session.

You can go anywhere you want in Money by clicking one of these buttons.

**Fig. 1.4**
The Report and Chart Gallery offers an array of ways to look at your finances.

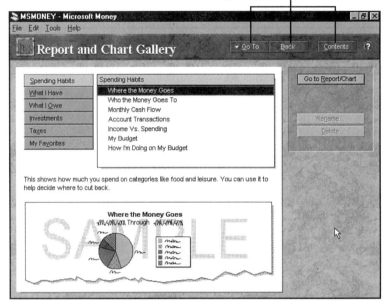

## Using menus and dialog boxes

If you've ever used a Windows program before, you are probably familiar with menus and dialog boxes. They're the standard controls that help you get around.

Money doesn't use a lot of menus or dialog boxes—it relies more heavily on on-screen buttons you click on, as you've seen. However, there is a small menu bar across the top with four menus on it, and some of those menu commands do bring up dialog boxes.

To select a command from a menu, just click on the menu to open it, then click on the command to select it. There are sometimes shortcut key combinations listed next to a menu command—for instance, next to Exit, there's Ctrl+F4. That means to hold down the Ctrl key while you press the F4 key. If you learn these shortcut keys, you can bypass the menu entirely.

Some menu commands have arrows next to them. That means that there's a submenu hiding there. When you select the command, a submenu with more commands appears to further narrow down your selection.

# All about dialog boxes

Some menu commands have ellipses (dots) next to them—it means that when you select the command, a dialog box will appear. This dialog box includes most of the controls you'll find in any Money dialog box. (FYI, I got this dialog box by selecting File, Print Setup, Report and Chart Setup, and then clicking on the Options button.)

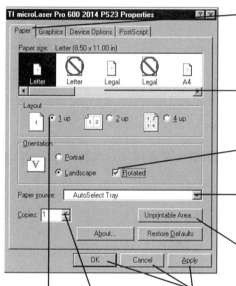

Some dialog boxes have tabs, which means the dialog box has more than one "page" of controls. To see the other controls, click on a different tab.

Scroll bars let you see more of a list than can be displayed on the screen at once. Drag the bar, or click the arrow buttons at either end. Just click on your selection on the list. (Here, I've clicked on Letter.)

A checkbox is an on/off switch. A checkmark means "on"; no checkmark means "off." Click to toggle between the two states.

A down-pointing arrow next to a box means there's a drop-down list to be had. Click the arrow to open the list, then click on an item in the list.

Option buttons are like radio buttons in your car—only one at a time in any group can be selected. When you click an option button, the previously selected one pops back out.

When a text box calls for a number, you can type it in, or you can use the up and down arrow buttons. Clicking on one of these tiny buttons increases or decreases the number in increments.

Command buttons take action. You can click on OK to accept your selections and close the dialog box, or Cancel to reject them and close. The Apply button accepts your changes without closing the dialog box.

Some command buttons have ellipses (dots) on them. This means they open another dialog box.

# There must be a Help system around here somewhere...

Where would we be without online help? Probably buried in a stack of technical reference manuals, fast asleep. Online help lets you look up the exact feature you need help with, and get the answer quickly.

 **TIP** **There are two reference manuals you will still want to consult.** One, obviously, is this book. The other is the Getting Started with Microsoft Money book that comes with the program. It's short enough to be readable, and can give you some hints and examples.

Like all Windows programs, Money comes with a fairly impressive Help system, and several ways of getting into it. The following sections show you the way.

## The Help triumvirate: Contents, Index, Find

All Windows 95 programs have some common features in their Help systems: Contents, Index, and Find. These are tabs in the Help window that you can use to locate the topic that you need help with. More on these momentarily—first we have to open up the Help window itself. To open Help, select <u>H</u>elp, <u>H</u>elp Topics, and you'll see a Help window pop up with tabs for Contents, Index, and Find.

### Contents lets you browse the Help system

Contents is a great help tool for browsing the Help system. It's arranged like a book with multiple chapters, so you can think of it as thumbing through a manual, looking for the heading for the section you want. Click on the Contents tab, and you'll see something resembling Figure 1.5.

**Fig. 1.5**

The Contents tab contains a series of books you can look up the topics in.

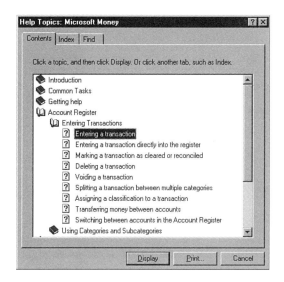

Pick a book, and click on it. More sub-books open up underneath it. Keep clicking on books and sub-books until you start seeing some icons that look like pieces of paper with question marks. These are actual help documents, which you can read by double-clicking on them.

## Index has all your help in order

Another way to use Help is the Index tab. You'll find it helpful if you know the name of the feature you want help on—it works like an index in the back of a book. Click on it from the main Help window, and you'll see all the topics in the entire help system, in alphabetical order.

Type the topic you're interested in (or at least the first few letters), and the alphabetical list will jump to the spot matching what you typed (see fig. 1.6). Click on the topic you want, then click the Display button to see it.

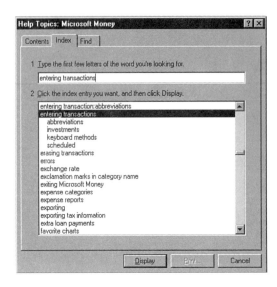

## Find helps you locate the help you need

The final way to use the Help system is the Find tab. This one is great if you aren't sure what the topic is called, because the Find tab looks through the contents of each help screen, not just the titles, to come up with a list of topics that match.

Click on the Find tab, and then type in what you want to find in the top text box in the tab (see fig. 1.7). To narrow Money's search, you can click on one of the matching words in the middle area of the tab—or you can leave them all selected to get a list of all related topics. The topics that match the word(s) you chose will appear at the bottom. Click on the one you want, then click Display.

# I have a Help document on-screen! What do I do, now?

Once you get a Help topic on-screen (see fig. 1.8), you have a variety of options:

**Fig. 1.7**
Another way to use
Help is to Find what
you want.

**Fig. 1.8**
You'll eventually arrive
at a help topic. What
you do next is up
to you.

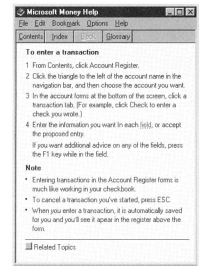

- Select File, Print Topic, then click OK, to print the topic.

- Select Edit, Copy to copy the topic to the Clipboard. (From there, you can paste it into a word processing program, or any other program that accepts text, by selecting Edit, Paste in that program.)

- Select Bookmark, Define, then click OK, to mark this topic as one you would like to come back to later. In the future you can select the topic directly from the Bookmark menu.

- Click the Close button (X) in the top right corner of the window to close it and go back to working in Money.

- Click the Contents buttons or Index buttons to go back to those tabs on the main Help window.

- Click the Back button to return to a previous Help topic you viewed, if any.

- Click the Glossary button to open a Glossary window, an alphabetical list of important terms you should know. Click on a letter button to move quickly to a certain letter if you want. Close the window by clicking the Close button when you're finished.

You can close any Help window (or any window at all, for that matter) at any time by clicking on the Close (X) button in its top right corner.

## Other ways to get help

Besides the main Help system, you can get help on a particular feature by clicking the little round question mark button at the top right corner of the Money window. (You can see it looking back at Figures 1.3 and 1.4.) No matter which feature you're using, you can click on this little button to see a description of that feature.

Also, when you're working in a dialog box, and you wonder what a particular control does, you can right-click on the item and then select What's This, or you can select the control (Tabbing to it is a good way) and press F1.

F1 works other places too, not just dialog boxes. For example, on the Contents screen, you can press Tab to select one of the features, then press F1 for a description of it.

**Q&A**   *I press Tab at the Contents screen, but nothing happens!*

Look closer. There's a thin dotted outline that surrounds the selected feature on the Contents screen. You move the outline from feature to feature by pressing the Tab key. Unfortunately, it is very hard to see— you have to really squint for it.

# Let's get out of here!

If you're ready for more, go on to Chapter 2 at this point, and begin setting up your accounts. But if you want to take a break and ponder all you've learned, or maybe just get a cup of coffee and some pie, exit the program:

**1** Select <u>F</u>ile, E<u>x</u>it or press Alt+F4.

**2** Money will give you a backup reminder (see fig. 1.9). Since we haven't done anything that warrants preserving yet, click No.

**Fig. 1.9**
Money reminds you to back up your file, even when you haven't done much that merits backing up.

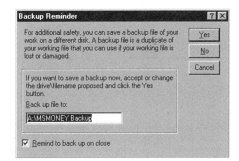

 **Q&A** *Should I ever answer Yes to the backup reminder?*

Eventually, yes. It's always a good idea to safeguard your important data. The backup will ensure that your financial information will not be lost if your hard disk fails.

I must admit, though, that I never back up my Money data to a floppy disk this way, and I usually turn this reminder off. (You can do so by deselecting the Remind me to back up on close check box in Figure 1.9.) That's because I use the Backup program that comes with Windows 95 occasionally to back up my entire hard disk, and because I would rather live dangerously than fumble with floppies.

Later, as you enter account information and transactions that you want to safeguard, you can answer Yes to this question, and insert a floppy disk on which to store the backup when prompted. You may not want to follow my lead on this particular issue—I've always been somewhat of a daredevil.

# 2

# The First Step: Setting Up Your Accounts

● **In this chapter:**

- **How do I know which account type I want?**

- **Creating a new account: just the facts, ma'am**

- **More accounts, please!**

- **How do I know when to start a new file?**

*Getting your account types straight is important. If you try to wedge an ATM transaction into an account designed for mutual funds, the result will be pretty ugly* . . . . . . . . . . . ▶

**H**ave you ever gone for a job interview where they made you fill out a huge, complicated application form before you could even talk to a human being? The application form they give you is carefully designed to ask all the right questions that will help these people decide if you're a desirable character with the skills they want.

Now, what if you went on a job interview, and the guy at the desk said, "Sorry, we're all out of application forms. Here, fill out this shipping invoice instead." So poor you sits there and tries to figure out how you're going to tell them that you have six years of college on the line marked Freight Terms.

The point is, it's extremely important to make sure you're filling out the right form for the right situation. In Chapter 3, you're going to learn about entering transactions into your Account Register, which is basically a big form. The blanks on the form are different for each account type—for instance, the checking account register has a blank for Check Number, and an investment account register has blanks for quantity and price. You wouldn't want to try to wedge your checking account info into an investment account register, or vice versa!

It's important to choose the right account type when you create an account so you'll have the right blanks later when you enter a transaction. This chapter focuses on getting the right accounts set up for future smooth sailing.

# What kinds of accounts can I keep track of in Money?

Money offers 11 account types, so you're sure to find one to meet your needs, no matter what kind of account you're trying to track. Table 2.1 gives a rundown on them, to help you decide.

**Table 2.1   Account types in Microsoft Money**

| Account type | Used for | Contains these blanks |
|---|---|---|
| Assets | Valuable things you own, such as your house or art collection. | Number<br>Date<br>Payee |

| Account type | Used for | Contains these blanks |
|---|---|---|
| | | Decrease<br>Increase<br>Value |
| Bank | A bank account that does not fall under Checking, Savings, or Line of Credit. | Number<br>Date<br>Payee<br>Payment<br>Deposit<br>Balance |
| Cash | Day-to-day expenditures that are not associated with a bank or financial institution (i.e. "pocket money"). | Number<br>Date<br>Payee<br>Spend<br>Receive<br>Balance |
| Checking | A checking account through a bank or other financial institution. You can track ATM transactions too. | Number<br>Date<br>Payee<br>Payment<br>Deposit<br>Balance |
| Credit Card | Any credit card you use. (It need not be associated with one of your bank accounts.) | Number<br>Date<br>Payee<br>Charge<br>Credit<br>Balance |
| Investment | Stocks, bonds, and mutual funds. Create one investment account for each brokerage statement you receive. | Date<br>Investment<br>Activity<br>Quantity<br>Price<br>Total |
| Liability | Money you owe that you don't pay interest on (for instance, money borrowed from a friend, short-term debt, taxes). | Number<br>Date<br>Payee<br>Increase<br>Decrease<br>Balance |

continues

**Table 2.1    Continued**

| Account type | Used for | Contains these blanks |
|---|---|---|
| Line of Credit | Charge cards that directly debit (deduct from) an account. | Number<br>Date<br>Payee<br>Charge<br>Credit<br>Balance |
| Loan | Amortized loans, such as car or house loans, or student loans. | Date<br>Payment Number<br>Payee<br>Payment<br>Principal<br>Balance |
| Other | Other expenses that do not fall into any other category. | Number<br>Date<br>Payee<br>Spend<br>Receive<br>Balance |
| Savings | Savings accounts (usually interest-earning). You can also keep track of checks and ATM transactions. | Number<br>Date<br>Payee<br>Payment<br>Deposit<br>Balance |

Don't be overwhelmed by the different account types—notice that most of the blanks are going to be the same no matter which account type you pick. There will always be a blank for the date and the balance, for instance, and usually one for a payee.

Most people will want to start out with a checking account, and maybe a savings account too. We'll get into some of the less common account types, like investments, in later chapters.

# First things first: entering info for an account

Once you've chosen the type of the first account you want to set up, you're ready to roll. For the examples in this section, I'm going to use a checking account, since that's the type that most people start with.

 **TIP** **If you want to set up a credit card, loan, investment, or line of credit,** there are a few more steps than the ones shown here. I'll go into these later in this chapter.

To start a new account:

**1** Click Account <u>M</u>anager on the Contents screen. The Account Manager screen appears (see fig. 2.1). There aren't any accounts set up yet, so the screen looks pretty barren.

**Fig. 2.1**
You can start creating new accounts from the Account Manager screen.

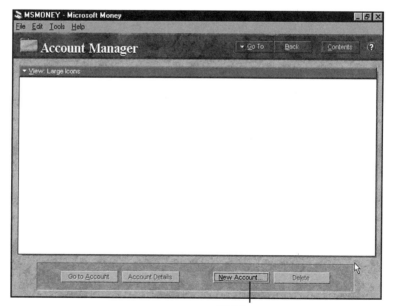

*Click here to start a new account.*

**2** Click the <u>N</u>ew Account button. The New Account Wizard dialog box appears (see fig. 2.2), asking you to select an account type.

**Fig. 2.2**
Select an account type from the list. (Check back at Table 2.1 if you aren't sure which to pick.)

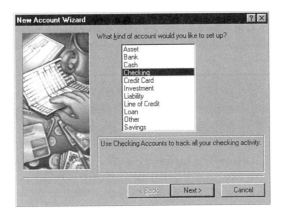

3  Click on the account type you want, then click the <u>N</u>ext button.

4  You're asked to name the account—type it in the text box. I'm going to give mine the name of my bank: "Union Federal Checking." Then click <u>N</u>ext.

5  Finally, you're asked for an account balance. Enter it into the text box. You can do this two ways:

  • You can enter the current balance from your checkbook. Then you don't have to enter any transactions that you've already made, but you also won't be able to reconcile your next bank statement with Money.

  • You can enter the ending balance from your last bank statement, and then in Chapter 3, enter all the transactions you've made since then. You can then reconcile your account with the next bank statement you receive. (This is what I'm going to do.)

6  Click Finish. The dialog box goes away, and you can see an icon in the Account Manager representing the account you just created.

You're done! Congratulations, you've just set up an account in your Money file. If you want to set up more accounts now, go right ahead and do it by repeating the preceding set of steps. Then, when you're finished with them all, click Contents to return to the Contents screen.

**Q&A** *How many accounts can a file hold?*

There's no fixed limit on the number of accounts you can have. Use as many as you need!

**Q&A** *When should I start a new file?*

Most people will never need to start a new file—the default file (MSMONEY) will satisfy all their needs. The only time you might want to create a new file would be to keep the finances completely separate for two people, or for your business and personal accounts. Chapter 9 goes into creating new files in more detail.

# What about credit cards and line of credit accounts?

You can set up a credit card or a line of credit account the exact same way that you did the other accounts (see the preceding procedure), except for one extra step. Right before the last step ( between steps 5 and 6), you're asked to enter an estimated monthly payment, enter the date that payments are due, and choose which account you'll pay the bill from. You can also set up Money to remind you when the bill is due.

For instance, as you can see in Figure 2.3, I usually pay $50 on my credit card, my payments are due on the 27th of the month, and I pay the bill out of my checking account.

**Fig. 2.3**
With a credit card or line of credit account, you need to enter a few more bits of information.

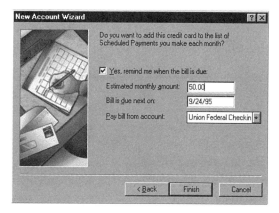

# And investment accounts?

Investment accounts are like savings accounts, except you can't count on the interest rate or profit staying stable. Set up an investment account the same as any other account, except for these differences:

- You're asked whether the account is tax-deferred or not. For instance, if it's an Individual Retirement Account (IRA), it's tax-deferred.

- You're asked whether this account has an associated cash account or not. Answer Yes if this is a brokerage account that you use to trade stocks. Answer No if this is a retirement plan or an account that does not involve a broker or bank.

If you answer Yes, that there's an associated cash account, Money will create two icons for this investment in the Account Manager window. One will have the name you give it, and the other will have the same name, followed by (Cash)—for example, Hutton Investments and Hutton Investments (Cash). You'll learn how to handle these accounts in Chapter 10.

# The ultimate wizard: setting up a loan account

Loan accounts are a whole different animal, and Money realizes this. There are a lot more factors that go into setting up a loan than any other account type! For instance, with your mortgage, there's principal and interest, escrow, taxes, insurance, and so on.

 *CAUTION* **Before you start setting up a loan in Money, make sure you have** all the information about the loan handy—the payment due date, payment amount, interest rate, number of payments left, and so on. You'll need these.

Money includes a special wizard for setting up loans. When you select Loan as the account type, this wizard kicks in. Because every loan has several unique factors, this wizard works hard—and requires a few more answers from you. Be patient and keep going, though, and Money will soon have your own personal loan information on-deck and ready to serve you. Follow these steps to set up a loan:

**1** From Account Manager, click the New Account button.

**2** At the New Account Wizard dialog box, click Loan, then click Next. A very different-looking wizard starts up, as shown in Figure 2.4.

**Fig. 2.4**
The Loan Wizard is different from the wizards for the other account types.

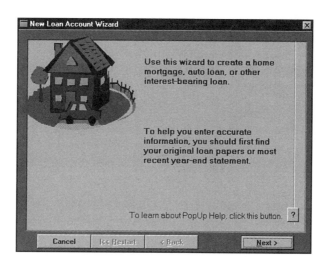

**3** Click Next to begin the Loan Wizard, then Next again to get past the information screen that describes the steps in the process.

**4** Click the Borrowing Money button (assuming you are borrowing money), then click Next.

 **TIP**    **Need help as you work with the wizard? Just click the question** mark for a pop-up Help menu.

 **TIP**    **You can also use this wizard to set up a loan you are giving to** someone else, but the steps are different. They're easy to follow, though— just enter the information it asks for.

**5** Next you're asked for the name of the loan (see fig. 2.5). Enter it in the Loan Name text box. This is for your own use only—I'm calling mine Home Mortgage.

**Fig. 2.5**
Enter the name of the loan and the institution that is lending the money.

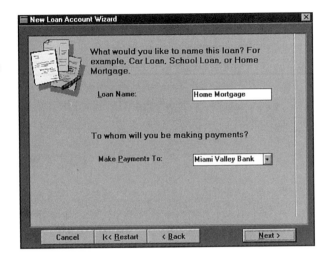

6  Enter the name of the lending institution in the Make Payments To text box. Mine is Miami Valley Bank. Then click Next.

7  Select Yes or No to indicate whether or not payments have already been made on the loan. (In my case, I'll answer Yes.) Then click Next.

8  Next you're asked whether Money should record all the payments you've made since the start of the loan, or if you would prefer to begin at the beginning of the current calendar year. Since I've had my loan for several years, I'm going to start with the current calendar year. Click the answer you want, then click Next.

9  Next, enter the due date of the first payment you made this year (or at the beginning of the loan, depending on what you selected in step 8). Then click Next.

10  Click Next again to get past the information screen that tells you it's time to calculate the loan.

11  Open the Paid How Often drop-down list and select the frequency of your payments. Monthly is the most common, and that's what I'm going to pick. Then click Next.

12  Choose how the interest is calculated on the loan. I'm not exactly sure of this on my loan, so I'm going to pick the default option, which is Based on Date Payment Is Due. Then click Next.

**TIP** **Steps 13-17 will ask you for information about your loan amount.** You can leave any one of these blank, and Money will calculate it for you.

**13** Enter the remaining loan amount as of the first of the year (or as of the beginning of the loan, depending on your answer in step 8). Then click Next.

**14** Enter the interest rate for the loan, as of the beginning of this year (or at the beginning of the loan, depending on step 8). Click Next.

**15** In the Loan Length box, enter the number of remaining payments or years. Then in the drop-down list to the right, select either Payments or Years. Click Next.

**16** Enter the amount that you pay each month in principal and interest. (This doesn't include your taxes and insurance.) Then click Next.

**17** If you have a balloon amount you must pay at the end of the loan, enter it in the Balloon Amount text box. Some car loans require this; most mortgages do not. Click Next.

**18** If you left one of the fields blank in steps 13 through 17, Money calculates that field for you and presents you with the answer in a dialog box. Click OK to clear the dialog box away.

**CAUTION** **If you don't leave any of the fields blank in steps 13-17, the values** you enter must work together exactly—otherwise, Money will tell you that they don't, and you'll need to reenter one or more numbers.

**19** Review the information about your loan on the screen (mine is shown in Figure 2.6). Click Next if everything is okay.

**TIP** **If you want to change anything, click the Back button to return to** the screen you want to change, make your changes, then click Next to get caught back up again.

**20** Click the Next button again to move past the info screen that tells you that you're now going to set up the payments (the Managing Payment screen).

**21** You're asked to enter categories and subcategories for your principal and interest. We haven't talked yet about categories—you'll learn about them in Chapter 5. However, for now, let's just accept the categories and subcategories that Money suggests, pressing Tab to move between text boxes:

**Fig. 2.6**
Here's a summary of the information you've entered so far; click Next to accept it.

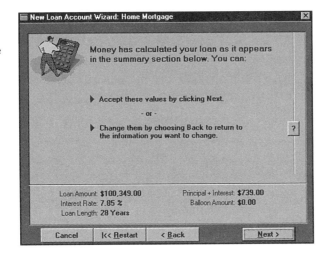

- In the Principal Category box, type Housing, or whatever is appropriate for the loan you're setting up.

- In the Principal Subcategory box, type Mortgage Principal (or another subcategory if it seems more appropriate).

- In the Interest Category, type Housing (or another category).

- In the Interest Subcategory box, type Mortgage Interest (or whatever category you want to use).

- Click Next when you're finished entering the categories and subcategories.

**22** If other payments (like escrow for taxes and insurance) are included in your payment amount for this loan, click the Other Fees button. If not, click Next and skip to step 24.

**23** In the Other Fees screen, enter categories and subcategories, descriptions, and amounts for other payments. Click Done when you're finished. For instance, here's what I did for my home mortgage, as you can see in Figure 2.7.

- I entered Insurance as a category. A list of choices popped up in the subcategory box, and from it I selected Homeowner's/Renter's Insurance.

- For my property taxes, I entered Taxes as the category. From the list of subcategories that popped up, I selected Real Estate Taxes.

- I entered my insurance company's name for the payee for the insurance line, and Marion County Tax Assessor as the payee for the tax line.

- I entered the amounts I pay for each of these on the respective lines.

- Click <u>N</u>ext to move on, after you've entered any other fees.

**Fig. 2.7**

My mortgage payment also includes taxes and insurance, as you can see.

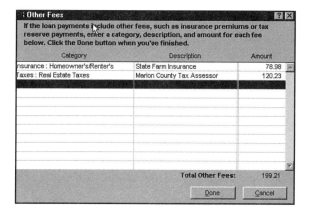

24  If you want to be reminded of the payment, click <u>Y</u>es, Remind Me. You'll need to enter the next payment's date and the account that you'll pay it from. Or, to skip the whole reminder affair, click <u>N</u>o, Do Not Remind Me. Click <u>N</u>ext to continue.

25  Read the summary that appears (mine's shown in fig. 2.8), then click <u>C</u>reate to create your loan account. Click Exit to return to Money.

Whew! Quite a process, eh? Setting up a loan is one of the most complicated things you'll do in Money, but it's well worth the effort. From now on, entering payments for your loan, and keeping track of your loan balance, will be as easy as clicking a few buttons.

**Fig. 2.8**
A summary of your
loan information.

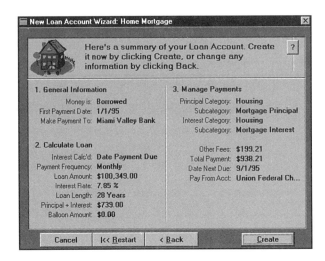

# Moving on...

In this chapter, we created the forms that we'll fill out later when we enter transactions. It wasn't exactly a thrill ride (that loan setup procedure was more like a morning commute in heavy traffic!), but setting up accounts is a big-time important step. Now, whenever you go to enter a transaction in one of your accounts, you'll be assured that the right blanks are available to hold your information. Now, if only someone could figure out a way to fill out those darned job applications on a computer...

# Part II: Making Money Work for You

# Money In, Money Out: Entering Transactions

● In this chapter:

- ● **Opening up an account register**

- ● **All about transaction types**

- ● **The ins and outs of entering transactions**

- ● **Categorizing a transaction**

- ● **Can a transaction be split among several categories?**

- ● **Transferring funds among accounts**

- ● **How can I get a different view of the register?**

*You and Money form a financial management team—you remember to enter every transaction into an account register, and Money will help you manage your way to financial success* . . . . . . . . . . . . . . . . . . . . . . . . . . . . . . . **>**

**M**y last job—the one that drove me to freelancing—was as a mid-level manager in a large company. As with most mid-level management positions, my main job was to keep track of things. Wherever I went, I carried a notebook, in which I was supposed to collect information about problems and delays on various projects. Then several times a week, I would go to meetings where I would present the information I had collected. Being a hands-on type of person, this drove me absolutely batty, which is why I am writing this book instead of sitting in some conference room right now. (Life is sweet.)

When it comes to my finances, though, I could sure use a manager—someone to keep track of each transaction, and then present it back to me or take action on it when asked. Fortunately, that's exactly what Microsoft Money does! When you enter transactions into an account register, it's like Money is dutifully writing them down in its notebook, for future reference.

Money can help you manage your way to financial success—provided that you remember to enter every transaction. In this chapter, you'll learn how to enter various types of transactions into your **account register**.

**TIP** **What can Money do once you've entered a transaction? Well, it** can print a check for you (Chapter 6), reconcile the account with your bank statement (Chapter 8), create a report or chart (Chapter 11), or even pay the bill electronically (Chapter 12).

 *Plain English, please!*

An **account register** in Money is just like a paper account register you might keep for an account, like the register in your checkbook or your savings account passbook.

# First, open up the register

When you write down a fact in a notebook, you have to make sure you turn to the right page first. For instance, my planning notebook had a page for each day, and I would always try to write down information on the page for the day when the meeting was going to be held where I would have to present the info.

In Money, transactions are entered into account registers, and there is a register (a "page") for each account you created (see Chapter 2 for info on creating accounts). When entering a transaction, you have to make sure you put it into the right account register.

Clicking the Account Register button on the Contents screen will open the last account you have worked with. If you have only one account, or if you want to reopen the register for the account you have most recently opened, this button is the way to go.

**TIP** **If the Account Register doesn't give you the register you wanted,** just click Contents to return to the Contents screen, then click Account Manager and select a different account, or click the account name at the top of the register and select a different account from the drop-down list that appears.

If you want to open a different account, you'll need to use the Account Manager. Click the Account Manager button on the Contents screen. The Account Manager appears, as shown in Figure 3.1. Then click on the icon for the account you want to use, and click Go to Account.

**TIP** **You'll learn a lot more about the Account Manager in Chapter 9,** "Account Management: Keeping Track of What You've Got."

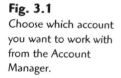

**Fig. 3.1**
Choose which account you want to work with from the Account Manager.

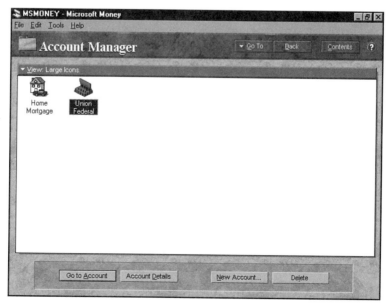

# Understanding an account register

The exact look of the Account Register screen will change somewhat depending on the type of account, but most of their features are the same.

*This shows how the register is currently displayed. Click here to open a drop-down list with many display choices. (We'll cover these later in the chapter.)*

*Here's the name of the account you opened. Change to a different account if you wish by clicking the name and selecting a different account from the drop-down list that appears.*

*This is the actual register. When you enter a transaction, it'll go here.*

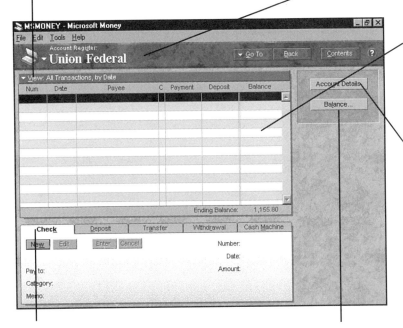

*Click here to bring up a screen where you can enter and change detailed information about the account. (We'll cover this in Chapter 9.)*

*There are tabs for each of the major transaction types in this account. When you enter a new transaction, you'll click on the appropriate tab as the first step. (More on this later.)*

*When you're ready to reconcile the account (see Chapter 8), you'll click this button.*

# Next, just type in the transaction

Entering a transaction is as easy as filling in the blanks. Of course, it helps if you have the right blanks on-screen to work with.

A Checking account register gives you five types of transactions you can enter, each represented by a tab at the bottom of the screen: Check, Deposit, Transfer, Withdrawal, and Cash Machine. Other account types give different types. It's important that you pick the right tab on which to enter a transaction, because there are different fields for each type.

 **Q&A** ***What do I do if I find that I've set up the wrong account type, after I've entered lots of transactions?***

You can change an account's type relatively easily, as you'll learn in Chapter 5. Here's a quick overview, though: from the Account Manager screen, click on the account, then click the Account <u>D</u>etails button. Click the <u>M</u>odify button, then select a different account type and click OK.

 *CAUTION* **If the transaction types do not seem right to you, you've probably** chosen the wrong account type. Turn back to Chapter 2 to learn about the available account types, and set up a new account of the correct type. It is much easier to do this now, rather than after you have entered transactions.

## How do I know which transaction type to use?

The transaction types should be fairly self-explanatory in most accounts. Types like Check, Cash Machine, Spend, Charge, and Decrease all refer to money that's going out. (The only exception is with a loan or liability. With these, a decrease is money coming *into* the account, since it's decreasing the amount still owed.) Types like increase, deposit, credit, and receive all refer to money that's coming in.

 *CAUTION* **If you deposit money at a cash machine, it's considered a Deposit.** The Cash Machine transaction type is only for cash machine withdrawals.

Transfer is the only transaction type that might give you any trouble. A **transfer** is only for money movements between two accounts, if both of them are set up in your Money account file. When you enter a transfer in Money, it makes two entries:

- one in the account that's losing the money,

- and the other in the account that's gaining the money.

We'll look at it in more detail later in the chapter.

**Q&A** ***If I'm making a payment on a loan, wouldn't that be considered a transfer?***

Yes. You can enter it that way in Money if you like. Just choose the loan account as the one that's gaining the money. Or, if you prefer, you can enter the payment as a normal transaction (a check you write, for instance), and select the loan account as the payee.

# Entering your basic, no-frills transaction

To enter any new transaction, open the register, then follow these steps:

**1** Click on the tab for the transaction type you want to enter.

**2** Click the <u>N</u>ew button. Fields appear in the tabbed area in which to enter the transaction (see fig. 3.2).

**Fig. 3.2**
When you click the New button, fields appear for you to enter a new transaction.

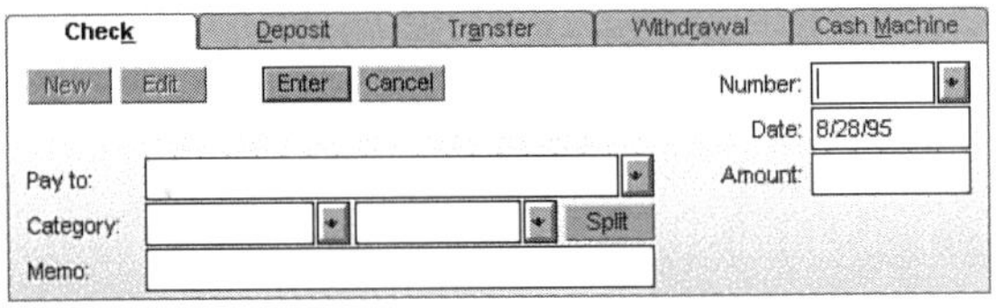

| Check | Deposit | Transfer | Withdrawal | Cash Machine |
|---|---|---|---|---|

New  Edit  Enter  Cancel  Number: [ ]
Date: 8/28/95
Pay to: [ ]  Amount: [ ]
Category: [ ] [ ]  Split
Memo: [ ]

**3** You'll see a blinking cursor in the first field. (If you're entering a check, like I am in Figure 3.2, it'll be the Number field.) Do one of the following:

- Type the information into the field. For example, I could type **101** in the Number field to enter check number 101.

**TIP** **Here's a nice feature: after you've entered the first check number** (when you enter your first transaction), Money takes over the check number by automatically displaying the next higher number when you enter your next transaction. Since I'm entering 101 this time, the next time I enter a check the number 102 is pre-entered in the Number field.

- If there's a down-arrow to the right of the field, a drop-down list is available. Click the down-arrow to open the list, and then click on a list item. If it's a long list, type the first few letters of the entry you want to move quickly to on the list.

**4** Click in the next field, or press Tab to move to it, and enter the information it requests. For instance, if you're entering a check, then the next field is Date. Today's date is already filled in, so you can Tab on past it unless the transaction you're entering occurred (or will occur) on a different date.

**5** Continue moving to fields and filling them out. (They'll be different depending on the account type and transaction type.) There is more information about many of the fields in the remainder of this chapter.

**6** When you are finished filling out all the fields for the transaction, click the Enter button or press Enter on the keyboard.

 **TIP** **Make use of the Memo field! In it, you can type reminders that** will help you remember what the transaction was for. For instance, I might enter "Bill's retirement party" to help me remember why I wrote a check for $100 to the local grocery store so I wouldn't panic later when looking at my food expenditures for the month.

After you've entered the transaction, it appears up above, in the register, as shown in Figure 3.3. You can enter more transactions the same way—just repeat the steps again.

# Why all the drop-down lists?

Money is very big on drop-down lists, as you have probably noticed by now. And with good reason: they come in very handy.

For instance, there's usually a drop-down list in a field where you're specifying a recipient (like Pay To) or a source (like From). You can set up payees to appear on these lists (see Chapter 7), or you can just type in the individuals and businesses. Once you've typed one in, it appears on the list, so you can reuse it by selecting it from the list when entering another transaction.

**Fig. 3.3**
Mission accomplished;
the transaction appears
in the register.

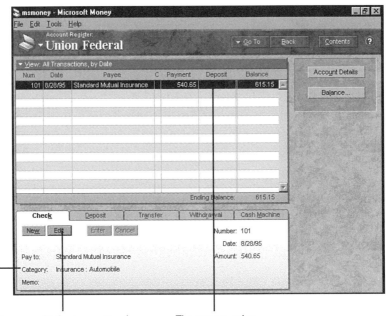

*The information
for the selected
transaction above
appears here.*

*You can edit the transaction by
clicking the Edit button or clicking
anywhere in the tabbed area.*

*The reverse-color
highlighting means this
transaction is selected.*

## Special uses for Number, Account, and Category drop-down lists

You can enter a check or transaction number in the Number field easily
enough, but when you open its drop-down list, you won't find additional
check or transaction numbers to choose from. Instead, you'll find these
items:

- **Electronic Payment** (Epay). Select this if you're going to pay electronically (as explained in Chapter 12) rather than writing a physical
check.

- **Electronic Transfer** (Xfer). Same as Epay, except it's for electronic
transfers from one bank account to another.

- **Print this transaction**. If you're going to print a check with Money
rather than write one with your old checkbook and a pen, choose this
instead of a check number.

Sometimes you'll see an Account field with a drop-down list. When you open
this list, you'll see all your other accounts. You can't add to this list by typing

in your own entries—if you want a new account, you need to set it up as you learned in Chapter 2.

There are two drop-down lists next to Category on most transactions too—you can select categories from them, or type in your own. The left one is for the category, and the right one is for the subcategory. Categories can be a little trickier than the other drop-down list items; they're the subject of the following section, and of Chapter 5 as well.

# How to enter categories and subcategories

When you set up your Money account, it created a few **categories** automatically, which are ready for your use. As you're entering a transaction, you can skip over the Category line completely, or you can open the drop-down list and choose one. (In Chapter 5, you'll learn much more about categories, including how to create your own.)

 *Plain English, please!*

> **Categories** are ways of classifying your income and expenses, so you can create reports and charts later that show how you are spending and receiving money. For instance, if you categorized each check you write to the grocery store as Groceries, you will be able to create a report that shows how much money you spent that month on groceries. **Subcategories** are further breakdowns of the categories—for instance, if Food is the category, you might have Groceries and Dining Out as two subcategories. Categories are optional; you don't have to use them. However, many of Money's powerful features, like reports, can't be used unless you use categories.

Notice in Figure 3.4 that there are two drop-down lists next to Category. That's because Money lets you hone down your categories in to subcategories. For instance, you might have an Insurance category, and several subcategories: Property, Life, Health, and Automobile. You would select the main category, Insurance, from the left drop-down list, and the subcategory (for instance, Automobile) from the right one.

You probably won't use both a category and a subcategory in every case. Some categories don't have subcategories, nor do they need them. If that's the case, just choose the category from the left drop-down list, and leave the right one blank.

**Fig. 3.4**
Categories go on the
left; subcategories on
the right.

Categories are a real blessing, especially at tax time, because they help you
see where your money has gone. There's much more to say about categories,
but let's wait until Chapter 5, where there's room to cover the subject the
way it deserves to be covered—in full detail.

## What does the Split button do?

Have you ever written a single check for lots of different household items at
one of those giant mega-superstores? It's oh-so-convenient to buy your
groceries, hardware, small appliances, lawn fertilizer, and home electronics
at a single store, isn't it?

But then you get home and try to enter the check into Money. Uh oh. In the
excitement of those low discount prices, you must have loaded up your cart
with lots of items, including a gallon-size jug of ketchup, a Thighmaster, and a
new VCR. How in the world can you fit all that stuff into a single category?

Of course, you can't. That's where the Split button (located at the right end of
the categories fields) comes in. Click it, and you'll open a Split Transaction
window.

 **TIP**    **Instead of clicking the Split button, you can select Split from the**
**Category drop-down list.**

In the Split Transaction window, you can enter lots of line-items that all roll
into a single transaction, and categorize each line separately. For instance,
you can put that keg-o-ketchup under Food:Groceries, the VCR under
Furnishings:Electronics, and the Thighmaster under Leisure:Equipment. Just
fill in the category, subcategory, description, and amount. Figure 3.5 shows
how I've apportioned my purchase in the various categories and subcategories. Don't forget the sales tax!

Click the Done button when you're finished to return to the register.

**Fig. 3.5**
In the Split Transaction window, each line has its own drop-down list for category and subcategory.

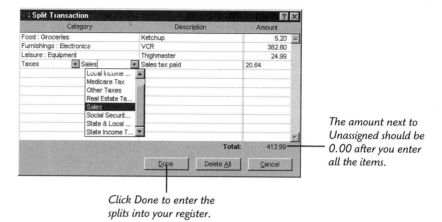

The amount next to Unassigned should be 0.00 after you enter all the items.

Click Done to enter the splits into your register.

**Q&A** ***The categories I want to use aren't listed in the drop-down list! What do I do?***

Money comes with a few categories, but probably not all the ones you'll want. For Figure 3.5, in fact, I've added some categories, such as Taxes:Sales Tax and Leisure:Equipment.

It's easy to add categories. You'll learn all about it in Chapter 5, but for now, if you want to add a category, just type it in the field and press Enter. A message will appear asking you to set up that category—just press Enter to do so.

# Handling transfers

A transfer is just like any other transaction, except that the payee is a bank account, not a person or business. To enter a transfer, click the Transfer button. Then fill in the following fields:

- **Number.** You can assign a number to the transaction if you want, but personally, I would skip it. If this is an electronic transfer (see Chapter 12), select Electronic Transfer (Xfer) from the Number drop-down list.

- **Date.** This should already be filled in with today's date.

- **Amount.** This one's a no-brainer. Just fill in the dollar amount of the transfer.

**Fig. 3.6**
As you can see, I'm
transferring funds from
my savings account
into checking.

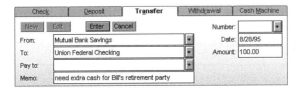

- **From.** This is probably the account that you have open right now. (If not, then the money is coming from another account, into this account.) Select the account that contains the money to be transferred, if it's not already correct.

- **To.** This is the account where the money is going. It has to be one of the accounts you've set up in Money. If you haven't set up this account yet in Money, click Cancel, then return to Chapter 2 and set it up.

- **Pay To.** In 99% of your transfers, you'll leave this blank, because it's just going from one of your own accounts to another. But Money offers the Pay To field to let you specify a different payee if needed—for instance, if you're transferring the money to your brother Earl's account, you could designate Earl as the payee, to keep your records straight in case you wanted to do a report (see Chapter 11) that showed how much money you've given Earl.

- **Memo.** This one is optional. If you want to write a note to yourself to explain why you transferred the money, do it here.

Click Enter when you've filled out all the fields to enter the transfer. An entry will be made in the registers of both accounts, and each account's balance will be adjusted accordingly.

## What about cash machine withdrawals?

Cash machine withdrawals (also known as Automatic Teller or ATM withdrawals) involve withdrawing cash from one of your bank accounts. There's a separate tab in the register for ATM withdrawals. Because it's always you paying yourself, there's no payee—or rather, the payee is always "Cash." Other than not being able to enter a payee, they're the same as other transactions.

# Viewing your register differently

By now, you've probably got several transactions entered in your account register. The default register view is all transactions, sorted by date and then by check number, with a single line for each transaction, and it works pretty well for most people.

However, there might be times when you want to view your register differently. For instance, you might want to see only the unreconciled transactions, or you might want them in a different order. Click the bar right above the register, where it says "View:", to open a drop-down list of your viewing options, as shown in Figure 3.7. From there, you can make these changes:

**Fig. 3.7**
You aren't limited to the default view of your register; there are several settings you can change.

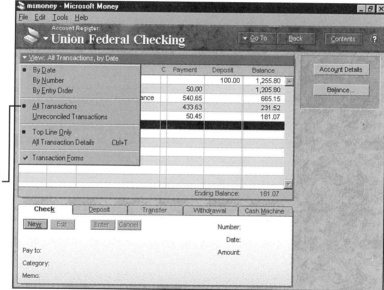

*A dot or check beside an option means it's on.*

- **Order.** You can choose to sort your transactions by <u>D</u>ate (i.e., what you entered in the Date field) by <u>N</u>umber (i.e. what you entered in the Number field), or by <u>E</u>ntry Order (the date/time at which the entry was actually made in the register, regardless of the date in the Date field).

- **Which transactions.** The default is <u>A</u>ll Transactions, but if you prefer, you can choose <u>U</u>nreconciled transactions. That means any transactions that have been cleared when you reconciled your account with the bank statement (see Chapter 8) won't be shown.

- **How much detail.** By default, you see the Top Line <u>O</u>nly. (This is good when you want to see lots of transactions at once without having to scroll down.) You can choose instead to see A<u>ll</u> Transaction Details, which shows everything you entered about a transaction, including categories and memo information. All Transaction Details gives more information, but fewer transactions can fit on the screen at once.

- **View or hide transaction forms.** By default, you see the tabbed forms at the bottom of the screen that help you enter your information. You can hide these if you like by selecting Transaction Forms from the menu. This lets you see more transactions on the screen at once; you might want this if you are viewing but not entering transactions. (You can also enter transactions without the forms, directly into the register, if you like.)

**Q&A** ***Why do some options on the menu in Figure 3.7 have dots and others have check marks?***

Notice that on the menu, there are some divider lines between groups of options. They form groups. Only one option in each group can be selected at a time—the dots indicate which one is selected. Other options stand alone, such as Transaction Forms. These can be on or off, independently of any other options, and they use check marks.

# Different account types—different transactions

Most of the account types have similar fields on their transactions, but here are a few special ones to look out for:

- In an Investment account, there is no transaction number, and you have an Activity drop-down list that lets you choose activities such as Buy, Sell, and Reinvest Dividends. There are also several special buttons to the right of the register, which you'll learn about in Chapter 10.

- With a Loan, you have a Payment Number field rather than Number, and the category is always Split. (You set up the split when you set up the loan; it's split between principal, interest, and any other categories you chose, such as taxes and insurance.)

# Do I need to save my work?

You don't need to worry about the entries you make in your register being saved—they're saved automatically as you enter them. Even if your computer loses power before you exit Money, all the transactions you entered will be there the next time you start the program. Notice that there's not even a Save command on any of the menus in Money! That's how automatic the saving really is.

# Making Changes to Transactions

● **In this chapter:**

● **I have to find this transaction so I can change it**

● **Changing a transaction without scrapping it completely**

● **How about moving it to a different account?**

● **Deleting and voiding: two ways to bag it**

*Need to change a transaction? Not a problem. Money makes change like a pro* . . . . . . . . . . . . . . . . . . . . . . . . . . . . . ▶

**E**verybody needs to make changes and corrections now and then. If you don't believe me, take a look at your paper checkbook register, and count how many times you've scratched something out and tried to write a correction in that tiny white space between the scratched-out part and the border. Pretty ugly, isn't it?

Fortunately, Microsoft Money makes great change, and with no unsightly pencil scratches. You can edit any transaction—change the payee, the category, the amount, the memo, or whatever you need. Can't find the transaction by browsing through the register? Money's search capabilities can help you locate just the one you're looking for.

# Where, oh where has my transaction gone?

Locating a certain transaction is easy if you have only a few transactions in your register. Just skim through, using the scroll bar or Page Up and Page Down keys, until you find the one you want. Then click on it to display its information in the tabbed area below. (Chapter 3 described the register screen in detail, so if you're a bit hazy on the details, turn back there for a quick refresher.)

But what if your register contains hundreds of transactions? If it doesn't yet, it will after a few months, or a year, of record-keeping. Even if you write less than a dozen checks every month, you'll be amazed at how quickly that account register bulks up.

 **TIP** **To make it easier to find the transaction you want by just** eyeballing it, you can change the register view so that it shows only unreconciled transactions (the ones you haven't yet matched with your bank statement). In the account register, click the <u>V</u>iew bar directly above the register. In the drop-down list that appears, select <u>U</u>nreconciled transactions. All cleared (reconciled) transactions will be hidden. This works for all account types that can be reconciled, such as checking and savings; it doesn't work with investment accounts or loans.

To find a transaction in an account register, select <u>T</u>ools, <u>F</u>ind, <u>T</u>ransactions, or just press Ctrl+F. (You can do this from any screen; you don't have to have the account register displayed.) Up pops the Find Transactions dialog box, as shown in Figure 4.1.

**Fig. 4.1**

Use the Find Transactions dialog box to locate any transaction you need.

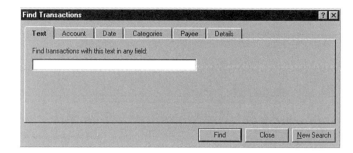

The beauty of finding a transaction with the Find Transaction dialog box is that you can search based on any part of the transaction that you happen to know, even the most bizarre bits. Notice the tabs across the top of the dialog box in Figure 4.1; click on the tab for the bit of information that you know about the transaction, and enter it into the blank there. You can enter information into the blanks on as many tabs as you can provide the information for, to narrow the search as much as possible. Here are your choices:

- **Text.** This is the most generic kind of search. If you remember certain words in the transaction, type the word(s) in the text box on this tab.

- **Accounts.** Here, you choose to search All Accounts or Selected Accounts. If you choose Selected Accounts, pick which accounts you want to search from the list of them that appears.

- **Dates.** On this tab, you can choose the time interval, as shown in Figure 4.2. Choose an interval from the Range drop-down list, and the dates appear in the From and To blanks. Or you can choose Custom Dates from the list and enter your own date range in the From and To blanks.

  For instance, if you know that the transaction occurred in the last 30 days, and contained the text "Quickie-Mart" in the payee line, you could click the Text tab, type Quickie-Mart, then click the Date tab and select Last 30 Days from the Range drop-down list.

**Fig. 4.2**
You can specify a date range to search; choose from one of many preset intervals, or create your own.

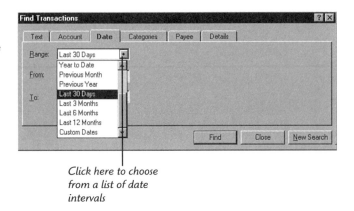

Click here to choose
from a list of date
intervals

- **Categories**. To find only transactions of a specific category, click this tab (see fig. 4.3), then click one of the options. (You'll learn more about categories in Chapter 5.) For instance, if you remember that the transaction had something to do with groceries, you could search the Food category. Here's a rundown on the options in this tab:

**Fig. 4.3**
If you want to search for transactions in a specific category (or categories), this tab lets you do that.

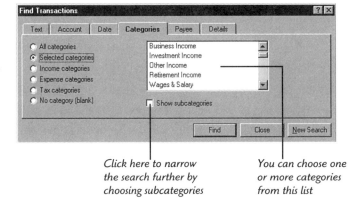

Click here to narrow
the search further by
choosing subcategories

You can choose one
or more categories
from this list

*All categories*—If you don't know which category the transaction was placed into, select this.

*Selected categories*—Click this option if you want to search a number of categories, then select each category you want to search. If you want to get more precise, you can use subcategories; click Show subcategories, and they'll appear on the list too.

*Income categories*—Select this if you're sure the transaction you are looking for was assigned one of the income categories.

*Expense categories*—Just the opposite of the above—select this if you're sure the transaction was assigned an expense category.

*Tax categories*—Some categories track information for taxes—you specify this when you set them up (see Chapter 5).

*No category (blank)*—The un-category—select this to narrow the search down to transactions which are not categorized.

**Payee.** Use this tab if you want to search by payee (you learn more about payees in Chapter 7). Your choices are All Payees (the default), Selected Payees, or No Payee (blank). The list box in this tab shows all the payees you've ever used in any of your registers. Choose Selected Payees, then click on the payees on the list that you want to select.

**Details.** The Details tab is a hodge-podge of transaction details. (Check out Figure 4.4 to see for yourself.) Here, you can specify a transaction type (Deposit, Check, Transfer, ATM, and so on), a check or transaction number range, and/or an amount range. You can also limit your search to Reconciled or Unreconciled transactions if you like.

**Fig. 4.4**

On the Details tab, you can specify a transaction type, status, number, or amount.

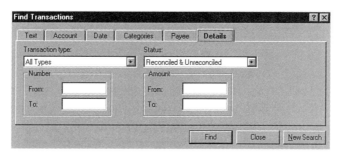

When you've entered as many criteria as you know about the transaction, click the Find button, and you're on your way. Presto, the transactions that match your criteria appear below the blanks, as shown in Figure 4.5.

**Fig. 4.5**
I was looking for all my deposits, and I found them; they're shown at the bottom.

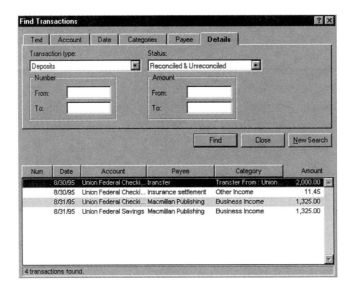

After you've got your list of found transactions, you can check out (and edit) any one of them—just double-click on it. An Edit Transaction window pops up with all the info for that transaction. But I'm getting ahead of myself here—editing a transaction is the subject of another section.

# How do I add a transaction?

You learned in Chapter 3 how to enter transactions into the register, and there's no separate procedure for inserting new transactions between existing ones. Really, there's no need. Why? Because your register automatically sorts transactions by date. If you want to insert a transaction between two others, just give it a date that's in-between the dates of the two you're inserting between, and Money will place the transaction in the right spot automatically.

# Can I change a transaction I've already entered?

The first step in editing a transaction is to find it. (You figured that out by reading the last section, though, right?) You can find it by eyeballing your register, or by using the Find procedure you just learned.

If you find the transaction on your own, you can edit right there in the register. To edit a transaction from the register, you can either double-click on it or single-click and then click the Edit button. (Or, you can right-click on the transaction and then choose Edit from the shortcut menu that appears.) The transaction's details appear on the tab at the bottom where you originally entered them. It looks just like when you entered the transaction, in Chapter 3. (Use Figure 4.6 to refresh your memory.)

**Fig. 4.6**
To edit a transaction from the register, double-click on it.

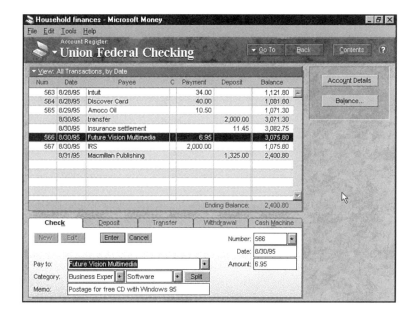

If you found the transaction by searching, it's listed at the bottom of the Find Transactions dialog box. Double-click on a transaction in that list, and a separate window pops up containing the info for that transaction, as shown in Figure 4.7.

**CAUTION** **When you edit a transaction in the Find Transactions list, as in** Figure 4.7, make sure that the account listed in the Account blank is the one you expected. You may have similar transactions in several accounts.

Either way, you can click in any blank and type your corrections. You can use the Delete and Backspace keys to remove individual characters, and use the arrow keys on the keyboard to move the cursor. Make your changes, then press Enter, or click the OK (see fig. 4.7) or Enter (refer to fig. 4.6) buttons.

**Fig. 4.7**
When you double-click on a transaction you found, it opens in the Edit Transaction window.

 **TIP** The one thing you can't change about a transaction is its transaction type. For instance, if you entered an ATM withdrawal as a check, you'll need to delete it and reenter it as the right type. You'll learn to delete transactions later in this chapter.

# Wait! This transaction belongs in a different account!

Moving a transaction to another account is as easy as any other edit you make to the transaction, as long as you're moving it to an account that you have set up in the same Microsoft Money file. (You'll learn about using more than one file in Chapter 9; usually you have only one file.)

 **CAUTION** You can't select more than one transaction at a time to move, no matter which method you're using. Sorry, but they have to be done one at a time.

How to do it? There are a couple of ways.

You may have already guessed one of them if you took a close look at Figure 4.7. That's right, the key is the Account drop-down list. When you edit a transaction directly from the register, you don't get to choose which account it goes in; it goes in the active account. However, when you find transactions with the Find Transactions command, it looks for transactions across all accounts—you aren't tied to just one.

Therefore, when you edit a transaction you've found (see fig. 4.7), there's a drop-down list for Account that tells which account the transaction is in. To move the transaction to a different account, just open this drop-down list and choose a different one. Then click OK and it's taken care of.

The other way to move a transaction is even more straightforward. Start in the account register for the account that contains the transaction. Select the transaction by clicking on it, then choose Edit, Move to. (Or, right-click on the transaction, and select Move to from the shortcut menu that appears.) A Move Transaction dialog box opens (see fig. 4.8), listing all your accounts; just click on the one you want to move the transaction to, then click OK. It's moved. You can open the account register for the destination account to check if you like.

**Fig. 4.8**
Use the Move Transaction dialog box to shuffle transactions between one account and another.

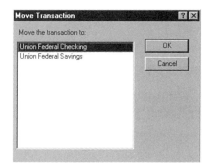

**CAUTION**    **Make sure that the transaction you're moving really belongs in the** different account—if you move transactions just to practice, move them back when you're done experimenting. Otherwise, when your bank statement comes you'll have a terrible time figuring out why your account doesn't balance.

# Deleting versus voiding: what's the difference?

There are two ways to cancel a transaction, and each method is good for a certain circumstance. Unfortunately, most people don't understand the difference between the two.

*Deleting* is for transactions that were a mistake from the first—like data entry errors. If you enter a transaction into the wrong account, for example, and you didn't want to move it to the correct account right away, you could delete that transaction and then reenter it later in the correct account. Or let's say you entered a few bogus transactions just to practice in Chapter 3, but they don't have any correlation to any real transactions you've ever made. Delete these and you'll never see any trace of them again.

*Voiding* is kind of like taking a big rubber stamp and a red inkpad, and stamping VOID (or UNDO, or CANCEL) on a contract or bill. With voiding, the transaction stays in your register, so you can be reminded that it existed, but its income or expense isn't reflected in your account balance, and the transaction won't affect any of your reports or charts (explained in Chapter 11). You might void a check that you started to write, then made a mistake on and tore up. That way, if you ever wonder what happened to check number 4122, you will be able to look at your register and see that it was voided. (No, it wasn't stolen.)

## Deleting a transaction

To delete a transaction, just select it, then press the Delete key on the keyboard, or select Edit, Delete. When asked if you want to delete the transaction, click Yes. It's gone immediately.

 **CAUTION** **If you delete a transaction that has been reconciled (or voided),** you'll get a warning message telling you this. Click OK to delete the transaction anyway. Be careful, however; deleting a reconciled transaction could mean creating an error in your account balance. (If your account balance matched your bank's balance for your account, and you delete a reconciled transaction, it will no longer match.)

## Voiding a transaction

Personally, I don't like voiding, because I don't like being reminded of my mistakes. I would rather be confused than depressed about my human fallibility. However, if your ego is less fragile than mine, you will appreciate the ability to void a transaction.

When you void a transaction, it stays in your register, but the word VOID appears in the balance column, as in Figure 4.9.

 **Q&A** *If I stop payment on a check, should I void it or delete it in my register?*

I would definitely recommend voiding it. That way, you'll be able to look back at your register later and remember the incident.

**Fig. 4.9**
Voided transactions don't leave—they just negate the monetary value so that they don't affect your balance.

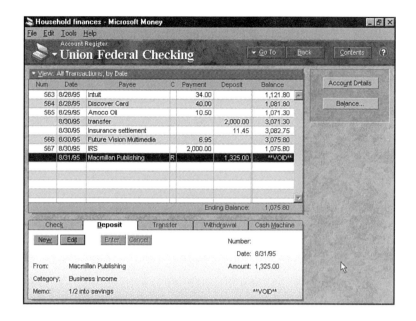

To void a transaction, select it in the register, then select Edit, Mark As, Void. As you can see in Figure 4.9, \*\*VOID\*\* appears in the Balance column, letting you know that this transaction doesn't affect the balance.

The nice thing about voiding is that, unlike deleting, it's reversible. Just repeat the procedure to un-void the transaction. (Edit, Mark As, Void). Void is a toggle that turns on or off each time you select it. When you're un-voiding a transaction, you'll get an error message telling you that this transaction is reconciled; click OK to get past it.

**Q&A    *What's that R doing in the C column in Figure 4.9?***

The C column in your register means 'cleared," and 'R stands for 'reconciled." You'll learn more about reconciliation in Chapter 8. For now, all you need to know is this: when you void a transaction, Money marks it as being reconciled. Why? It's for your own convenience, so it doesn't show up in the list of unreconciled transactions that you'll work with when you sit down to reconcile your account, which we'll cover in Chapter 8.

# Slicing it Up With Categories and Classifications

● **In this chapter:**

● What's a category, and why should I use one?

● Roll-your-own categories

● Creating a classification

● Okay, how do I apply these things?

*Categories and classifications require some extra planning, but you'll thank yourself later.* . . . . . . . . . . . . . . . . . . >

**M**y mother used to say, "don't lump people together—everyone's an individual." Rather than relying on religion, politics, race, or bank accounts, she insisted on getting to know each of my friends personally before passing judgment on them. (This was in the 1960s and '70s; she was way ahead of her time.)

Well, that philosophy is great when dealing with people, but when dealing with your transactions in Microsoft Money, lumping things together based on some criteria or other is one of the handiest things you can do. By grouping transactions under certain classifications or categories, you can get a big-picture look at your financial situation.

# What are categories, and what can they do for me?

You've already seen categories (and subcategories too) at work in Chapters 3 and 4. When you enter or change a transaction, you have the opportunity to select a category and subcategory for the transaction, and to even split a transaction among several categories. But what is this category thing all about, really?

**Categories** are a method of sorting out your transactions according to their purpose. Think about it—every transaction has a purpose—you don't just give away your money for no reason, and you certainly don't get income out of the clear blue sky. For instance, your income might include salary, inheritance, lottery winnings, alimony, an insurance settlement, and probably some other categories too. Your expenses probably include rent or mortgage, utility bills, food, clothing, and entertainment.

 *Plain English, please!*

**Subcategories** are just what they sound like: categories that are subordinate to other categories. For instance, under the Utilities category, you might have the subcategories of Telephone, Electricity, Gas, and Cable.

# They help you see where your money is going

By categorizing each transaction, you can see where your money is going, and where it's coming from. In Chapter 11, you'll learn about Money's reports and charts, which give you an easy-to-understand look at your finances broken down by categories. These reports and charts are one excellent reason to use categories; they show breakdowns of your finances based on certain categories. You can see from a report or chart, for instance, what percentage of your expenses fall into the Food category. Without categories, the reports and charts won't be nearly as useful or meaningful.

# They help you at tax time

In Money, you can designate certain categories as Tax-related. When you do this, the transactions in these categories appear on special reports that deal with taxes. For instance, if you categorize your income and expenses carefully, you'll be able to use a tax report to find out what amounts to enter on the various blanks of your income tax form at the end of the year. I categorize my charitable donations as such every time I write a check, and Money gives me a grand total for my donations on a tax report. I'll teach you later in this chapter how to tell Money that a certain category is tax-related. You'll get the full story on dealing with old Uncle Sam in Chapter 15.

# Let's set up some categories!

There are a couple of ways to set up categories. One is to do it "on-the-fly" as you enter transactions. I like this method because it ensures that I only create the categories that I'll really use.

Other people may prefer to set up all their categories and subcategories before they enter transactions (or before they enter any more). With this method, you can carefully plan your categories by looking at the complete list of existing ones and filling in the gaps for your own situation. This method also enables you to enter more detailed tax and description information about a category than the quicker "on-the-fly" method allows.

# Creating categories: the "categorize-as-you-go" method

Technically, you have already seen this way of setting up a category. In Chapter 3, as you were entering a transaction, you had the opportunity to type a new category and/or subcategory directly into the register. Let's review this procedure:

1 Open the account register, and begin a new transaction. (Refer to Chapter 3 if needed.)

2 Move the cursor to the Category blank (click there or use the Tab key), and type a new category. Then press Tab to move to the next blank.

**TIP** **When inventing names for your categories, be as descriptive as** possible. The more precisely you categorize your transactions, the more useful your reports and charts will be. For instance, "Pay" is not the greatest category name, especially if you have more than one job. "Salary XYZ Corp." is better.

3 Before the cursor moves to the next blank, a dialog box appears asking for information about the new category. If you're entering a category (in the left blank), Figure 5.1 appears; if you're entering a subcategory (in the right blank), Figure 5.2 appears.

**Fig. 5.1**
Create a new category for either income or expense transactions from this dialog box.

*Type in a new category name here*

*Click here to include the category on tax reports.*

**Fig. 5.2**
Use this dialog box if the category you're creating is a subcategory—subordinate to another category.

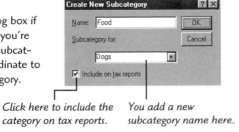

*Click here to include the category on tax reports.*

*You add a new subcategory name here.*

**4** Verify the name you typed for the category; it appears in the Name blank. Change it if needed.

**5** If creating a new category (see fig. 5.1), choose Income or Expense to indicate which type of transaction will use this category. If creating a subcategory, choose which category it should be subordinate to from the Subcategory for: drop-down list (see fig. 5.2).

**CAUTION**    **You can't use the same category for both income and expenses.** However, you can create two categories with similar names, one for income and one for expense.

**6** Select the Include on tax reports check box if this category is tax-related.

**7** Click OK or press Enter. The category is created, and you can finish entering the transaction.

**Q&A**    ***How do I know if a category should be tax-related?***

See Chapter 15 for full info on this, but in general, a category is tax-related if you can deduct it on your taxes (like charitable contributions), or if you owe taxes on it (like income).

**Q&A**    ***How do I enter more specific tax information about a category, such as the tax form it's associated with?***

That's part of the Details info for the category, and you can set or change it by displaying the list of categories, clicking on the category, and then clicking the Details button. Don't worry about that now, though—we'll cover it later in this chapter, under "Details, details, details."

# Creating categories: the careful planning method

If you're one of those people who likes everything neat and orderly, you may want to create all your categories at once, with some master structure in mind.

To do this, you'll need to work with the Payees and Categories screen. From the Contents screen, click on Payees and Categories. Then on the screen that appears, click the Categories button, and you'll see the display in figure 5.3.

If your display doesn't look like this one,
make sure this button is selected.

**Fig. 5.3**
Get an aerial view of
your categories from
this screen.

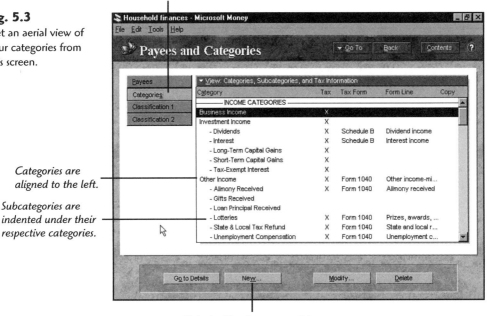

Categories are
aligned to the left.

Subcategories are
indented under their
respective categories.

Click the New button to add a
new category or subcategory.

From here, follow these steps to create a new category or subcategory:

**1** If you want to create a subcategory, first click on the category that it
should be subordinate to. If you're creating a category, it doesn't matter
which category is selected when you start.

**2** Click the New button. The New Category or Subcategory dialog box
appears.

**3** Click on one of the option buttons:

  • Click **Category** if you are creating a new category.

  • Click on **Subcategory for *Category*** if you are creating a
    subcategory of the category listed.

**CAUTION** **If the category listed next to Subcategory for is not the one you** wish to use, click Cancel to end the procedure. Then make sure the category you want is selected and start over.

**4** Type a name in the <u>N</u>ame blank, then click Next.

**5** If you're creating a category, select Income or Expense to indicate what type of transactions will use this category. Then click Next. (If creating a subcategory, you won't see this dialog box.)

**6** Click Yes or No to choose whether the category is tax-related. Then click Finish.

When you've finished this procedure, the new category or subcategory appears on this list. It'll also appear on the drop-down list of categories or subcategories whenever you're entering a transaction.

**TIP** **You can right-click on any category or subcategory to get a** shortcut menu. On this menu, you'll find commands equivalent to the four buttons at the bottom of the Payees and Categories screen. It's just another way to issue the commands—entirely optional.

# How do I rename a category?

You might want to change the name of a category to make it more accurately reflect the transactions you're using it with. For instance, you might start out with a category called "Dog Expense" but then you buy a cat too and want its expenses to be included, so you could change the category name to "Pet Expense."

Making name changes is easy; just select the category you want to modify, then click the Modify button. (Or, you can right-click on the category and select Rename from the shortcut menu that appears.) A dialog box opens up. From here, you can enter a new name (in the New Name text box), and (if it's a category, rather than a subcategory), change whether the category is Income or Expense related.

*How do I make other changes to the category, such as whether or not it appears on the tax reports?*

You can make lots of detail-level changes like that to a category through the Category Details screen. Stay tuned to the very next section for full info about that.

## Details, details, details

You might have noticed in the Payees and Categories screen (refer to fig. 5.3) that some categories have more information about them than others. For instance, notice that Dividends not only has an X in the Tax column, but it also lists the tax form that the dividends are reported on (Schedule B) and the line on that form (Interest Income). Quite naturally, you may be wondering how that information got there.

The pre-designed categories that Money sets up for you when you create your accounts all have this extra detail information automatically. You can change it, or add details to the categories you create yourself, on the Details screen.

To see the Details screen for a particular category, click on the category (or subcategory) to select it, then click the Go to Details button at the bottom of the screen. (Or, right-click on the category, then select Go to Details from the shortcut menu that appears.) A Category Details screen appears, in which you fill in various details about the category. See the page "Add more information about a category on the Details Screen," for the full scoop on using this screen.

# Add more information about a category on the Category Details screen

This is the Category Details screen for a category called Business Income that I set up earlier. Here's what you can do on this category details screen:

*You can choose whether or not the category appears on tax reports by selecting or deselecting this check box.*

*You can specify which Tax Form and Form Line the category is associated with. Chapter 15 has more information about taxes.*

*If you file multiple copies of the form you chose, you can indicate which copy this category belongs with in the Form Copy blank. (See Chapter 15 for more details.)*

*You can add subcategories by clicking the New button, typing a name, then clicking OK. (This isn't available when viewing the details for a subcategory.)*

*You can rename the category. Just click the Rename button and type a new name, then click OK.*

*You can add an abbreviation for the category in the Abbreviation blank. Then, when you enter transactions, you can just type the abbreviation and Money will fill in the category for you.*

*When you're finished working with the category's details, click here to return to the Payees and Categories screen.*

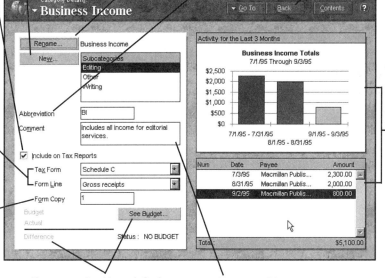

*You can also see a graph of the category's activity for the last 3 months (a grand total of all the transactions that used it), and see a list of each transaction, too.*

*If you are using Money's Budget feature (see Chapter 14), you can access your budget by clicking this button. If any budget information is set up for this category, it appears at the bottom of the screen, to the left of this button.*

*You can add comments or notes about the category here, in case someone else will be using the program, or to remind yourself.*

# How do I get rid of a category?

Deleting a category from the list is easy. You have to do it from the Payees and Categories list, though; you can't do it on-the-fly as you're working in the account register.

To delete a category, just select it and click the <u>D</u>elete button. If the category has subcategories, you'll get a warning that they'll be deleted, too. If this is okay, click OK to continue.

If some transactions use this category or subcategory, a dialog box will appear asking you to choose a new category to convert those transactions to (see fig. 5.4). Open the drop-down lists in this dialog box and select a new category (and subcategory if desired), then click OK, or leave them blank to have no category assigned to the transactions.

**Fig. 5.4**
If some transactions use the category, you'll need to assign them to another category here.

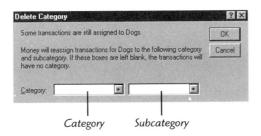

Category    Subcategory

**CAUTION** **If there are no subcategories beneath the category you choose,** and it's not assigned to any transactions, you won't get any kind of warning; the category will just disappear, and you can't use the usual Edit, Undo to get it back. You have to re-create it from scratch.

# What is a classification, and how do I work with it?

A classification is like a category, in that it's another way to divide up your transactions. What's the difference between categories and classifications? Well, in the previous section you learned that categories divide your transaction list up by purpose: you may have expense categories, for example, for Food, Rent, Utilities, and so on. A classification can divide transactions up in other ways—any that you choose. I know—that's not a very good definition, and it's probably still not clear to you what a classification can do. So let's look at an example.

Let's say you have four rental properties (houses I, II, III, and IV, for simplicity's sake) for which you pay the utility bills, and from which you receive income (rent). You might set up the following categories:

| Category | Subcategory |
| --- | --- |
| Rent | |
| Utility | Gas |
| Utility | Electric |
| Utility | Water/Sewer |
| Repairs | Parts |
| Repairs | Labor |

These categories will work great to keep track of the money you spend in each category—for example, they'll let you know exactly how much money you pay to the electric company every month. But what if you wanted to keep track of the expenses and income for a single house? You could create a separate account, but that seems excessive, especially since all the money for the houses comes out of one general business checking account.

A better way is to create a classification called Properties, and then set up four entries in it, one for each house. Then for each transaction, you could specify not only the category/subcategory, but also which property the transaction pertains to. It might look something like this:

Classification 1: Properties

House I

House II

House III

House IV

So, for example, for a new gutter for house I, you would choose House I from the Properties drop-down list, then select Repairs:Parts as the category and subcategory.

Keep in mind, that classifications are entirely optional; lots of people go through their entire financial lives without ever needing one. They're simply another way of dividing up your transactions.

**TIP**   **Money lets you have up to two classifications in use at once, so** you could also add a second classification if you wanted. However, there are not many financial situations that would really warrant two classifications; most breakdowns can be achieved with a combination of one classification and many categories.

**Q&A**   In Chapter 3, when we entered transactions, there was no blank for classification, but that's only because we hadn't set up any classifications yet. After a classification has been set up, an extra line appears in the form when entering a transaction, on which to enter the classification. You'll see this up-close later in this chapter (check out Figure 5.7 if you want to see it now).

# Create-your-own classifications

You can create up to two classifications, as I said earlier, but most people will only ever need one. (Actually, most people will never need any, but don't let that stop you from experimenting with it.)

There are a couple of steps for setting up classifications. First, you create the classification itself, and then you fill it with the possible values for that classification. Ready? Let's do it.

## Step 1: creating the classification itself

To create a classification, start at the Payees and Categories dialog box that we've been working with in this chapter, then click the Classification 1 button. When you do so, the Add Classification dialog box appears (see fig. 5.5).

**Fig. 5.5**
The first step in creating a classification is deciding what you're going to classify.

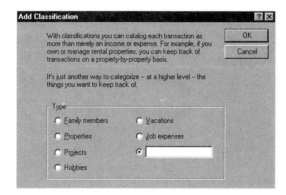

Click on one of the helpful suggestions in the Add Classification dialog box (I'm going to go with Properties, for the rental properties example), or type your own in the blank text box. Then click OK, and you're back at the Payees and Categories screen, just like nothing happened. But wait—something did happen. The Classification 1 button is now replaced with a button for the classification you just created.

**Fig. 5.6**
The Classification 1 button is replaced by the new classification you've chosen.

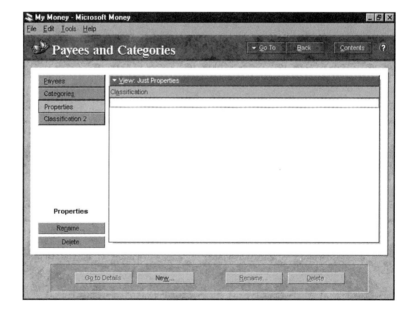

## Step 2: giving the classification some values

No, not family values. (Unless, of course, you picked Family as the classification type back in figure 5.5, in which case you've just been subjected to a very bad pun.)

 **TIP** **Just as you can add new categories on-the-fly as you enter**
transactions, you can also enter new values for your classification then, from the register, instead of doing it now.

Click the New button to add a value to your classification. You'll get a dialog box that's name matches the type of classification you set up. For example, since I'm doing properties, mine says New Properties or Sub-Properties (see Fig. 5.6). If you chose Family, it might say New Family or Sub-Family. You get the idea. Type the name for the new classification, then click OK. You'll see the new classification on the on-screen list.

 *Plain English, please!*

A classification isn't equivalent to a category. Rather, a single classification is like a whole separate list of categories, and each of the items on that list is a value. For instance, in the Property classification, you might have several values: House I, House II, House III, and so on.

**Fig. 5.7**
Adding a new value to the classification is as simple as filling in the blank.

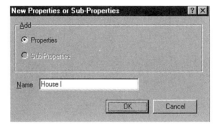

 **TIP** **After you've set up a classification, you can create**
subclassifications, just like subcategories. For instance, if each of my houses had two apartments, I could have subclassifications for each apartment under each building. Just select the classification that the new one should be subordinate to before you click the New button, then select Subclassification from the dialog box that appears.

# How do I apply categories or classifications transactions?

Now comes the moment that the whole chapter has been in preparation for—using the categories and/or classifications in a transaction. You've already seen this—sort of—in Chapter 3, but let's do it up right.

Open the Account register and begin entering the transaction. Next to the Category line there are two drop-down lists. In the left one, select the category. In the right one, select the subcategory.

If you have set up any classifications, there will be a drop-down list box immediately below the Category line for it. For instance, in figure 5.7, notice mine is labeled Properties because that's the name of my classification. Open the drop-down list and choose the value for the classification. Continue entering the transaction as usual.

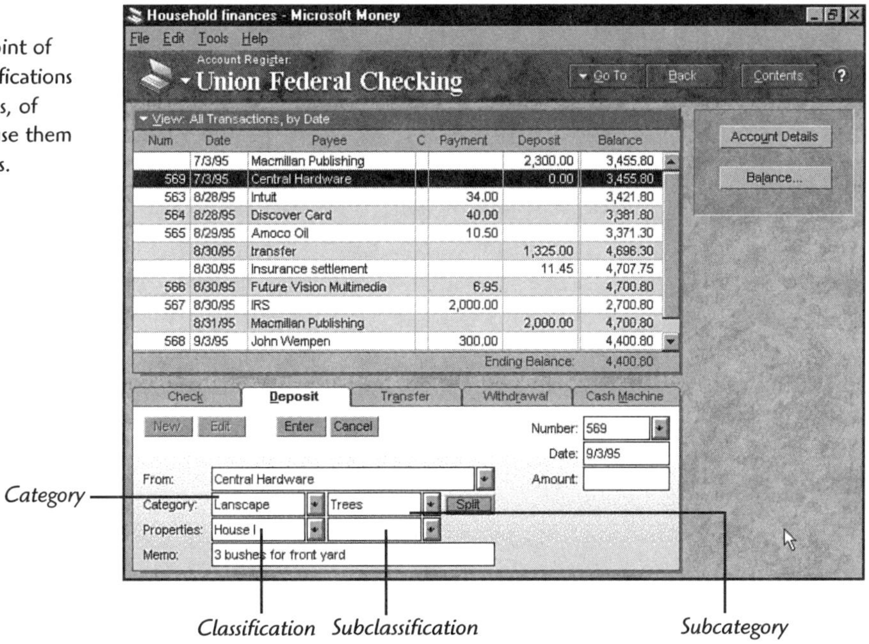

**Fig. 5.8**
The whole point of creating classifications and categories, of course, is to use them in transactions.

Category

Classification    Subclassification          Subcategory

Voila! Your transaction is sliced, diced, labelled, and pureed. (Okay, maybe not pureed.) It may not seem like much at the moment, but when you get to the reports and charts in Chapter 11, or to dealing with taxes in Chapter 15, you're going to be very, very glad that you took the time.

# 6

# Easy Hard-Copy: Printing Checks

● **In this chapter:**

- **Letting Money print checks—the pros and cons**

- **How do I get a supply of "printable" checks?**

- **The big event: printing the checks**

- **What if I made a mistake?**

*Does your hand cramp thinking of paying the monthly bills? Then let Money write out all those checks for you. All you do is sign your name . . . . . . . . . . . . . . . . . . . . . . . . . . . . ▶*

t may have occurred to you as you were entering all those transactions into Money in Chapter 3: "Hey, I'm writing out every
check twice! Once by hand, in my checkbook, and then once in Money, to
enter it into the account register."

It's true—if you're writing checks with your good old checkbook, you're
going about it the hard way. By letting Money print your checks for you,
you can enter each transaction once—and only once—and Money uses the
information both on the check it prints and in the register it keeps.

"Sounds too good to be true!" you're probably thinking. "What's the catch?"
Well, there's always a catch, of course. You can't feed your regular checks
into the printer—you have to purchase special checks from Microsoft, and of
course they're more expensive than your normal checks. A *lot* more expensive. Is the convenience of having Money print your checks worth the extra
expense? Well, take a look at the process in this chapter, and then decide for
yourself.

 **TIP** **You may be able to find a manufacturer who will sell you cheaper**
checks that will work just as well with Microsoft Money. Most check sizes
are fairly standard among financial programs that print checks (like Quicken,
Money, Managing Your Money, and so on). Check with your bank to find
out if their check printer offers these checks at a cheaper price than
Microsoft.

# Reality check: should you use Money to print checks?

Having Money print your checks for you is a great convenience—in fact,
it's the feature that a lot of people buy the program especially to use. Just
imagine—no more hand cramps from writing all those checks each month.
All you have to do is sign your name to the neatly printed check. No more
spelling errors, or having checks returned because the bank couldn't read
your writing, or because you left a line blank by accident. It's a real dream
come true, for a lot of people.

But unless you have lots of expendable income to burn, stop a minute and
let's have a reality check. Microsoft Money is a really inexpensive program,

but some of the goodies that you can use with it, such as the special checks for printing and the online banking services, can be very pricey. In fact, the prices for the checks that will work with Money are as much as 10 times higher than the price of regular checks. (We'll get into the exact costs later in the chapter.)

 **TIP** **Online bill paying is another way to avoid writing out checks by** hand. There are some extra costs involved with it too, but they're partially offset by not having to buy stamps to mail your bills. If you're interested in the online banking services, check out Chapter 12.

This practice of marketing free or very inexpensive software and then charging richly for the accessories is not really mercenary—it's just good business sense, and a pretty common practice. For instance, you've probably received free software from online services like America Online and Prodigy, with which you can connect to those services. It's not that the software is worthless—it's great software! The online service companies give it away free so that you'll sign up for their service, and they'll recoup the cost of the software through the fees you pay for using their service.

# What should I expect to pay for checks?

By the time you read this, the exact prices may have changed, but here's a rough look at what you'll expect to pay for checks. For the latest brochure and prices, call 1-800-432-1285.

There are two check designs available: Basic Value and Standard. The main difference is that the Basic Value check has a plain border around it, and only comes in blue, while the Standard has a fancier border, and comes in blue, green, or burgundy.

Of course, all your checks are printed with your name, address, phone number (if you want it), and checking account number, plus your bank's name, address, phone number, and ID number. You can get a monogram or graphic on either design.

Checks are sold in quantities of 250, 500, 1000, and 2000. The cheapest checks are the wallet size. Here are the prices as of late 1995 for regular, single-sheet wallet-size checks (suitable for laser or inkjet printers). These checks are 6"×2 5/6" each, and come three to a page.

| | 250 | 500 | 1000 | 2000 |
|---|---|---|---|---|
| **Basic Value** | $41.50 | $56.50 | $75.50 | $114.00 |
| **Standard** | $48.50 | $65.95 | $87.95 | $132.00 |

They also sell form-feed checks that are suitable for dot-matrix printer use, at approximately the same prices listed above.

If you need multi-part checks (for instance, to keep carbon copies for your reference), these are available too—of course, they cost more. Also available: business size checks (larger than wallet size: 8 1/2"×3 1/2"), and voucher checks (the kind that businesses use to itemize what a check is for). All of these cost more than the wallet size checks, as you might expect.

You can also order envelopes that are custom-sized to exactly fit the various types of checks. This is totally optional—any envelope works fine to mail your payment, and most bills come with preaddressed envelopes anyway. But if you're the type of person who likes to have an orderly matched set of everything (for instance, matching stationery, envelopes, and sealing wax), you may want to purchase envelopes too. They're rather expensive, as you might expect: about $30 for 250 of them.

# How to get your checks

If you're in a hurry, the best way to get checks is to call 1-800-432-1285. Have a deposit slip from your checking account ready, because you'll need to read off the information to the operator. You'll also need a major credit card to order by phone.

Another speedy way to order is to fax or mail in an order form. With both mail and fax, you fill out an order form, which you might prefer to reading off all your information over the phone. If you mail your order form, you can pay by check (no credit card needed.)

**TIP** **If mailing in your form, it's best to include one of your checks or a** deposit slip from your current checking account, to ensure that you don't make an error copying the numbers onto the order form.

Where do you get an order form? There's one included with Money. You can access it by selecting <u>H</u>elp, <u>O</u>rdering Checks. Click the line at the bottom of the help screen labeled **Click here to order checks**. Then, in the Ordering Microsoft Money Checks screen that appears, click on the line that says **Click here to open a Microsft Money checks order form**. The order form opens in Microsoft Word (if you have it) or WordPad. Fill it out on-screen, or print it out and fill it out by hand, then fax it to 800-531-1931, or mail it to:

Microsoft Money

Checks Box 64181 St.

Paul, MN 55164-0181

Personally, I hate to buy anything without considering all the options. That's why instead of using the order form in Money, I called 800-432-1285 and requested a brochure. In about a week, I got an attractive color brochure in the mail with the current prices and an order form. I also requested sample checks, so I could see what I was ordering.

# The big event: Printing the checks

Normally, when you enter a check into your register, you enter a check number in the Number blank of the Account register. If you want to print the check using Money, instead of entering a check number, open the drop-down list in the Number blank and select Print this transaction. When you click Enter, the check number will show Print, as shown in figure 6.1.

**Fig. 6.1**
This check is ready to
print.

*Notice the reminder here.*

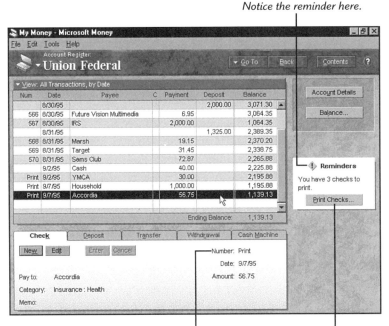

*Checks to be printed show "Print"
instead of a check number.*

*Click here when you're
ready to print.*

# Testing how your printer feeds paper

To avoid wasting valuable checks, you should be certain how your printer accepts paper. For instance, do you have to turn it upside down? Feed it in bottom-first?

To test without risk, take a blank sheet of paper and draw an upward-pointing arrow on one side. Then feed the sheet of paper into your printer, arrow up, point first, and print any document from any program (not necessarily Money). If the document comes out with the arrow on top, right-side-up, you know that you should feed your checks in exactly as you fed the test paper in. If not, the test sheet demonstrates how you

need to feed the paper (and thus, your page of blank checks) into the printer.

If you still aren't sure whether your checks are inserted properly into your printer, and you don't mind wasting a check, click the Print Test button to make sure that your checks will print correctly. One sheet of checks will feed through, with a voided check printed, and the Print Checks dialog box will reappear (see fig. 6.2), with 2 entered in the For a partial sheet text box, indicating that there are now 2 checks left on the sheet you just used. Tear off the void check, and insert the remaining two checks into your printer's manual feed.

After you've set "Print" as the check number for the transactions you want to print, you're ready to go. Follow these steps.

**1** Either click the Print Checks button next to the reminder in the register (refer to fig. 6.1), or select File, Print Checks. The Print Checks dialog box appears.

**2** Open the What type of checks will you print? Drop-down list, and choose the check style that you purchased. For instance, I bought Laser Wallet, so that's what I'll pick. Then click Next to continue.

**3** In the next Print Checks dialog box that appears (see fig. 6.2), click All Checks to print all the checks that have not been printed yet, or Selected checks to open a dialog box that will enable you to pick which ones are to be printed.

**Fig. 6.2**
On this screen you can specify exactly how you want your checks to be printed.

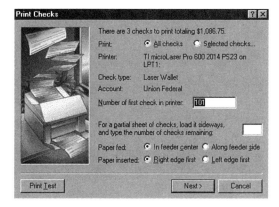

**4** If you choose Selected checks, the Select Checks dialog box opens (see fig. 6.3). Click the checks you want to print, then click OK to continue.

**5** Type the number of the first check in your printer in the Number of first check in printer text box. If you have printed checks before, Money remembers the number of the last check you printed, and suggests the next sequential number, but you can change it if the number isn't right. (After the checks have been printed, Money enters the actual numbers into the register.)

**Fig. 6.3**

If you don't want to print all the checks right now, select the ones you do want to print.

This check is not selected.

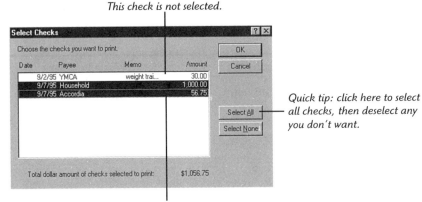

Quick tip: click here to select all checks, then deselect any you don't want.

These checks are selected.

6 If you want to print a partial sheet (for instance, you've already printed one check and torn it off, and now you have 2/3 or 1/3 of a sheet left), type the number of blank checks remaining on that sheet in the For a partial sheet text box. (You'll need to feed the partial sheet in sideways, manually; you won't be able to use the paper tray or document feeder.)

7 Select the option buttons that describe how your paper is positioned: In feeder <u>c</u>enter or Along feeder <u>s</u>ide, and <u>R</u>ight edge first or <u>L</u>eft edge first. (The print test I talked about earlier in this section will help you determine this.)

8 Click Next when you're ready to print, and wait for the checks to come out of your printer.

9 If the checks printed satisfactorily, click Finish, and you're done. If not, click <u>R</u>eprint.

10 If you're reprinting, a Reprint dialog box appears, very similar to the Select Checks dialog box of Figure 6.3. Click the checks you want to reprint, then click OK and return to step 9.

**Q&A** *I messed up the checks I was printing! Now what?*

If a check doesn't print correctly, just click the Reprint button (see step 9) and try again. Money automatically changes the check number for you to the next unused check number. For instance, if you messed up check 109, it enables you to reprint that same check on check 110 (see Figure 6.3).

If you don't discover the printing problem until after you've already clicked Finish (step 9), simply return to the register, open the Number drop-down list, and select Print this Transaction again. Then reprint the check as if you had not printed it yet.

# What else can I print?

With all the fuss about printing checks in Money, you might think that checks are the only thing Money prints. Not so. You can also print reports and charts. We'll cover this kind of printing in Chapter 11, where you learn about the reports and charts themselves, so stay tuned.

**Q&A** *Can I print my account register for a certain account?*

Yes, but it's considered a report. When you're in an account register, you can select File, Print, to get a Print Report dialog box. Click OK, and a report will print showing your register's transactions broken down by month, in date order. You'll learn how to customize the report to get different results in Chapter 11.

# 7

# Who Ya Gonna Pay?
# Setting Up Payments

● **In this chapter:**

- **Why should I bother setting up payees?**

- **Let Money memorize your recurring payments**

- **Payment reminders: Money does wake-up calls**

- **Automatic checking account deductions—never forget again**

*Sure, you can enter payments and payees on-the-fly, but with just a bit of extra effort now, you can save yourself hours in the long run.* . . . . . . . . . . . . . . . . . . . . . . . . . . . . . ●

**R**emember that story of the Ant and the Grasshopper that they told us as kids to frighten us into having a strong work ethic? The good and diligent Ant worked hard, preparing for the future. The lazy dilettante Grasshopper had a good time, heedless of the cold winter ahead. Then when winter came, the Ant was safe and cozy, and the Grasshopper was miserable. In some versions of the story, the Ant took pity on him—in other versions, the Grasshopper starved or froze to death. (Of course, both ants and grasshoppers die in the winter, no matter what—but that information ruins the whole lesson about the benefits of devoting your life to hard work, hmm?)

With MS Money, two philosophies reign: the Grasshopper faction says "I don't need to set anything up in advance! Whenever I need to enter a payee, or a category, or whatever, I'll just do it as I write the check." Those of the Ant persuasion, however, believe "I should set up all the payees I'm going to need right away, so that my job will be a lot easier and my information more complete when it comes time to enter transactions."

If you're a Grasshopper, you can just skip right over this chapter. It doesn't contain anything essential to your financial success. Meanwhile, all of us Ant-types are going to do a little planning and organizing. We'll whip our list of payees into shape, set up some automatic payments and payment reminders, and tell Money to memorize some of the payments we make each month. Then later, when we enter transactions again, we'll be a lot more efficient than those devil-may-care Grasshopper folks.

 *Plain English, please!*

> A *payee* is a financial jargon term for the person or organization who is receiving your payment. In Money, "payee" takes on a broader meaning—it refers to any person or business that a transaction involves, whether they are paying you or you are paying them. That's why, as you will see, people who you receive money from appear on the Payees list alongside the "real" payees, those you pay. **99**

# Why can't I just write a check and be done with it?

To be honest, there's no reason why you need to set up payees, if you're just doing enough record keeping to "get by." Plenty of people use Money as little more than a glorified calculator—they enter their transactions, and it keeps an accurate running balance. And that's fine.

Besides, Money generates a rough payee list automatically as you work. Whenever you write a check or enter a transaction, Money remembers the name you wrote in the Payee blank, and keeps it on file. The list of payees is nothing more than a complete list of everyone you've ever doled out your money to using MS Money.

 **TIP** **It's handy that Money records payee names, for a couple of** reasons. One is that you can look back and see how a certain name was spelled, so you don't have to look it up again. (This comes in handy when you're writing recurring payments to a company like Kreutzcampftz's Plumbing.) The other is that it can save you some typing. When you go to write another check to the same payee, and you start typing the payee name, Money searches the list. If it finds an entry that matches what you've typed so far, it enters it for you. So, assuming I didn't have any other payees that began with "Kreu," I could just enter those letters and Money would type out the rest of the payee, "Kreutzcampftz's Plumbing," for me.

But all of this is done automatically, without any special setup on your part. So why would you want to go to the trouble of setting up a payee formally, as you'll learn in the following section of this chapter? Here are a few reasons:

- You can enter the payee's address, so that it automatically prints on the check. This is great if you have to address an envelope for the payment—no more fumbling around with your files to find the correct mailing address.

- You can record the payee's phone number, so it's handy in case you have a question. Also, in the case of credit card companies, if you ever lose the card, the phone number that you would call to cancel the card is right there. You won't lose valuable time searching for it.

- You can have Money remember your account number, if you have one, for that payee. This can be valuable for your own records, and also for printing on the check. (Some companies ask you to write your account number on the check.)

- By entering payees upfront, you ensure that you don't have several variations of the same payee on your list. Since you can create some reports by payee (see Chapter 11), it's important that all payments to the same payee be recorded as such. You won't have separate entries for Amoco, Amoco Oil, and Amoco Credit Card, for instance, when they all refer to the same bill that you pay every month.

# Entering payees for future convenience

Well, I hope I've convinced you that entering payee information is a good thing. (If I haven't, you're probably not even reading this; you've probably either dozed off or skipped to the next chapter.)

There are two procedures I'd like to go over with you—entering new payees, and adding/modifying details for the ones you already have. If you have entered any transactions in Money (see Chapter 3), you probably have several payees already on your list. I do, as you can see in Fig. 7.1. You can see your own list by clicking the Payees and Categories button on the Contents screen, and then clicking the P̲ayees button if it's not already selected.

**Fig. 7.1**
After only a month of record keeping with Money, I've already accumulated quite a list of payees.

*Click here if Payees is not already selected.*

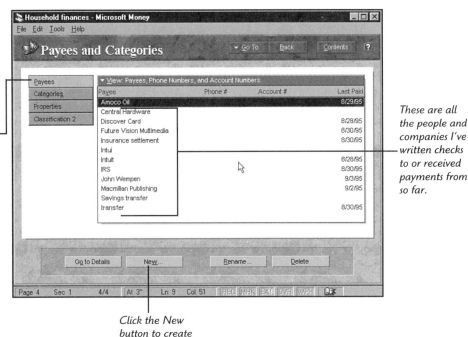

*These are all the people and companies I've written checks to or received payments from so far.*

*Click the New button to create a new payee.*

Although I've accumulated this list, there are a few more payees I would like to enter—people I sometimes write checks to, but haven't yet with Money. And of course, I have this long list of payees that don't have many details associated with them yet (you can see in figure 7.1 that the Phone # and Account # columns are blank).

## Entering a new payee

As I've said before, one way to enter a new payee is just to write a check to that person or organization, or deposit a check from them. Presto, the new payee shows up on the Payees and Categories list the next time you open it.

The other, more formal way, is to do the following:

**1** If you're not there already, click the Payees and Categories button on the Contents screen to go there. Click on the Payees button if it's not already selected.

**2** Click the New button. The Create New Payee dialog box appears (see fig. 7.2).

**3** Enter the name of the person or organization in the text box, then click OK. The new payee shows up on the list.

**Fig. 7.2**
The Create New Payee dialog box asks you for the one piece of information it needs: the Name.

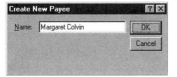

Pretty simple, eh? You were expecting the opportunity to enter phone numbers, addresses, and the like? Well, that's a separate step, as you'll learn in the next section.

## Entering or changing details about a payee

The real extra value of formally setting up a payee comes when you enter the details. On the Details screen, you can enter address, phone number, account number, and more, as shown in Figure 7.3.

**Fig. 7.3**
All the information I'll probably ever need for this payee is listed here in one convenient format.

*Click here to rename the payee.*

Just enter the information you know into the blanks.

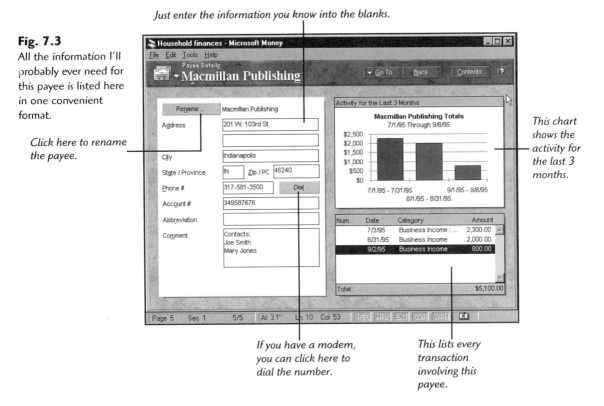

*This chart shows the activity for the last 3 months.*

*If you have a modem, you can click here to dial the number.*

*This lists every transaction involving this payee.*

To see the Payee Details screen for a payee (like the one in fig. 7.3), double-click on the payee's name in the Payees and Categories list, or click on the name and then click the Go to Details button at the bottom of the screen. (Or, right click the payee, then select Go to Details from the shortcut menu that appears.) From there, just enter any information you have into the appropriate blanks.

Besides the blanks to enter detail information, there are a few other features on the Payee Details screen:

- The Rename button enables you to rename the payee. If you want a payee to have a different name, it's better to rename it with the Rename button than to delete it and create a new one. Why? Because all the transaction history of that payee will be preserved under the new name. Any payments you made to the payee under its old name will continue to be recognized under the new name.

- The chart at the top right corner shows the amount you have paid to or received from the payee in the last three months. For instance, in Figure 7.3, I can see at a glance that the income from this source has been steadily declining!

- The transaction list at the bottom right corner lists every transaction I've ever had with this payee. Since I've only been using Money since July, there aren't very many on the list yet. When the list fills up the window, the scroll bar next to it will activate, and I'll be able to use it to scroll through the list.

# You're outa here! Deleting a payee

If you find that your list of payees is cluttered up with people or organizations that you did business with once, but will never deal with again, go ahead and delete them (it may make you feel better to have a tidy list).

Deleting a payee will not affect any transactions you have already entered—that payee will still appear for that transaction. (This is *unlike* categories, where deleting a category wiped it out from all existing transactions too.)

For instance, let's say you used to buy all your groceries at the local Big-Mart, but the store went belly-up and closed its doors. You will obviously never write another check to Big-Mart, so you might as well delete Big-Mart from your payee list.

## Dialing your phone with Money

If you have a modem connected to your primary phone line, you can dial the number listed in the Phone Number text box by clicking the Dial button. You might want to place a quick call to your credit card's company, for example, to discuss a bill that's due.

Money uses the Phone Dialer feature of Windows 95 to dial the phone, but it happens behind the scenes, so you don't have to open Phone Dialer yourself. Just click the Dial button in the Payee Details screen. You'll hear your phone dialing (through your modem's speaker). When you see the Call Status dialog box (shown below), lift the telephone receiver and click the Talk button.

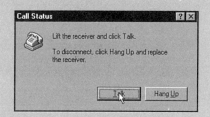

To delete a payee, select it from the Payees and Categories screen, then click the Delete button. You'll get a message asking you if you really want to delete it, and reassuring you that the deletion won't affect past transactions. Click Yes, and it's out of there.

**CAUTION**   **Be careful! Make sure you really want to delete a payee before** you do it. You can't get the payee back once it's been deleted; you have to recreate it. And although previous transactions will still show the old payee, even if you create a replacement with exactly the same name, the old transactions won't show up as related to the new payee.

# Making Money memorize your payments

If you have lots of payments that you make on a regular basis, like mortgage, car payments, or gym dues, you'll appreciate Money's Payment Calendar feature. If you set up a loan with Money's New Loan Account Wizard (in Chapter 2), you had the opportunity to create a scheduled payment at the end of the setup process. If you did so, you already have a scheduled payment!

Like a wake-up call in a hotel, a scheduled payment helps you meet your obligation. It reminds you five days in advance of the due date, and will even print the check for you, or make the payment via modem. Believe me, it's a lot better than tacking up a Post-it note reminder on your refrigerator and hoping it doesn't fall off!

**TIP**   **If you want to be reminded earlier or later than 5 days in advance,** see the note at the end of this chapter.

The Payment Calendar is the place where all scheduled transactions are created and modified. To see it, click the Payment Calendar button on the Contents screen. Figure 7.4 shows my payment calendar. Notice that there's already a payment listed there, since I chose to have a reminder when I set up my mortgage loan in Chapter 2.

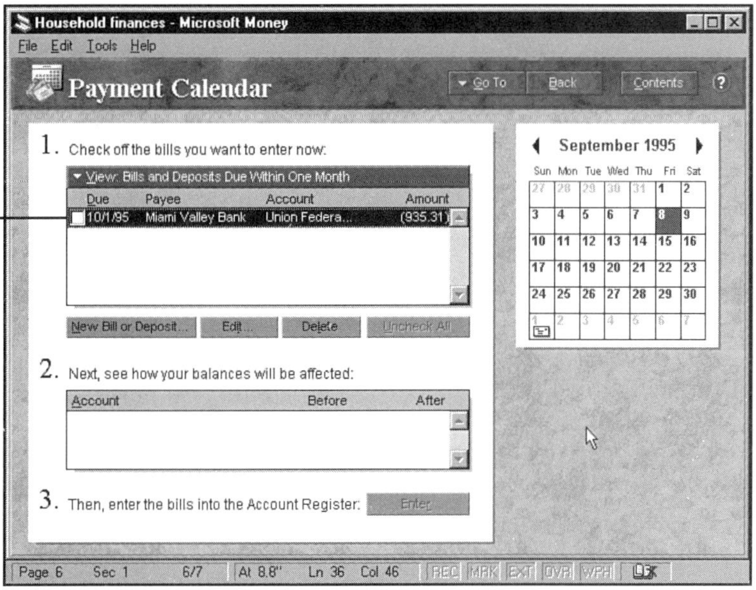

**Fig. 7.4**
The Payment Calendar helps you pay all your bills on time, to improve your credit rating!

*Here's a scheduled payment I set up earlier.*

# Let's create a new scheduled payment

Besides my mortgage payment, I have several other payments that I make regularly. For instance, I'm a member of the local YMCA, and they deduct my $35 monthly membership fee directly from my checking account. Before I started using Money, it was easy to forget to write down that automatic deduction each month in my checkbook, and I would invariably be $35 off each time I reconciled my bank statements. But no more—I created a scheduled payment to take care of it.

Here's how you can do the same thing:

**1** From the Payment Calendar, click the New Bill or Deposit button. The Create New Scheduled Payment dialog box appears (see fig. 7.5).

**2** Select the type of payment (Bill, Deposit, or Transfer), then click Next, and an editing screen appears, similar to the form you fill out in the account register. If you chose Bill or Deposit in step 1, you'll see a screen like the one in Figure 7.6; the transfer screen looks slightly different.

**Fig. 7.5**
The first step in creating a scheduled payment is to choose which type you want: Bill, Deposit, or Transfer.

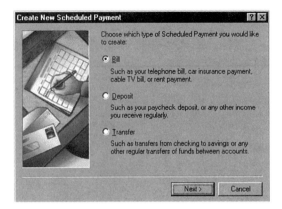

**Fig. 7.6**
When you enter a transaction here, it gets placed on the Payment Calendar. The blanks are all the same as in your account register.

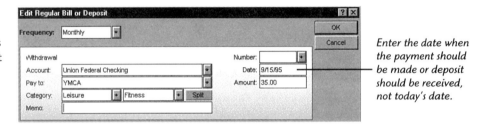

*Enter the date when the payment should be made or deposit should be received, not today's date.*

3 Enter the transaction details, just as you would in your account register. By default the date is today's date, but you'll want to change it to the date on which the transaction should happen (in the future).

4 Click OK when you're finished. The transaction appears on the list (see fig. 7.7), and a little envelope shows on the calendar to indicate that a payment is due that day.

*Click here to open a drop-down list that can change your view of this listing.*

**Fig. 7.7**
The new payment shows up in two places—as a transaction on the list, and as a symbol on the calendar.

*Here's some information about the new transaction.*

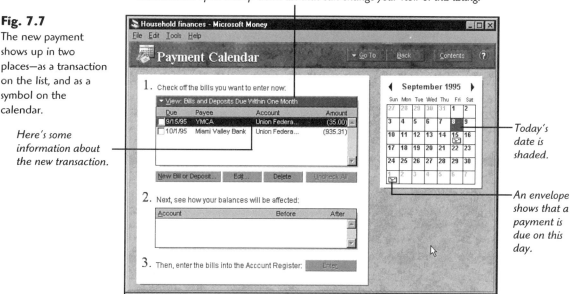

*Today's date is shaded.*

*An envelope shows that a payment is due on this day.*

# How do I tell Money it's okay to pay the bill?

Money will remind you five days before a payment is due. It's nothing too obtrusive—certainly nothing as jarring as a telephone wake-up call out of a dead sleep. Instead, there will just be a little message over the Payment Calendar button on the Contents screen, telling you which payment is due. Figure 7.8 shows an example.

**CAUTION**  Here's something important to remember—unless you're using online bill paying, the payment isn't automatically made just because you've entered it into Money. You must remember to write the check with your paper checkbook, or to print the check using Money's checks (see Chapter 6).

When you see that reminder message, that's your cue to open up the Payment Calendar and authorize Money to pay the bill. Money doesn't pay the bill automatically—it just reminds you to do so. Click the Payment Calendar button to go to that screen, and you'll see a check mark next to each payment that's due (see fig. 7.9). Money places that check mark there beside each payment that's due. You can pay payments that aren't quite due yet at the same time by manually adding the check mark next to them too.

**Fig. 7.8**
When a payment is
due, Money offers this
gentle reminder note.

*This payment is due.*

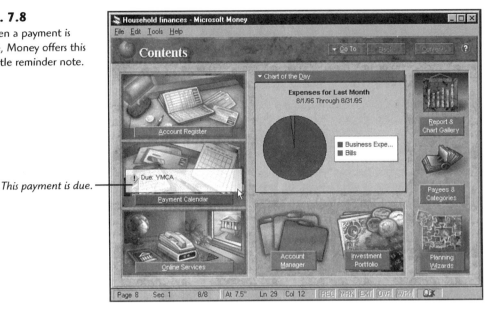

**Fig. 7.9**
When it's time to make
a payment, Money
shows you how it will
affect your account
balance.

*The payment has a
check mark here,
indicating it should
be paid.*

*This area shows
how your finances
will be affected by
the payment.*

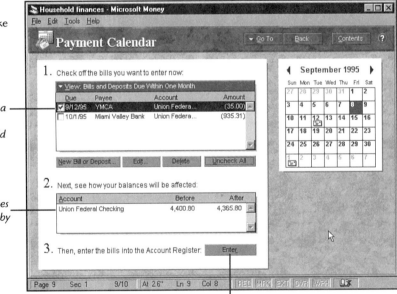

*When you're
ready to pay
the selected
bills, click the
Enter button.*

**TIP** **You can pay other payments that aren't due yet by clicking the** check box next to each one. This forces them to be "due" now. You might want to pre-pay a bill, for instance, if you're going to be out of town during the time when it'll be due.

Examine the effect on your account in the "2" area of the Payment Calendar screen, then click the Enter button when you're ready to make the payment(s). All of the payments with check marks beside them will be entered into your register as paid.

When you click Enter, for each bill you've selected you'll see an Enter Scheduled Payment dialog box. Make any last-minute changes to the transaction, then click the Enter button to enter it into your register.

 **Q&A** ***I want to be reminded earlier. Is there any way I can change that "five day in advance" thing?***

Sure. The five-day warning is just a default interval. You're free to change it to be warned earlier or later if you wish, or not at all.

Just select Tools, Options, and click the Payment Calendar tab. In the Bill Reminders section, change 5 to some other number, then click OK.

There are lots more setting changes you can make, not only for the payment calendar but for other parts of Money. See Appendix B to learn all about them.

# Part III: Routine Money Maintenance

**8**

# The Day of Reckoning: Reconciling an Account

● **In this chapter:**

- **The bank statement came today now what?**

- **Handling bank fees, service charges, and interest**

- **How do I add a transaction while I'm reconciling?**

- **Help! It didn't balance!**

*There's no reason to dread that bank statement anymore! With Money, account reconciliation can be simple and painless . . . . . . . . . . . . . . . . . . . . . . . . . . . . .* ⊙

**W**hen I hear the word "reconciliation" I always think of some horrible family feud that's being patched up, like in some made-for-TV movie—something like "A Walton's Mountain Easter," maybe. Jim-Bob and Jason finally see that their two points of view on what to do with the old sawmill aren't so far apart after all, and they hug and say "I love you" and the whole family sits down for an Easter feast. (Sniff.)

Actually, that definition is not far from what it means to reconcile a bank account, except there's no "I love you" and no homemade pie. When you reconcile an account, you sit down with the bank statement on one side of the table (figuratively) and your MS Money records on the other side, and you find out that the two sides aren't that different. You identify any points on which they disagree, figure out who is right, and iron out the differences, until both sides are in complete harmony.

 *Plain English, please!*

**Reconciling an account** means you check your record-keeping against the bank's, and try to come to an agreement about how much money is in the account. Another word that's sometimes used in place of reconcile is **balance**. **"**

Personally, I used to dread getting a bank statement in the mail, because it meant an hour or more of frustration. I would find all the math errors I had made over the previous month. The bank statement would get littered with scribbles and checkmarks from trying over and over to compare my poor, sloppy records with the bank's printout.

But with Money, reconciling is considerably easier, and takes only a few minutes. In this chapter, I'll show you step-by-step how to handle those incoming bank statements in Money, and save yourself a lot of time and frustration.

# Account reconciliation basics

If you've ever had a bank account, you've probably reconciled an account before. Here are the things you need to do:

- You compare each of the statement's withdrawals and deposits to the checks, withdrawals, deposits, and transfers that you have recorded (in your checkbook, passbook, in Money, or elsewhere), and mark each one as "cleared."

- You add any bank service charges and interest earned to your records, and adjust your balance accordingly.

- You figure out how to account for the differences between your records and the bank's, and make corrections in your records (or call the bank to dispute the statement) as needed.

- You enter a new, corrected balance into your records, or verify that your existing balance is accurate.

This is the exact same process that you go through when reconciling an account with MS Money—the only difference is that some of the steps are handled automatically for you. For instance, when you add service charges and interest, Money corrects your balance for you.

# Telling Money that you're ready to reconcile

When you receive a bank statement, it's usually for one particular bank account. (At least it's that way with my bank—if I have three accounts, they send me three separate statements, in three separate envelopes. Talk about a waste of postage!) That's why you start the reconciliation process from inside an account register.

The first step to reconciling an account is opening up its account register. You learned how to do that in Chapter 3, remember? Click the Account Manager button on the Contents screen, then double-click the account you want. Or, to open the most recently used account, click the Account Register button on the Contents screen.

From here, click the Balance button, and you're on your way. (Remember, as I mentioned earlier, Balance is another word for Reconcile.)

# Entering bank fees, service charges, and interest

The first thing you'll see when you click the Balance button is the Balance dialog box (see fig. 8.1). Here's where you take some basic information from the bank statement and enter it into the blanks:

*Enter the date from the bank statement here, not today's date.*

**Fig. 8.1**
When reconciling an account, you start by entering the ending balance off the bank statement, so you'll have something to compare your own ending balance to.

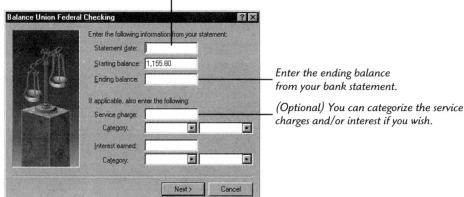

*Enter the ending balance from your bank statement.*

*(Optional) You can categorize the service charges and/or interest if you wish.*

- **Statement date**: Enter the date from your bank statement.

- **Starting balance**: Don't change this; it's the ending balance from last month's bank statement. If it's blank, fill it in with the starting balance from the current bank statement. If your starting balance is wrong, call your bank.

- **Ending balance**: Fill this in with the ending balance on your current bank statement.

- **Service charge**: If you were charged any service charges, enter them. You can categorize them if you want to.

- **Interest earned**: If you earned any interest, enter it. You can categorize it, too.

**TIP** **Although you can enter service charges and interest as separate** transactions in your account register, and then mark them as cleared, it's much more efficient to enter them on the Balance dialog box instead.

When you've entered all the requested information, click Next to move on to the next step: clearing individual transactions.

# Marking transactions "cleared"

After the preliminaries you just went through, you're ready to tackle the transactions.

You'll start from the balancing screen shown in Figure 8.2. Notice that it looks a lot like your account register, except the transaction entry forms have been removed, so you can see more of the transaction listing.

**Fig. 8.2**
Click in the C column for each transaction which matches one listed on your bank statement.

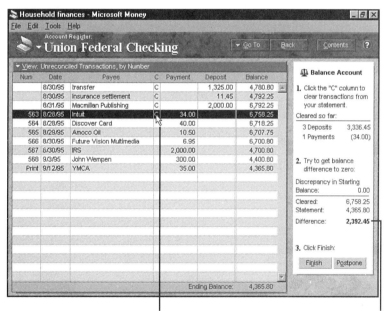

*Click in the C column to clear a transaction.*

*You can see how close you are to balancing here. When this number is 0.00, you're balanced.*

To reconcile the account, match up each transaction listed on your bank statement to a transaction in Money. When you find a match, click in the C column in Money to mark that transaction "cleared" and place a check mark next to that line on your bank statement with a pencil or pen.

# I missed one! Adding transactions while reconciling

If you find a transaction that appears on your bank statement, but not in MS Money, then one of two things is going on: either the bank made a mistake (less likely), or you forgot to enter a transaction into Money (more likely).

To enter a transaction while you're reconciling, just type it right into the register that you're using to clear the transactions. Click in the Num column on the first blank line and type the number, then press Tab to visit each column one-by-one, typing in the necessary data. When you're finished, press Enter and that transaction is added to your register without delay.

## Clearing versus reconciling a transaction

In general, both clearing and reconciling individual transactions refer to the same thing—matching up a transaction with the bank statement. However, if you open the Edit menu, and select Mark As, you'll see that there are four choices: Unreconciled, Cleared, Reconciled, and Void. If Reconciled and Cleared are the same thing, why are there two separate options?

Cleared is a temporary state, while Reconciled is more permanent. If you click in the C column on the balancing screen (see fig. 8.2), the transaction is marked as Cleared. It stays on the screen for you to see it, because it's cleared, but not yet

reconciled. When the entire bank statement has been balanced, and you click Finish to finish the process, each C will change to an R.

While balancing your account, do not change a transaction's status to Reconciled with the Edit, Mark As, Reconciled command. When you do so, the transaction is immediately marked as Reconciled and removed from the list you're working with. Then, since that transaction is no longer part of the balancing process you're going through, but needs to be, your account will not balance correctly.

**TIP** **Although they're not visible by default while you're balancing, you** can use transaction forms to enter the additional transactions if you wish. It's simply a matter of personal preference. Just click the colored bar across the top of the register or press Alt+V and select Transaction Forms from the drop-down list that appears.

# Finishing up...

When all the transactions on your bank statement have been matched to transactions in Money, the number next to Difference in figure 8.2 should be 0.00. Click Finish, and you're done. If it's not...well, see the final sections of this chapter for some things to check.

**TIP** **You'll want to file away your paper bank statements neatly, for** future use. For instance, if you apply for a mortgage, they'll want to see your last 3 months of bank statements, and they won't accept your MS Money record. They'll need copies of the actual papers you got from your bank.

### Can I come back to this later?

If you're in the middle of reconciling your account, and something comes up requiring that you exit from Money, or use a different Money feature, you can postpone your balancing act. Just click the Postpone button. Then later, start again by clicking the Balance button, the same as if you were doing it for the first time.

If you're coming back after postponing, you won't be able to change the service charges or interest, but everything else should be editable, including the ending balance. This brings up an excellent use for the Postpone feature—if you find after you started that you entered the ending balance incorrectly, you can Postpone the reconciliation, then change the ending balance when you return.

# Help! It didn't balance!

It's everyone's nightmare—the account that simply will not balance, no matter what you do. Before you tear your bank statements into little shreds and use it as confetti at your pity party, check the following things:

*Does the ending balance you entered match the one on your bank statement?* Check the number next to Statement on the balancing screen (refer to fig. 8.2). If it's not the same as your statement's ending balance, click Postpone, then click the Balance button again to return to reconciliation, but enter the correct ending balance this time.

*Does the starting balance match that of your bank statement?* In general, you shouldn't change the entry in the Starting balance blank (refer to fig. 8.1). It comes from the ending balance of last month's bank statement, or the starting balance you entered for the account if this is the first month. If there's a discrepancy, it may be a bank error, but if you're sure it's your own error, go ahead and change it.

*Did you enter all the transactions?* Every transaction on your bank statement must match a transaction in Money. You may need to add transactions that don't appear in Money but should. (Just type them in, as explained earlier in the chapter.) Note that the reverse is not true, though—you may have transactions that appear in Money, but not on your bank statement. That just means that those transactions have not been sent to your bank yet from the payee.

*Did you remember the service charges and interest?* Not all bank statements label these clearly. Look closely at your bank statement to see if these small additions or subtractions apply to your account.

*How about ATM withdrawals?* ATM transactions are very handy, but it's also easy to forget to record them in Money, since there's no check stub to help remind you. Go through your pockets and/or purse to see if you can find any unrecorded ATM receipts.

# Maybe SmartReconcile can help

You can also try Money's SmartReconcile feature to help you find the problem. SmartReconcile looks for likely transactions that you may have marked incorrectly, and reports them to you.

To use SmartReconcile, click the Finish button, even though your account does not yet balance. You'll see a Balance Account dialog box like the one in figure 8.3, warning you that your account doesn't balance (yes, you knew that) and asking what to do about it. Click the middle option (Use SmartReconcile to help find the error), then click Next.

**Fig. 8.3**
If your account doesn't balance, SmartReconcile may be able to help you find the problem.

What happens next depends on what SmartReconcile finds. If it can't find any obvious errors, it lets you know. Click OK to return to the Balance Account dialog box (refer to fig. 8.3) and then return to your reconciliation attempt by clicking G̲o back to balancing the account. Finally, click next.

If SmartReconcile finds a possible problem, it lets you know. Figure 8.4 shows a problem it found with my register. My mistake—I forgot to clear this transaction. Since it was for exactly the same amount as my balance was off by, SmartReconcile noticed it. To correct the problem, I can just click Yes. If SmartReconcile were mistaken, I could click No to tell it to keep looking for problems, or Cancel to tell it to give up.

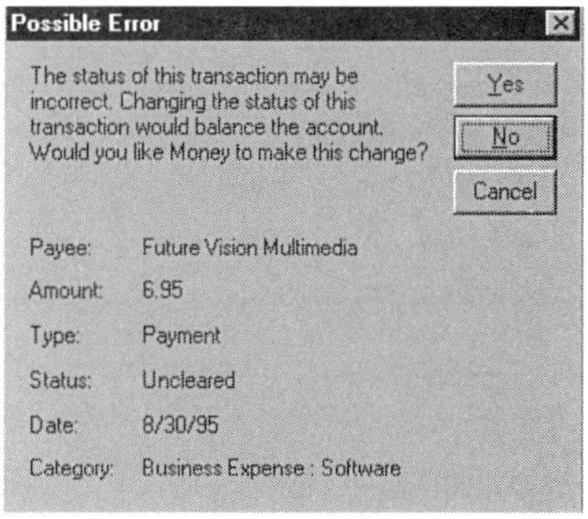

**Fig. 8.4**
SmartReconcile alerts you of a possible problem.

# I've tried everything, and it still won't balance!

There are only two things you can do if you've checked and double-checked every line and your account still won't balance.

The first is easy, and sort of a cop-out, but it may be the best thing if the difference is minor. That's to accept the bank's version of the story and make an adjustment in your register. To do this, click the Finish button even though the Difference is still not $0.00. You'll see the Balance Account dialog box shown in Figure 8.3. From here, click Automatically adjust the account balance. You can enter a category for the adjustment if you wish. Then click Next, and you'll get a message saying that an adjustment has been made. Click OK and you're done.

The second is to print out a copy of your Money account register (Chapter 6 explains how) and march down to your local bank. One of the bank representatives can go through your records with you and help identify where the discrepancy lies. You may even catch an error that the bank made!

 **TIP** **Here's my general rule for allowing discrepancies: if the** unsolvable error is in my favor, and is less than $50, I accept it and chalk it up to my careless recordkeeping. I do the same thing if the error is in the bank's favor and under $10. I figure my time is worth more than $10 an hour, and it would take me at least an hour to go to the bank and talk with someone.

# 9

# Account Management: Keeping Track of What You've Got

● **In this chapter:**

- **Should I even bother creating a new file?**

- **Keep it clean—archive your old transactions**

- **Changing the account type—without losing all your work**

- **How do I get rid of accounts I don't want anymore?**

*Even if your office file cabinet is a mess, your Money files will stay tidy and compact with a minimum of care . . . . . . .* ❯

**W**hen I was a kid, one of the great wonders of the household to me was Mom's file cabinet. It was a big dark-green metal thing, circa 1930, stuffed with file folders that contained everything from Appliance Warranties to Zoo Photos. The alphabetical order made things easy to find—if you could manage to pull out the folder you wanted from the tightly-stuffed drawer.

Hindsight is 20/20: as our family's paper trail grew, Mom should have spread the folders out between two filing cabinets, based on some logical division (like "Mom's Stuff" and "Dad's Stuff"). She could have also weeded out many of those folders by throwing away the booklets for the appliances that had long ago been discarded. As it was, her once-efficient system got out of hand.

And it can happen to you, too. Your Money file is like a file cabinet, and every account you have is like a file folder you store in that filing cabinet. You don't want Money stuffed full of bulky files like that old green filing cabinet of Mom's—it's too hard to find what you want.

In this chapter, you're going to learn some important "file cabinet" skills that will keep your organizational system tidy and easy to use. You'll learn to create a new file (like buying a new filing cabinet), how to archive certain transactions to trim down an overstuffed file, and even how to delete certain accounts entirely if they've outlived their usefulness.

# What's this about different files?

So far in this book, we've been talking mostly about transactions—your money comes in, your money goes out, and Microsoft Money keeps track of it all in neat folders called accounts. Seems like a pretty good system!

Back in Chapter 2, when you were creating your accounts, I mentioned that accounts are stored in files. All the accounts you've created and worked with so far have been in the Msmoney.mny file, which is the default storage location. One way of thinking about it is that all your folders (accounts) are contained in a single file cabinet drawer (a file).

*Plain English, please!*

> The .mny on the end of the Money file is its extension. Almost all files have an extension that tells which program they belong to. All Money data files have an .mny extension to show that they belong to the Microsoft Money program. **99**

Okay, it may seem a little confusing, but it's actually a very well-thought-out system. Since all your accounts are in one file, you can work seamlessly between them, transferring funds, borrowing from one account to pay another, creating reports based on all accounts together.

Sometimes, however, you might not want seamless connectivity between some accounts. In those cases, you're wise to create a brand-new Money file and build a new group of accounts to handle the separate finances ( you'll learn to do this later in this chapter).

# Why a new file might make sense

Why might you want a new file? Basically, any time you have two sets of finances that you want to keep absolutely separate. Some "for instances" might be:

- Parents might keep separate finances for each of their children. Each child might have a savings account for college at a bank and an "allowance" cash fund that the parent keeps.

 **TIP** An alternative to creating a separate file for each child is to create separate accounts in one file, and then use Classifications (see Chapter 5) to classify each transaction individually for the child it pertains to.

- If you are a trustee for a disabled person's finances (such as an elderly relative in a nursing home), it is very wise to keep the finances separate, to avoid confusing that person's income and expense with your own.

- If you run a small business or home business, it makes sense to keep the business records separated from your personal ones. Since most business expenses are tax deductible, and most home/personal expenses aren't, you'll want to set up separate categories for business and home—the business ones tax-related, the home ones not so.

- Most married people keep joint finances in a single file. However, if you prefer to keep your finances separate, it's perfectly legitimate to create a separate file for each person.

**TIP**   **If you are married or in a live-in relationship, and one person** owns more of the assets or makes a lot more money than the other, you might consider keeping the finances separate, and having a third account for joint expenses into which both parties contribute. That way, if there's a divorce or breakup, you'll know exactly what's yours. Most divorce courts split everything 50/50 unless there are clear records to the contrary.

## DON'T start a new file for these reasons

Sometimes folks will start new files without realizing that their end result could be accomplished more easily in another way. After all, when you create a new file, you don't have access to your special categories and classifications that you've set up, and you have to enter each account from scratch, just as you did in Chapter 2. That's a lot of work!

Here are some situations where a new file is probably not what you need:

- Don't think that you have to create a separate file if you have more than one of a particular kind of account—you don't. A single Money file can handle lots of different checking accounts, for instance, as long as you name each one uniquely.

- If you manage rental property, don't create a separate file for each property. They're not separate businesses—they're just separate assets in the same business. Instead, create a classification called Properties (see Chapter 5) and classify each transaction according to which property it pertains to.

- If you've got money that you never touch, like a retirement fund, you might be tempted to stick it in its own file, so you don't have to look at it. This is a mistake, because it's part of your total assets. Keep it in the same file as your other personal accounts—it's okay that you never use it.

# The big moment: creating a new file

Now that you know why you're creating a new file, let's do it. (Don't you feel good knowing you're doing this for the right reasons?)

From anywhere in Money, select <u>F</u>ile, <u>N</u>ew or press Ctrl+N. The New dialog box appears (see fig. 9.1). From here, just type a name for the new account in the File <u>n</u>ame text box, and click OK.

**TIP** **Naming rules? You can use up to 255 characters for the name,** and you can include spaces, upper- and lower-case letters, and some special symbols (for example, a dash and an underline are both perfectly acceptable, as is an exclamation point).

**Fig. 9.1**
To create a new Money file, just assign a name and click OK.

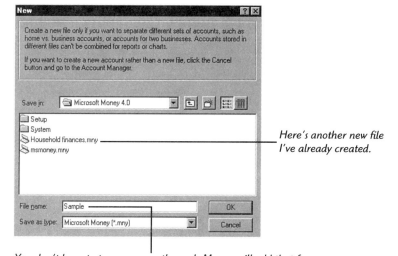

Here's another new file I've already created.

You don't have to type .mny on the end; Money will add that for you.

**CAUTION** **In the New dialog box, there are the standard Windows 95 type** controls for changing the drive and folder that the file will be saved in. I don't recommend changing these in this case—it's better to keep your Money data files in the Money folder, so you'll always know where they are.

After you've created a new file, it's opened automatically in Money, and the New Account Wizard opens so you can start creating the new file's accounts. (Money assumes that you wouldn't have created it if you didn't want to work with it right now.) If you don't want to create new accounts yet, just click Cancel.

So now you've created a new file. In the next section, you'll learn how to choose which one to work with, among all the files you've created.

# How do I pick which file to work with?

When you start Money, it always loads the file that was loaded the last time you exited the program. Up until this point, it's always been Msmoney.mny. But let's say the last thing you did yesterday was create a new file called Sample (Sample.mny). When you start Money again, Sample.mny will load instead of Msmoney.mny.

**TIP** **If you don't see extensions like .mny, they're probably turned off** in Windows 95. You can turn them on again by selecting View, Options from the My Computer or Windows Explorer windows, clicking the View tab, and clicking to remove the check mark next to Hide MS-DOS file extensions for file types that are registered. It's a matter of personal preference, but I like them on.

## Getting rid of Money files you don't need

You can delete unwanted files from within Money. Just select File, Open to see the Open dialog box. Then right-click on the file you want to delete and select Delete from the shortcut menu that appears. You can delete any Money file this way, as long as it's not currently open.

You also can do it from Windows Explorer or My Computer—just locate the file, select it, and press the Delete key on your keyboard or drag the file to the Recycle Bin.

Where to look for the file to delete? That's simple if you took my advice earlier about saving all your Money files in the Money folder. On my com-

puter, it's in C:\Program Files\Microsoft Money 4.0. That's probably where it is on your computer too, unless you chose a different folder when you installed the program. (See Appendix A for installation aid.)

Another way to find and delete all the Money files you don't want anymore is with the Find feature in Windows 95. Click the Start button, then move the mouse over Find. Then click Files and Folders. In the Named text box of the Name & Location tab, type *.mny and then click Find Now. You'll get a list of all the Money data files on your hard disk. You can delete the ones you don't want by clicking on one and then pressing the Delete key.

As you can see, you need a way of telling Money which file you want to use. Select File, Open, or press Ctrl+O. The Open dialog box appears (see fig. 9.2). From here, just double-click on the file you want to open, or click on it once and then click the Open button.

**Fig. 9.2**
Choose which Money
file you want to open.

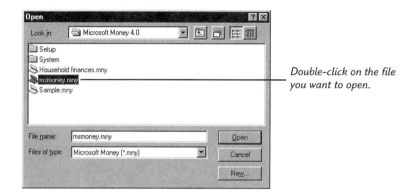

*Double-click on the file
you want to open.*

# The end of an era: archiving a file

If you let your transactions accumulate in your file indefinitely, the file is going to get fairly huge. That's not bad, except that big files take longer to load (which means Money will start more slowly) and take up more space on your hard disk. (And hard disk space is like cash—it doesn't matter until the day that you don't have enough of it.)

One way to decrease the size of your file is to archive it. When you archive a file, you have the option of removing all the transactions that fit certain criteria. The transactions are backed up in the archive, so they're still there if you ever need them, but they aren't hogging up space in your everyday Money file.

To archive a file, make sure you've opened the one you want to archive, and then follow these steps:

**1** Select <u>F</u>ile, <u>A</u>rchive. You'll see an Archive dialog box like the one in Figure 9.3.

**Fig. 9.3**

Your entire file will be backed up (archived), and then any transactions before the date you choose will be deleted from the original file you work with.

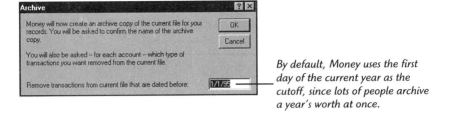

By default, Money uses the first day of the current year as the cutoff, since lots of people archive a year's worth at once.

2 Enter a date, or accept the one that's there, then click OK. An Archive dialog box appears that looks almost exactly like the New dialog box shown in Figure 9.1.

3 (Optional) If you want to save the file to a different drive and/or folder, select it from the Save in drop-down list. For instance, you might want to archive to a floppy disk.

4 Type a name in the File name text box. Money suggests the previous year as the name—for instance, 1994. This name looks good to me, since I'm deleting all the transactions before 1/1/95, so I'll stick with it. If you have more than one file for that year, you might include a designation in the name to indicate which file it is—for instance, Business 1994 or Personal 1994.

5 Click OK. A dialog box appears for the first account in your file, asking how you want the transactions archived. Its look varies depending on the account type, but it will resemble Figure 9.4.

**Fig. 9.4**

You can specify how you want each of your accounts handled individually.

```
┌─ Archive Union Federal Checking ──── ? X ─┐
│                                            │
│ Choose which type of transactions dated    ┌────────┐ │
│ before 1/1/95 you want removed from your    │   OK   │ │
│ account records.                            └────────┘ │
│                                             ┌────────┐ │
│ Account:   Union Federal Checking           │ Cancel │ │
│                                             └────────┘ │
│ ○ Remove all transactions.                 │
│ ○ Remove only cleared and reconciled transactions. │
│ ◉ Remove only reconciled transactions.     │
│ ○ Don't remove any transactions.           │
└────────────────────────────────────────────┘
```

6 Continue through the dialog boxes for each account in your file. When you've responded to the last one, Money archives your file, and you're finished.

If you ever need to open the archive file (perhaps to verify a payment or check your records), it's easy to do so, because it's just an ordinary Money file. Open it using the File, Open command, the same as you learned to do earlier in this chapter.

# Managing individual accounts in a file

Now that you've learned how to create new files and switch which one you're using, what about the individual accounts in each file? Well, you can manage them too. With Money, it's not a problem to make changes to accounts, or even delete them entirely.

Any change that you make to an account starts with the Account Manager. Click the Account Manager icon on the Contents screen to get there. (You worked with the Account Manager in Chapter 3, so it should look familiar.) From there, right-click on the icon for the account you want to change, and then click the command you want from the shortcut menu (see fig. 9.5).

**Fig. 9.5**
Right-click on an account icon for a shortcut menu of commands.

The first command on the shortcut menu is Go To. This opens the register, the same as double-clicking the icon. (This was also covered in Chapter 3.) Our first stop, however, is the Details command, which opens a window that lets you enter and change details about the account. (We'll cover the other two options, Rename and Delete, at the end of this chapter.)

## What are *Details*?

To open up the Details screen, select Details from the account icon shortcut menu (refer to fig. 9.5). The Details screen is shown in Figure 9.6.

*This chart shows a bit of balance history for the account.*

**Fig. 9.6**
You can enter all kinds of extra information about your account here—information that might be useful later.

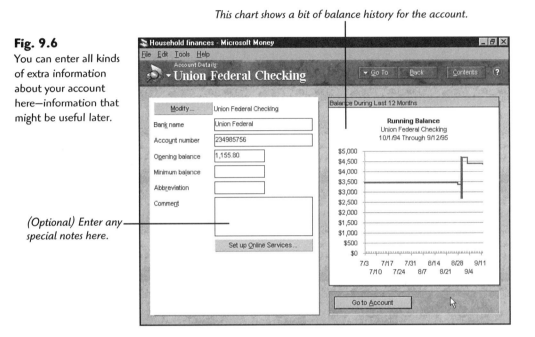

*(Optional) Enter any special notes here.*

Just like with a payee (see Chapter 7), you can enter any pertinent details you wish about your account on the Details screen. The Opening balance is already filled in, but you may want to add a Bank name (if it's not part of the account name itself) and an Account number. You can also add a Minimum balance (for your own reference only), an Abbreviation (you type the abbreviation anywhere in Money, and Money fills in the complete account name for you), or some Comments.

**CAUTION**   **Money allows you to change the Opening balance on the Details**
screen, but don't do it unless you're certain that it was wrong before. When you change the opening balance, Money goes through your entire register and recalculates each total based on the new opening balance—your current balance will definitely be affected.

# Can I change the account type?

Sure you can, and you won't lose any of your transactions you've already entered, either. From the Details screen, click the Modify button next to the account name, and you'll see the Modify Account dialog box (see fig. 9.7). From here, you can change the account name (type it in the New name text box), and/or select a different account type (click one of the option buttons). Then click OK.

**Fig. 9.7**
This dialog box changes your account name and account type in one fell swoop—but leaves all the existing transactions intact.

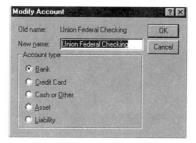

Notice in figure 9.7 that there are only certain account types you can change to. Money identifies the account types that are similar enough to the current type in order for the existing transactions to translate properly to the new form, and limits you to the ones that will work. Nice feature—it keeps you out of trouble.

**CAUTION**    **If you have a cash account that's associated with an investment** account, you can't change the cash account's type.

# What if I just want to change the name of an account?

If a simple rename is all you want, you don't have to wade through all the stuff in the Details screen. From the Account Manager, just select the account you want to rename, then do either of the following:

- Press F2.

- Right-click the account's icon, then select Rename from the shortcut menu.

A cursor appears in the name; you can just type a totally new name, or use the Backspace, Delete, and arrow keys to delete parts of the old name and enter your edits.

## Saying good-bye to an account

If you're very sure you want to delete an account (you *are* sure, aren't you?), you'll be pleased to see how easy it is. Just select the account in the Account Manager, and then do any of the following:

- Press the Delete key on the keyboard.

- Click the Delete button.

- Select Edit, Delete.

**CAUTION** **Be careful when deleting accounts! You can't get an account back** once you've deleted it, and all its transactions will be lost.

No matter which way you do it, you'll get a warning box telling you that deletion is permanent and will delete all the transactions. If you're sure that's what you want, click Yes. If not, click No.

# 10

# Letting Money Handle Your Investments

● **In this chapter:**

● **SEP? T-Bill? What do all these confusing terms mean?**

● **Creating easy investment accounts in Money**

● **How do I track individual transactions?**

● **Stock sales, splits, and prices**

● **What about tracking my retirement plan?**

*Money can't minimize your investment risk, but it can make tracking your investments as easy and painless as possible* . . . . . . . . . . . . . . . . . . . . . . . . . . . . . ▶

**W**hy would any sane person take money out of a regular savings account, earning an ample 3% per year, and invest in stock for some fledgling company that might take the software industry by storm—or might go swirling down the toilet? For the same reason that people gamble in Vegas, or buy lottery tickets. The thrill of the game. The potential for getting rich.

In this chapter, I'm not going to try to sell you on the benefits of investing—you're probably already interested in it, or you wouldn't be reading this chapter. Instead, I'll try to offer a bit of overview for the new investor, and then explain how Money tracks your investments.

Money excels at tracking your investments. It can handle almost any kind of investment you're into (or want to be into). You can enter stocks, bonds, CDs, mutual funds, T-Bills, Money Market funds, and all kinds of retirement plans, and track them like a pro. You can even use your modem to get stock price updates online, as you'll see in Chapter 12.

# A quick look at the investing game

With investments, as with Vegas, the higher the risk, the larger the potential prize. You can probably guess that the odds of winning the $100,000 slot machine are not as good as winning the $10 one. Similarly, if you buy the stock of a company that's doing very poorly, you can get a great deal, but there's a bigger chance that the stock's value will drop even further than there is with a company that is doing well (and has a higher stock price).

 **TIP** **If you're serious about investing, get yourself some professional** help! There are investment brokers and managers who will not only buy and sell for you, but they'll give you advice on the best investments to buy and sell.

Actually, not all investments involve risk. There are two kinds of investments—those that carry a risk, and those that tie up your money for a certain period of time. Certificates of Deposit, or CDs, are an example of the latter. You buy a CD at a certain interest rate for a certain period of time. At the end of that time period, you get your money back, plus the amount of interest that you agreed upon. (Money Market funds and bonds are other variations on this theme.) These investments don't risk your principal (your original money you put in). The only risk here is that you might need the money for something else during that time period, or that the interest rate will go up substantially and you'll have all your cash tied up in the lower-rate investment.

 **TIP** **United States Treasury Bonds are arguably the safest investment around.** They pay a respectable rate, and unless the U.S. Government collapses, you can count on getting your money back at the end of the allotted time period.

You'll do your investing through your bank or investment broker, so why would you want to enter the information into Money? There are a couple of reasons. One is that your investments are part of your larger financial picture, and you can't really understand how much you're worth unless you take them into consideration. (In Chapter 11, you'll learn how to generate reports and charts that show your financial situation.) A second reason is convenience. If you buy stock for instance, and write a check for it, you can enter a single transaction in Money to show that the cash was moved from one account (your checking account) to another (your stock brokerage account).

# Okay, how do I start setting up my investments?

You can set up an investment account through the Account Manager, as you saw in Chapter 2, and you may have already done so. If so, you can skip this section, unless you want to review the procedure.

 *Plain English, please!*
You need to understand some Money terminology here: investment accounts versus investments. An *investment account* is analogous to the other accounts you set up in Money—it's a blank "page" used to hold information about a particular brokerage or bank that handles your investments. An *investment* is the actual item you bought or sold—for instance, the CD, the stock shares, or the savings bond.

You'll want to create an investment account for each of the following:

- Each statement you receive from a brokerage
- Each bank you buy CDs or other investments from
- Each retirement plan you participate in

# Some basic investment terminology

Investing has its own special vocabulary. Here are some terms to help you along the way.

**401(k)** A retirement plan through your employer. You make contributions, and sometimes the employer does too. Contributions are not taxed, but withdrawals are.

**Bond** An agreement to borrow money and then pay it back with interest on a certain date. Bonds are often issued by governments, and sometimes by companies.

**Certificate of Deposit (CD)** Sort of like a bond, but purchased from a bank. You agree to let the bank use your money for a certain period of time, and the bank agrees to return it with interest on a certain date.

**Dividend** Profit-sharing that you get from the company in which you hold stock. In addition to the profit you might make by buying stock at a low price and selling it at a high price, you also receive quarterly dividend payments from the company for each share you hold, if the company is doing well.

**Individual Retirement Account (IRA)** A generic term that covers a wide variety of tax-deferred retirement plans. An individual can open an IRA for himself through a bank or brokerage, or an employer can provide an IRA plan. Contributions may be tax-deductible.

**Keogh** A retirement plan for self-employed people. It works much like other IRAs—contributions are tax-deductible and earnings are tax-deferred, but withdrawals are taxable.

**Money market fund** A type of mutual fund that invests in short-term securities, such as T-bills.

**Mutual fund** A collection of stocks, bonds, and other securities managed by an investment professional. You buy shares in a mutual fund as if it were a single stock.

**Rollover** A direct transfer of funds from one investment to another. For instance, when changing retirement plans, you roll over the funds to the new plan rather than cashing out the old one, to avoid paying taxes on the withdrawal.

**Registered Retirement Savings Plan (RRSP)** A Canadian retirement savings plan. Like the other plans, contributions are tax-deferred, but withdrawals are taxed.

**Simplified Employee Pension (SEP)** A retirement plan for small business owners and the self employed. Contributions to it are tax-deductible, and earnings are tax-deferred.

**Stock** Shares of ownership in a company. Stocks fluctuate in value on a daily basis, and usually pay quarterly dividends.

**Tax-deductible** You can deduct the amount from your income you report to the IRS.

**Tax-deferred** You don't have to pay taxes on the income until you withdraw it from the plan.

**Treasury Bills (T-Bills)** Money that the US government borrows from the purchaser for exactly one year.

**Treasury Note (T-note)** Like a treasury bill, except the duration is 2 to 10 years.

**Treasury Bond (T-bond)** Like a treasury bill, except the duration is 10 or more years.

Investment accounts in Money are designed to hold investments which fluctuate in value. If you're tracking an asset which does not fluctuate regularly, such as real estate or valuable collections, use an Asset account instead. (Refer to Chapter 2 to set up an Asset account.)

To create an investment account, follow these steps:

**1** From the Contents screen, click the Investment <u>P</u>ortfolio button. Then the Investment Portfolio screen appears.

**2** Click the Ne<u>w</u> button. The New dialog box opens, asking what you want to create (see fig. 10.1).

**Fig. 10.1**
Choose what you want to create. In this case, we're creating a new Investment Account.

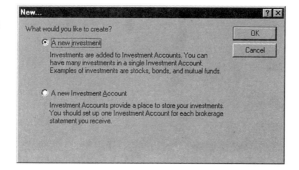

**3.** Click A new Investment <u>A</u>ccount, and then click OK. The New Account Wizard starts, and you're asked for a name for the investment.

**4.** Type the name (for instance, E. F. Hutton, or whatever company sends you your statement), and click Next.

**5.** When asked (see fig. 10.2), choose whether or not the account is tax-deferred. Most retirement plans are; most others are not. Check with your investment brokerage or bank to be sure. Then click Next.

 **TIP** **If you receive both tax deferred and non-tax-deferred invest-** ments on the same statement, it's best to create two separate investment accounts in Money to handle them.

**6.** Next you're asked whether the account has an **associated cash account**. Click <u>Y</u>es or <u>N</u>o, then click Next or Finish. (If you select No, the Next button turns to a Finish button.)

**Fig. 10.2**

It's important to answer accurately whether your account is tax-deferred, especially if you're going to use data from Money to prepare your taxes (see Chapter 15).

**66** *Plain English, please!*

An **associated cash account** is a holding tank where unused funds are kept—for example, your brokerage might keep the cash from your stock sale in a cash account for you until you decide what stock you want to buy with it. Retirement investments normally do not have these, nor do banks; brokerages normally do. **99**

**7.** If you answered Yes in step 6, enter the amount of money currently in your cash account, and click Finish. (You won't see this dialog box if you selected No in step 6.)

Now you have an account set up, and it appears in your Money Investment Portfolio, as shown in Figure 10.3. Now it's time to add your individual investments to the account.

**Fig. 10.3**
I've entered my brokerage account into Money, and now I'm ready to enter my investments.

If you don't see your account on the list, click here, and make sure you select Portfolio from the menu.

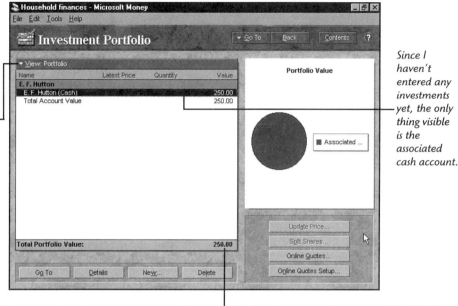

*Since I haven't entered any investments yet, the only thing visible is the associated cash account.*

*If you created an investment account with no associated cash account, this amount will be $0.00.*

# Specifying what you'll invest in

Remember in earlier chapters, you learned about creating payees and categories? You could do it up front, before you entered transactions, or you could do it on-the-fly, as you entered the transactions. It's the same thing with the information about each thing you're investing in. You can plug them in as you go, or you can create them ahead of time.

This business of setting up an investment confused me when I first started entering investments in Money, because the term "investment" applies to two different things:

- an investment is the stock or CD or bond or whatever that you want to buy—for instance, Illinois Power, a stock, is an investment;

- an investment is also the particular transaction you make—for instance, buying 40 shares of Illinois Power is an investment.

You can enter the info about Illinois Power first, before you enter the transaction, or you can just type in "Illinois Power" when you type your first transaction.

If you want to set up the investment in advance, you'll "create a new investment." (Yes, I know it's confusing, but just follow along.) From the Investment Portfolio screen, click the New button. The New dialog box appears, as in Figure 10.1. But this time, you're going to choose A new investment. Do so, then click OK, and you'll see the Create New Investment dialog box shown in Figure 10.4.

**Fig. 10.4**

Here's where you tell Money what kinds of investments you'll be making, for easy fill-in later, when you're entering the transaction.

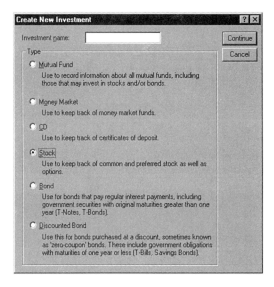

Type the investment name in the Investment name text box, and choose the type of investment you want (I'm choosing Stock, for instance). Then click Continue.

A dialog box appears that varies depending on the type of investment you chose. The New Stock dialog box shown in Figure 10.5 is what I got after choosing Stock as the type. Enter the stock symbol in the Symbol text box (this is important if you're going to be getting price updates online in Chapter 12). Next, click the Tax exempt check box if the item is tax-exempt (unlikely in the case of a stock), and add any comments you wish in the Comment text box. When you're done, click Continue.

 **Plain English, please!**

A stock symbol is the code for the stock that's used by the New York Stock Exchange to track the stock. It's usually some abbreviation of the name—for instance, Apple Computer is AAPL, and Microsoft Corporation is MSFT. 🙶🙶

**Fig. 10.5**
Enter the details about
the investment you're
setting up here.

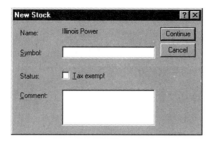

You can repeat this process for each investment you want to set up. If you
have your statements in front of you, you can work through the list of
investments there, and get them all entered at once.

# Buy! Sell! Entering an investment transaction

Now it's time to enter the actual investment in Money—for instance, buying
40 shares of Illinois Power stock. To keep our terms straight, I'll call this
entering a *transaction*. It's a lot like entering a transaction in any other
account register—you just pick which account you want to work with,
and go!

Start from the Investment Portfolio screen (refer to fig. 10.3), and select the
account you want to use. Then click the Go To button, and a register opens
for that investment account (see fig. 10.6). If you don't see the data entry
form at the bottom of the screen, as shown in Figure 10.4, click the View bar,
then select Transaction Form from the menu.

**CAUTION**   **If you have an associated cash account, make sure you're not**
entering the transaction into it when you mean to enter it into your
investment account. If you enter the register and see a button off to the
right labeled Investment Account, you know that you're in the cash
account. Click that button to go to the investment account's register.

To enter a new transaction, click the New button on the form at the bottom
of the register, and fill in the blanks, the same as you would with any transaction. Here are some things to watch for:

- Choose the investment you want from the Investment drop-down list. The investments that appear here are the ones you set up in the previous section. If you try to enter an investment that's not on the list, the Create New Investment dialog box pops up (refer to fig. 10.4) asking you to create it now.

- The blanks that appear depend on which investment you chose. For instance, in Figure 10.7, I chose a stock (Illinois Power), so the blanks for Quantity and Commission are available. They wouldn't be if I chose a type of investment that didn't require those (for instance, a CD).

- Make sure you enter the actual transaction date, not today's date.

- If there's an associated cash account, by default it will be filled in in the Transfer From blank. If the money for the purchase is coming from a different account, select it instead from the Transfer From drop-down list. If the money isn't coming from any account (or one not set up in Money), delete what's in the Transfer From text box and leave it blank.

- The Activity drop-down list shows all the activities you could perform on an investment. I've chosen Buy in Figure 10.7.

**Fig. 10.6**
Enter investment transactions basically the same way you enter any transaction into a register.

*Click here and select Transaction Forms if you don't see the form at the bottom of the screen.*

*Click here to enter a new transaction.*

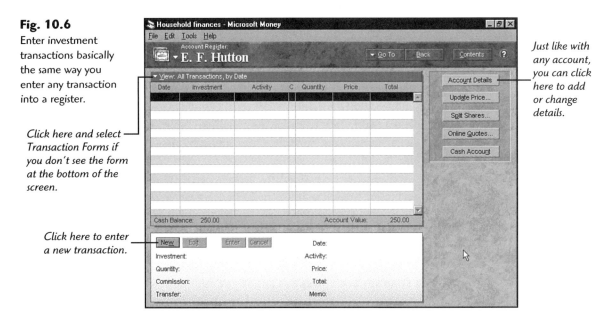

*Just like with any account, you can click here to add or change details.*

**Fig. 10.7**
Here's the form for entering a stock transaction. Yours may look different if you're entering a different kind of investment.

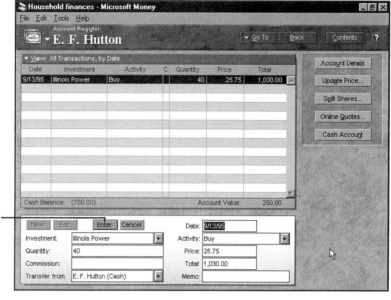

*When you finish entering information in this form, click here*

When you finish entering all the details about the transaction, click the Enter button or press Enter. The transaction appears in the register.

You can work with investment transactions the same as with any other transaction, including editing, moving, deleting, and so on. Refer to Chapters 3 and 4 for complete instructions.

The most fun you can have with your investment portfolio, though, is to admire it. You'll find some awesome charts and reports in Chapter 11 that will show you how your investments have performed over time, to help you plan them in the future, and to just plain show off to yourself!

 **Q&A** *When I get my statement from my brokerage, it lists interest and dividends. How do I tell Money about that incoming income?*

Enter any interest and/or dividends you receive as a separate deposit in your associated cash account. Just click the New button to create a new transaction, then plug it in. Make sure you select Interest or Dividend from the Activity drop-down list. If you don't have an associated cash account, and the dividends/interest are automatically reinvested, your statement should reflect additional stock or other purchases made with the money—enter those as regular investment transactions.

# I got a statement in the mail—now what?

The regular Balance button isn't available for investment accounts, so you can't reconcile your account using the techniques you learned in Chapter 8. However, you can mark individual transactions as "reconciled." In the investment account register, select the transaction that matches the one shown on your statement, and press Ctrl+Shift+M to mark it Reconciled. (Or, right-click on it, then choose Mark As, then Cleared or Reconciled). An "R" appears in the Cleared column. Repeat this for each transaction that you want to reconcile.

# Some special stock-tracking techniques

Stocks are a bit more volatile than your average investment, so you may want to pay a bit of special attention to them. The next section covers some of the actions you can take in Money to keep your stock portfolio up-to-date.

## Keeping your prices up-to-date

In Chapter 12, you'll learn how to get the latest stock prices online, which is pretty darned cool. However, if you have only a few stocks, it's almost as easy to grab a copy of your local paper (or the Wall Street Journal) and find the current price for a stock, and then enter it into Money.

From the Investment Portfolio screen or the account register, click Update Price. The Update Price dialog box appears (see fig. 10.8).

**Fig. 10.8**
You can enter the new price for your stock here, and your portfolio will be updated in value accordingly.

Choose which stock you want to update from the Investment drop-down list. Then enter the new price in the Price text box, and click the Update button. You're done! Your portfolio will now show the new value. You can choose a different stock from the Investment drop-down list and update its price too, or click Close when you're done.

## Splitting hairs (er, *shares*)

Sometimes when a stock price gets very high, the company that issued it announces a stock split. That means that they are "splitting" a high-priced share into two or more pieces, in an attempt to bring the price into a range that is attractive to buyers. For instance, let's say I have 10 shares of XYZ Corp. stock and each one is worth $120. The company announces a 3-for-1 split. I now have 30 shares, and each one is worth $40. I still have the same amount of money, but the number of shares is different.

Money understands stock splitting, and can automatically recalculate your number of shares and each share's value for you. Just click the Split Shares button from the Investment Portfolio screen. The Split Shares dialog box appears (see fig. 10.9).

**Fig. 10.9**
Money can help you calculate your new portfolio contents after a stock split.

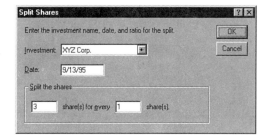

Choose which stock is splitting from the Investment drop-down list. Then enter the date that the split occurred (not today's date), and the ratio. For instance, in Figure 10.9, you can see I've entered a 3 to 1 ratio. Click OK, and Money updates your portfolio. You'll get a message saying it's been successfully done—click OK at it.

# Is there anything special about tracking a retirement plan?

A retirement plan (such as an IRA, 401(k), SEP, and so on) is basically just a tax-deferred investment account. It can include stocks, mutual funds, bonds, or any combination of investments, or it can be as simple as a fixed-rate IRA account at your local bank.

You'll create an Investment Account for each retirement plan you participate in. When you receive your statement from it, update the account by adding the transactions from the statement. (Make sure you enter the correct dates from the statement, not the date you make the entries.) If you're using an investment account, it would be considered a "Buy" transaction.

## Part of my paycheck goes into my retirement plan

When you get a paycheck, you can itemize it using split categories to track how much of your gross pay you're not receiving for one reason or another (taxes, insurance, whatever.) That way, you have a running total that matches your paycheck stub of how much you've paid into various funds.

 *Plain English, please!*

As you may remember from Chapter 3, you can use more than one category for a transaction with a Split. You click the Split button on the transaction form, then enter the various categories and subcategories, and amounts for each.

You can also include your retirement plan contributions in this split. Here's how:

First, set up a new subcategory under Wages & Salary, and call it Deferred Income. Clear the Include on Tax Reports check box as you're setting it up, since you don't have to pay taxes on the money that's set aside for your retirement. This will be the subcategory that keeps track of your retirement plan contributions.

Next, enter your paycheck into your account register. If you usually deposit it into your checking account, for instance, use that account register. Enter the amount of the check you're actually receiving in the Amount text box, and your employers' name in the From text box. Then click the Split button and enter separate categories for each itemized line on your paycheck stub.

Here's where it gets a little bit tricky. Normally, you would enter your gross pay as Wages & Salary:Gross Pay, and then you would categorize each of the deductions separately as negative amounts, as in Figure 10.10, until the Unassigned amount was $0.00.

**Fig. 10.10**
Here's how you would split the categories if you weren't contributing to a retirement plan.

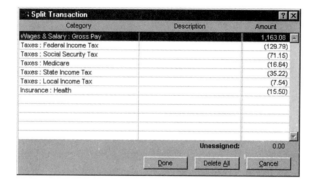

If you want to track retirement contributions, you must subtract the amount of the contribution from the Wages & Salary:Gross Pay line, and enter it as a separate line: Wages & Salary:Deferred Income. It would look something like Figure 10.11. (Note that the check issued to this person would be $130.24 smaller than the check issued to the person in fig. 10.10.)

**Fig. 10.11**
The portion of your income that's earmarked for your retirement fund must be categorized separately from your gross pay, as shown here.

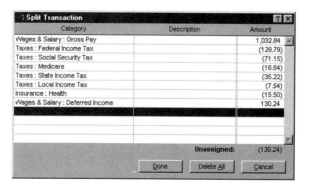

But we're not done yet. Notice in Figure 10.11 that the Unassigned amount is (130.24). We have earmarked that amount for investment, but we haven't told Money where we're investing! So add another line to the Split box with the category Buy Investment. When you choose that category, a Buy Investment dialog box pops up, as shown in Figure 10.12. Choose the investment account you'll be using from the Inv Account drop-down list, and then choose the investment from the Investment drop-down list.

**Fig. 10.12**
In the Buy Investment dialog box, you indicate where your retirement money will be invested.

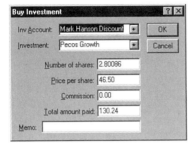

The amount of the investment is already filled in, so you need to enter a number of shares, or a price. You can enter either one, and Money will fill in the other one to equal your investment amount. In Figure 10.12, I've entered the share price, and Money has filled in the number of shares.

**TIP**    **If you don't know the exact price, just guess, and then correct the** figure when you get your next statement.

When you're finished, click OK, and your Split box will show the amount you just entered as a negative number, offsetting the positive Deferred Income and making the Unassigned amount $0.00 (see fig. 10.13).

**Fig. 10.13**
The invested money comes in (the Deferred Income line) and goes out (the Buy Investment line).

| Category | Description | Amount |
|---|---|---|
| Wages & Salary : Gross Pay | | 1,032.84 |
| Taxes : Federal Income Tax | | (129.79) |
| Taxes : Social Security Tax | | (71.15) |
| Taxes : Medicare | | (16.64) |
| Taxes : State Income Tax | | (35.22) |
| Taxes : Local Income Tax | | (7.54) |
| Insurance : Health | | (15.50) |
| Wages & Salary : Deferred Income | | 130.24 |
| Buy Investment : Mark Hanson Discount | Buy : Pecos Growth 2.801 @ 46.5( | (130.24) |
| | Unassigned: | 0.00 |

**TIP**    **If you don't know the details of each contribution to your** retirement plan, such as price and quantity, you may want to use an asset account rather than an investment account to track your retirement plan. However, you won't be able to include the plan's money on your investment reports (Chapter 11), and your tax reports won't be quite complete.

# My employer contributes to my retirement plan, too

If your employer makes matching contributions, you can enter those too. It's not done while entering your paycheck, as your own contributions are, because the money is not coming out of your paycheck—it's coming directly from your employer. Open the account that tracks your retirement plan, and enter a Buy transaction for each investment that your employer's contribution purchased, as shown in Figure 10.14. (Again, if you aren't sure of the number of shares or price per share in a stock transaction, guess, and then update it with the statement later.)

**Fig. 10.14**
If your employer contributes to your retirement plan, you can add that income directly to your retirement plan account as a separate transaction from your paycheck entry.

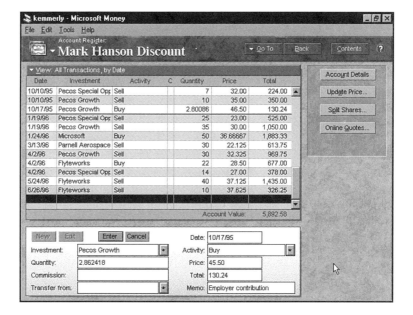

# The Big Picture: Reports and Charts

● **In this chapter:**

- Getting around in the Report and Chart Gallery

- What kinds of charts and reports can I create?

- Customizing: when the default just isn't enough

- I want to see this thing on paper!

*Charts and reports sum up your transactions neatly and make the bottom line easier to understand* . . . . . . . . . . . . . . ➤

One of the reasons to keep your finances in Microsoft Money, of course, is to avoid making math errors and help you balance your accounts. (That's one of my favorite reasons, personally, since I'm such a klutz at math.) But an even more interesting and compelling reason to use Money are the reports and charts.

Have you ever been in a meeting for a club, church, or business where you were presented with a long list of numbers or statistics? Probably. It happens a lot. Did you understand what you were given immediately and easily? Probably not. More likely, your eyes glazed over and your mind started wandering to your vacation plans or your dog's flea problem. That's because big collections of data (like your account register, for instance) aren't easy to fathom. Sure, you can see the individual transactions, but what's the big picture?

That's where Money's reports and charts come in—they neatly summarize your financial information in easy-to-understand reports and charts. Rather than staring at your complete account register, you can see a report or chart that summarizes the info, and quickly make some sense of those long columns of numbers.

 *Plain English, please!*

Reports are text-based summaries of your data—for instance, a report could add up all the transactions that were categorized as food:groceries and tell you how much you spent last month for groceries. Charts are graphical summaries of the same data. I'll tend to talk about reports and charts as a single entity in this chapter—that's because (at least in Money) they're just two different views of the same data—every Money report can be viewed as a chart, and vice versa.

What's the point of creating reports and charts? You can create them for yourself, to help you understand your finances and find ways to improve your spending and saving habits, or you can create them for other people, to convince them of your financial stability (perhaps to get a business loan or a mortgage). As I outline the various reports and charts that Money offers, you'll see dozens of ways that a report or chart can be helpful.

# Introducing Money's reports and charts

Money's reports and charts are both simple and powerful. It's very easy to display a simple chart or report—just a couple of mouse clicks, and you're done. You don't even have to do any typing. But you can also customize any report or chart to provide the exact information that you want to see, and save your customized report or chart for future use.

## The Report and Chart Gallery: a first look

To start looking at reports and charts, just click the Report and Chart Gallery button on the Contents screen. The Report and Chart Gallery window opens (see Figure 11.1).

*This symbol means the report or chart has been customized.*

*The reports and charts in the category you chose appear here.*

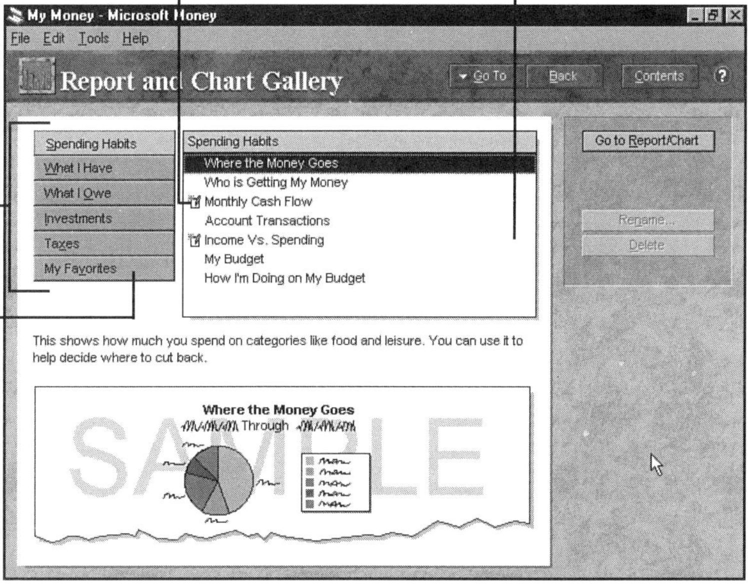

**Fig. 11.1**
Here's where you select which reports and charts you want to work with.

*Click one of these buttons to select a category.*

*You'll learn to add charts and reports to this category later.*

As you can see in Figure 11.1, the report and chart categories are listed on a series of buttons on the left. When you select a category, a list of the reports and charts available in that category appear in the list box to the right of the buttons.

Take a look at the names of the categories and reports/charts. Money's reports and charts are easy to understand because they have such sensible names. There's none of that confusing financial terminology like "accounts receivable" or "debits." Instead, the reports have immediately recognizable names like "Who is Getting My Money?" and "Upcoming Bills." Nice, eh?

**TIP** **Notice the little icon next to two of the reports/charts in Figure** 11.1. It indicates that the item has been customized. You'll learn how to customize a report or chart later in this chapter.

## Let's take a look at a chart

Let's jump right in and have a look, shall we? We can start with the Spending Habits category, since it's already selected (see Figure 11.1). If it's not, click the Spending Habits button on the Report and Chart Gallery screen, to see a list of the available reports and charts.

From here, click on the report or chart you want to see, then click the Go to Report/Chart button. The report or chart appears. For instance, in Figure 11.2, I've chosen the Where the Money Goes item, and I've been presented with this handsome chart.

**Fig. 11.2**
This chart shows me a breakdown of my expenditures by category.

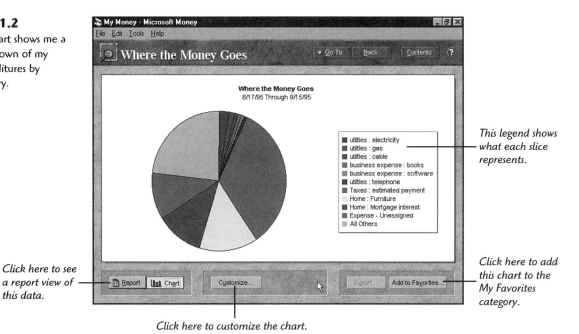

This legend shows what each slice represents.

Click here to see a report view of this data.

Click here to add this chart to the My Favorites category.

Click here to customize the chart.

**TIP** **If you haven't been using categories with your transactions, you** won't get much value out of the reports and charts, because most reports and charts are based on categories. (Some are based on payees.) You might want to review Chapter 5 and begin using categories in your future transactions.

The chart in Figure 11.2 relies on the various colors of each division, so this picture doesn't really do it justice. However, you can see that my largest expense this year has been my estimated income tax payments (that huge chunk on the right). Ouch!

When you're finished looking at the report or chart, click the Back button to return to the Report and Chart Gallery, or click Contents to return to the Contents screen.

## Want a closer look?

Since each part of a report or chart is based on your account register, there are real transactions behind each line of text and each piece of a chart.

When you move your mouse pointer over an area of the report or chart that's based on one or more transactions (that is, almost anywhere except the headings or title), your mouse pointer changes to a magnifying glass with a plus sign on it. If you let the pointer rest on a particular area for a few seconds, an information box pops up to tell you what you're looking at. For instance, in Figure 11.3, I'm checking out that large slice of pie on my chart from Figure 11.2.

Want an even *closer* look? You can see what's behind any item on a report or chart by double-clicking on it to open the View Transactions window. For instance, in Figure 11.2, if I click on that largest slice of the pie, I can see the transaction(s) that comprise it, as shown in Figure 11.4.

From the View Transactions window, you can double-click on a transaction to edit it (see Chapter 4 for editing details). You can also create a new report, based only on the transactions shown in the dialog box, by clicking the Create a Report button. (The report you were previously looking at closes, but you can reopen it later.) Or, if you just want to return to your chart or report, click Close.

**Fig. 11.3**
Just point at an area of your chart or report, and Money tells you what it represents.

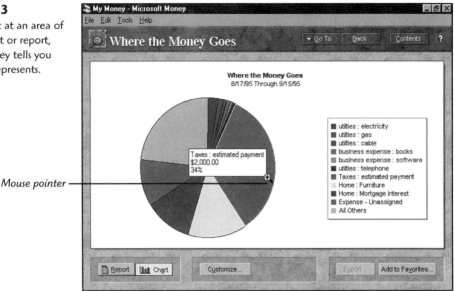

Mouse pointer ────

In this case, there's only one transaction.

**Fig. 11.4**
To see the complete breakdown of the transactions that make up a part of your report or chart, double-click on it to get this View Transactions window.

Click here to return to your chart or report.

You can create a separate report based only on the listed transactions by clicking here.

# Changing a chart into a report (or vice versa)

Although almost all of the reports/charts listed in the Report and Chart gallery can be viewed either as a report or as a chart, certain ones lend themselves naturally to one form or the other. The "natural" form of any item is what you see by default. For instance, Account Transactions is naturally suited to be a report—it's highly detailed and text-oriented. Who Is Getting My Money, on the other hand, is more suited to graphical format, because the whole point is to see a breakdown of where the money is going, not to read about individual transactions.

That's why sometimes you'll see a report, while other times you'll see a chart, when you first view an item. To change to the alternate form (for instance, in Figure 11.2 to change to a report), click on the appropriate button (Report or Chart) at the bottom left corner of the screen; for instance, I'll click Report, and the report in Figure 11.5 appears.

**Fig. 11.5**
Here's the same info you saw in the chart in Figure 11.2, but in Report format.

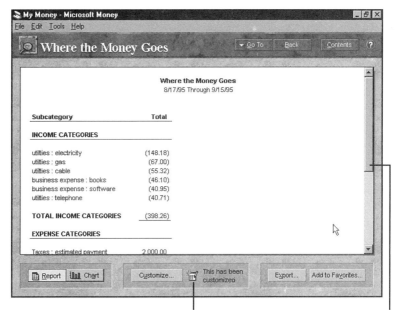

When you switch a chart to a report, or vice versa, it's considered "customizing."

Use the scroll bar to view the rest of the report.

**TIP**    **When you switch to the alternate form (for instance, from a chart to a report),** Money considers that a customization, and you'll see a reminder at the bottom of the screen (see Figure 11.5) that the report or chart has been customized. To get rid of that message, simply switch back to the original form.

# What reports and charts does Money offer?

The skills you've learned in this chapter so far apply to any report or chart you will work with. Now that you've got the basics under your belt, how about a tour of the various charts and reports that Money offers?

## Analyzing your spending habits

Let's start with the Spending Habits category, since that's the one we've been working with in our example so far. The reports and charts in this category are designed to help you "baseline" your spending—in other words, to figure out what your current habits and patterns are, so you can focus on improving them.

The Spending Habits category contains:

> **Where the Money Goes.** A pie chart that shows the breakdown of your expenditures by category, so you can see which expenses are eating up the largest portion of your income. You saw this one in Figure 11.2.

> **Who Is Getting My Money.** A bar chart showing all your payees. This shows you which payees are receiving the largest shares of your income—for instance, to compare your spending habits at one store versus another.

> **Monthly Cash Flow.** A report of the transactions for the last month, summarized by category, from your bank, credit card, and cash accounts. You can use this to plan how much you can save. Figure 11.6 shows part of my Monthly Cash Flow report for August.

> **Account Transactions**. This report shows all the transactions in a particular account. By default, the last account you worked with is used, but you can change which account is shown. (See "How do I customize a report or chart?" later in this chapter to learn how.). You can also change the date range for the transactions shown to limit the report to a particular time period.

> **Income Vs. Spending.** This very handy report can tell you at a glance if you are spending more than you're earning. It combines all your income from all accounts, and compares it to all your expenses, arriving

at a grand total. If the total is positive, you're doing fine; if negative, you'd better put yourself on a budget. (Chapter 14 talks about budgeting.)

**Fig. 11.6**
This monthly cash flow report tells me where my income is coming from, and where my money is going, all organized by category.

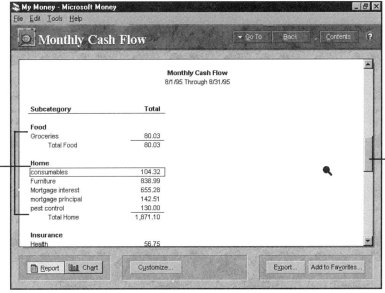

*Subcategories are broken down under each category.*

*You can't see the whole report onscreen at once—use the scroll bar to view different parts.*

**How I'm Doing on My Budget.** This bar chart shows your actual spending compared with your budget, by category. (It doesn't list every single category—it just shows the biggest ones, with an "All Others" category that it dumps the small stuff into.) You can use this to tell at a glance how well you're doing in your "big-money" budget categories.

**My Budget.** This detailed report breaks down every category and compares it against the budgeted amount for that category, so you can analyze your budget closely. We'll cover more of this in Chapter 14.

# What do I have?

The "What do I have?" reports and charts tell you about your assets—the money, valuables, equity, and investments you own. Sometimes when it seems like you're drowning in bills, it can make you feel better to take a look at what you've accumulated in your financial struggle—I like to look at a chart showing the money I've got socked away in my IRA, for instance.

These charts and reports can also be helpful if you're trying to convince someone that you're financially responsible, or have accumulated enough wealth to be good for a loan. Most institutions will insist on your actual bank statements, rather than just a Money-generated report, but the Money report or chart can help you begin your own planning before you go to the bank.

The reports and charts in this category include:

**Net Worth.** This bar chart shows your assets (what you own) and liabilities (what you still owe) in one compact graph. Mine is shown in Figure 11.7. Notice the depressingly high bar in the Liabilities section— that's my mortgage.

**Fig. 11.7**
This Net Worth chart shows your total financial picture in a single glance.

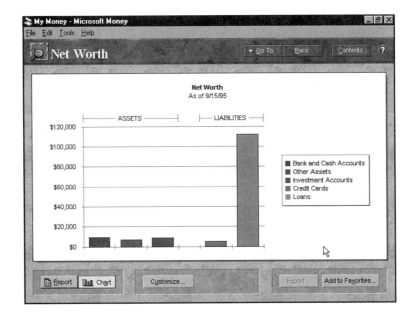

**Account Balances.** If you're wondering exactly how much money you have in each of your accounts, here's the place to look. This report neatly summarizes the information, showing you the current balance of every Money account in the file.

**Account Balance History.** Want a historical picture of the ups and downs of your account balance? Look no further. This line chart shows how your account balance has progressed over time. (Figure 11.8 shows an example.) This chart shows only one account at a time—by default it shows the last account you worked with. You can change which account is shown (see "How do I customize a report or chart?" later in this chapter).

**Fig. 11.8**
Here's a historical retrospective of my account balance. Looks like, on the average, the balance hovers around $1500.

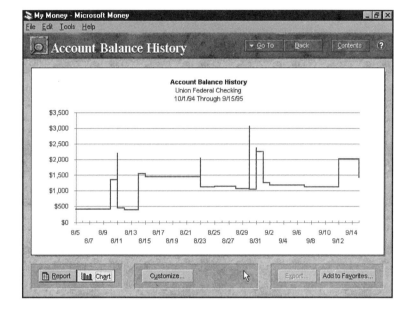

**Account Details.** If you took the time to enter details about each account (in Chapter 9), you can get a handy summary with this report. It lists each account and all the details you've entered for it. By the way, this report can't be converted into a chart.

# What do I owe?

The "What I Owe" category is not quite as upbeat as the previous one, because instead of focusing on your assets, it targets your liabilities—your debts. If you're wondering whether or not you can afford to take on additional debt (for instance, to buy a new house or car), these reports and charts can give you a realistic picture of the payments you're already committed to make.

The reports and charts you'll find here are:

**Upcoming Bills**. This report shows all the payments that you set up on your payment calendar that are due in the next 30 days. (Check out Chapter 7 if you need help using the payment calendar.) If you're planning a purchase in the near future, this report can help you figure out how much money you'll have left over after you meet your upcoming obligations.

**Upcoming Bills and Deposits This Month**. This report is a lot like the preceding one, except that it shows only the bills that are due between now and the end of the current month. If you get paid at the end of the month, this report can help you see what obligations you'll have to meet before your next paycheck.

**Credit Card Debt**. This pie chart shows what percentage of your total credit card debt is made up by each credit card. For instance, Figure 11.9 shows that I owe the largest amount (70%) to Capital One Visa. (I just used this card to by a new laptop computer!) You might use this data to decide which card to pay off first.

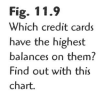

**Fig. 11.9**
Which credit cards have the highest balances on them? Find out with this chart.

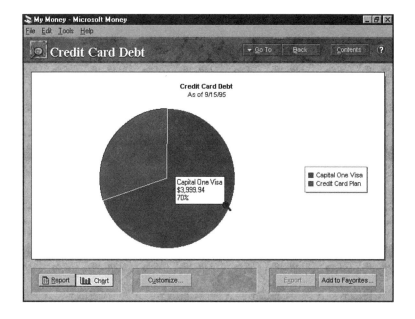

**Loan Terms**. If you're filling out a loan application, you'll probably need to include information about other loans you currently have. This report can provide that information in a neatly-summarized format—it lists the loan number, the outstanding balance, the payment amounts, and more. (This one has no chart option.)

**Loan Amortization**. Want to see what portion of each payment goes toward principal, and what portion toward interest? It's all here in a loan amortization report. You can see each payment's split of principal and interest, and the remaining loan balance after each one. This report doesn't have a chart option.

# A quick look at your investments

In Chapter 10, we talked about how setting up your investments in Money can help you plan your next strategic move in the investing game. One of the best investment tools in Money are the investment reports and charts. You can use them to see how your investment portfolio has gained in value over time, and to tell which investment types are the strongest performers. (You can dump the investments that aren't making any money!) Money also helps you see where your favorite stocks are price-wise, in comparison to their historical averages.

Here are the investment charts and reports you have to work with:

**Portfolio Value by Investment Account.** This report shows the value of each of your investment accounts, neatly summarized. At a glance you can see which accounts make up the bulk of your investment plan.

**Portfolio Value by Investment Type.** This pie chart shows how your investments are diversified. For instance, if you have money in stocks, CDs, and mutual funds, this chart shows a pie slice for each type, and tells you what percentage each slice makes up of the entire pie (er, *portfolio*).

**Performance by Investment Account**. This report is like the first one, except its primary purpose is to show gain or loss. You can target your top-performing investments here by seeing which ones are sky-rocketing and which ones plummeting.

**Performance by Investment Type**. The same as Performance by Investment Account, except broken down by investment type instead. For instance, you can see at a glance if mutual funds are gaining but CDs are taking a blow.

**Price History.** This line chart shows the performance of your stocks. For instance, you can see in Figure 11.10 that my Illinois Power stock is on the rise. Looks like a good time to sell, rather than buy.

**Fig. 11.10**
This chart shows stock price over time. You can position your mouse pointer at any spot on the line to see what the price was on that day.

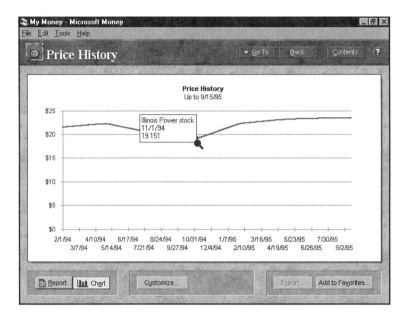

**Investment Transactions**. This is like an account register listing all your investment transactions, but it's formatted in a way that looks good when printed. You can use this to compare against a brokerage or bank statement if you prefer to work on paper instead of on the screen. There's no associated chart for this report.

# Taxes, taxes, taxes

Did you know that the United States income tax system is one of the most complicated in the world? In Chapter 15, we'll be delving into the mysteries of paying your taxes, and learning how Money can help. But for now, let's take a quick look at the reports and charts Money provides for handling your taxes. (We'll look at some of these in more detail in Chapter 15.) By the way, none of the tax reports have charts—they're all in report format only.

**Tax-Related Transactions**. Remember how, when you set up a category in Chapter 5, you indicated whether it was tax-related or not? Well, every transaction that uses a category that you set up to be tax-related appears on this report. You can use it to distill your account register down to only the transactions that are pertinent to your taxes.

**Capital Gains**. This report shows your gains and losses on your investments. Use it to determine whether you've gained or lost more on your investments this year. If you've gained, you have to pay taxes on your income!

### ❝ *Plain English, please!*

A capital gain is nothing more than income you receive from smart (or lucky) investing. For instance, if I buy stock at $20 a share and sell it at $40 a share, I've just acquired $20 in capital gain, and I have to report that $20 as income on my taxes. ❞

**Loan Interest.** Some loan interest is tax-deductible. (Check with your accountant.) For instance, the interest I pay on my mortgage is deductible (at least until the tax laws change again). To see how much interest you've paid this year on a particular loan, use this report. By default it shows the loan you most recently worked with, but you can customize the report to show any loan.

**Tax Software Report**. If you use special tax software to prepare your taxes, this Money report can help. It summarizes your income and expenses according to which form, schedule, and line the items belong on. From there, it's a snap to copy the data to your tax software. (You'll learn in Chapter 15 how to export this report directly into the tax program, in a special format.)

# A few of your favorite reports...

So what's that last category, "My Favorites?" That's where you can assemble copies of the reports and charts you use most often. From any chart or report, just click the Add to Favorites button. From then on, you can select the report from either its original location or from the My Favorites category.

**TIP** **If you want to customize a report or chart, but also keep the** original form of it, do the customization (see the next section) and then save the customized version with the Add to Favorites button. Then reset the original to its normal format (you'll learn this in the next section, too); the version in My Favorites will remain customized.

# How do I customize a report or chart?

As we looked at the various reports and charts, there were several instances where the data is taken from the account you used most recently. But what if you want to use a different account? Or a different timeframe? Not a problem.

Money's reports are extremely versatile. You can change the report name, the timeframe it encompasses, the chart type, the account(s) it accesses, and even the colors and patterns used, if you think any of those changes would make the report more useful to you.

To customize any chart or report, just click the Customize button at the bottom of the chart or report's display. A dialog box appears showing you your customization options for the chart or report you're working with.

## Fixing up that report the way you want it

Let's start by looking at the report options, because you set these for both reports and charts. (Actually, when you get down to it, a chart is just a picture of a report.)

To customize your report, start by displaying the report, then click the Customize button. The Customize Report dialog box appears, as shown in Figure 11.11.

**TIP** **When you're customizing a chart, you can access this Customize** Report dialog box by clicking the More Options button in the Customize Chart dialog box. This dialog box's controls will vary depending on the chart or report you're working with.

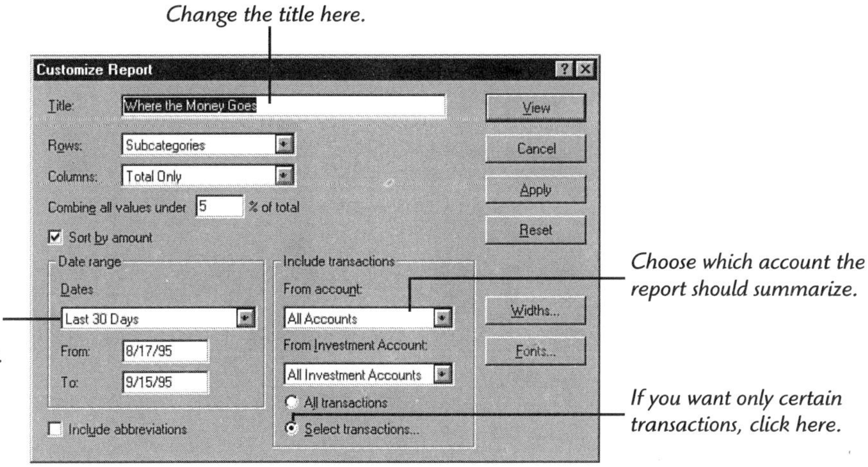

*Change the title here.*

**Fig. 11.11**
Make your changes to
your report here.

*Open this drop-down
list and select a date
range, or type one in
the From and To boxes.*

*Choose which account the
report should summarize.*

*If you want only certain
transactions, click here.*

I won't go into every detail of this dialog box, but here are some highlights:

- Title. Enter a new title for the report in this text box.

- Change the date range that's included in the report by selecting one of the preset ranges from the Dates drop-down list. Or, if you prefer, type a range in the From and To text boxes.

- To use a different account, select it from the From account drop-down list.

- If you want to include investment accounts, select them from the From Investment Account drop-down list. You can select No investment accounts to exclude them all.

- If you don't want to include all the transactions, select the Select transactions option button. A dialog box will appear, in which you can select which transactions to include.

- You can change the width of each column by clicking the Widths button (Customize Reports dialog box only). You can't set an exact width, but you can choose among Automatic (usually the best choice), Narrow, Standard, Wide, or Extra Wide.

- To change the fonts used in the report, click the Fonts button. The Fonts dialog box opens (Figure 11.12). From here, you can choose a different font and font size.

Make your selections, then click View to close the dialog box and apply your changes.

**Fig. 11.12**
Want a different font?
Change it here. You
have access to all the
fonts that are installed
in Windows 95.

Select a font here.

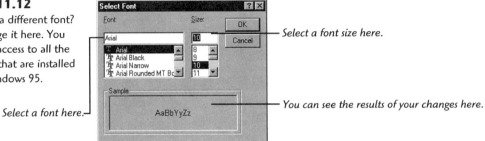

— Select a font size here.

— You can see the results of your changes here.

**TIP** **If you change your mind and want to return to the default settings** for the report or chart, click the Reset button in the Customize Report or Customize Chart dialog box.

## Let's look at the chart options

You can change all the same things on a chart that you can change on a report—plus more. For instance, you can choose a different chart type, if you think another type would be more appropriate, you can show percentages on pie charts, and you can switch between using colors or patterns on a chart, if any of these changes make sense for your situation.

When you click the Customize button for a chart, the Customize Chart dialog box appears (see Figure 11.13). Here are some of the things you can change here:

**Fig. 11.13**
Charts have some
special options all their
own; you can change
them from here, or
click the More Options
button to access the
Customize Report
dialog box.

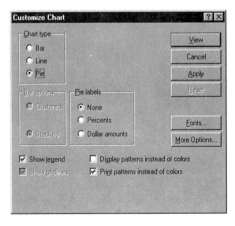

- Chart type. Your choices are Bar (as in Figure 11.7), Line (Figure 11.8), and Pie (Figure 11.9).

**CAUTION** **Changing the chart type is fine if you have a definite motive for** doing so. Usually, however, the most appropriate type of chart has already been selected for the data; you may not get very useful results if you change the chart type.

- Bar options. If you choose a bar chart, you can choose between Clustered (one next to another) or Stacked (one on top of the other) bars, if the chart has more than one data series. Figure 11.14 shows the difference between the two.

66 *Plain English, please!*
A data series on a chart can represent an account, payee, or category. For instance, if you were plotting the performance of several stocks in Figure 11.10, each stock's line would be a data series. 99

- Pie labels. If you choose a pie chart, you can choose to have the Percents or Dollar amounts appear on each slice.

- Show legend. The legend is the "key" that tells what each bar or line means. (It's pointed out back in Figure 11.2). It's very useful in most charts, but if you don't want it, deselect this check box.

- Show gridlines. On some charts (like Figure 11.10 for example), gridlines help your eye follow the line or bar across the page. Turn it on or off with this check box.

- Display patterns instead of colors. If you're showing the chart on a monochrome monitor, the colors may not show up well. (Check out Figure 11.2 and you'll see what I mean!) Change the colors to patterns by selecting this check box.

- Print patterns instead of colors. This is just like the preceding option, except it applies to your printer, not your monitor. If you haven't got a color printer, select this check box for better chart printouts.

But wait—there's more! You can click the Fonts button (it works the same as it did from the Customize Report dialog box), or click More Options to display the Customize Report dialog box itself. When you're finished, click the View button to close the dialog box and apply your changes.

 **TIP** **In both the Customize Chart and Customize Report dialog boxes,** you'll find an Apply button. You can apply your changes without closing the dialog box by clicking this button.

# Let's see it on paper!

Once you've got your chart or report exactly the way you want it, you'll probably want to share it with others (unless you were just creating it for your own satisfaction, which is fine too.) One way to share it is to gather everyone around your computer while you display the chart or report onscreen, but nobody wants to do that! For one thing, as you've seen, reports don't usually fit neatly on the screen—you're forever messing with the scroll bar to see different parts of the document.

A better way is to print your chart or document, and then make copies of the printout to share. It's easy to print a report or chart:

**1** Display the report or chart on-screen.

**2** Select File, Print, or press Ctrl+P, or right-click on the report or chart and select Print. The Print dialog box appears. It will either say "Print Report" or "Print Chart" at the top, depending on which you're printing. (The Print Chart dialog box is shown in Figure 11.14.)

**Fig. 11.14**
The Print Chart dialog box lets you choose how many copies, what page range you're going to print, and the print quality.

**3** If you want a number of copies other than 1, type it in the Copies text box.

**4** If you want a different print quality, select it from the Print quality drop-down list.

**TIP** **The lower the print quality, the faster the document will print.**
Use the highest print quality for a final draft. Some printers only have one print quality available—in that case, you're stuck with whatever is offered.

**5** If you're printing a report, you can select All to print all pages, or select Pages and then type in a From and To page number. For instance, to print pages 2 and 3, type 2 in the From box and 3 in the To box. This feature isn't available when printing a chart.

**6** Click OK. The report or chart prints, and you've got a handsome printout to share with the world!

**Q&A** ***What does that Setup button do in the Print dialog box?***

You can use it to set some additional options for your printer. The exact options available will vary depending on what kind of printer you have. You may be able to choose between Portrait and Landscape orientation, change the paper size, and choose which paper tray to use. You can also select a different printer, if you have more than one, from the Name drop-down list in this dialog box. Check out your Windows 95 documentation for more info about setting up a printer.

# 12

# Online Banking and Bill Paying

● **In this chapter:**

- **What kinds of things can I do online?**

- **Do I need any special equipment?**

- **How much is this going to cost me?**

- **Paying your bills online**

- **Getting the latest stock quotes**

- **Online banking: statements and more**

*With a modem and Money, your days of waiting in line at the bank drive-through are over* . . . . . . . . . . . . . . . . . . ➤

read the other day in the paper that some bank actually charged a customer a $2 fee because she talked with a real bank representative on the phone instead of using some automated service. Two dollars to talk to a real person—can you believe it?? That's how far financial automation has come (or how low it's sunk, depending on how you look at it).

It used to be that banking was a friendly, personal affair. You'd stroll into your hometown bank to deposit your paycheck, make a mortgage payment, chit-chat awhile with the teller (who you went to high school with and whose parents play bridge with your parents), then stroll out to do the rest of your errands—maybe stop by the electric company office and pay that bill too.

But today, who has the time to make a special trip to the bank? Not me, even if I did know the tellers by name (which I don't). Instead, I have my paycheck direct-deposited, I make withdrawals from an ATM machine, and I pay my bills by mail or telephone. Banking is purely a business thing.

Online banking isn't for everyone—if you're one of those people who likes the ritual of visiting the bank branch every Friday, or paying your bills by check every payday, you'll miss that. But if you're a busy person like me who is tired of standing in line and licking stamps, online banking may be the best reason yet to use Microsoft Money.

# What kind of banking can I do online?

Money offers three kinds of online banking. You can do any one of these individually, or all three—the choice is up to you:

- **Pay On-Line**   With this feature, you can pay all your bills through Money each month, instead of printing out checks and mailing them. You enter the bills to be paid in Money, then connect with a service which debits your checking account and pays your bills. You can use this feature with any bank.

- **Bank On-Line**   If you have an account at a participating bank, you can download current bank statements to reconcile your Money records. You can also check balances and transfer money between accounts.

- **Quotes On-Line**   Update the prices of your stock holdings by modem with this feature. You can call at any time during the day to transfer the most recent closing prices to your Money investment portfolio.

# Sounds great! How does it work?

The online banking system is administered by a company called On Line Services, Inc., located in Lisle, Illinois. Microsoft doesn't have any involvement in this—it's a separate, private company that Microsoft has made a deal with to handle your banking needs.

Even though you're doing online banking, you perform all your upfront work in Money *offline*—while you're not actually connected to the On-Line Services computer. You're only online long enough for Money to send the preprepared information and retrieve any info that's waiting for you—then it disconnects.

 **TIP** **Money minimizes your connect time in order to save you the** expense of a long distance phone call. However, if you live in a major metropolitan area, you don't have to worry about long distance charges at all, because On-Line Services has a local access number in most large cities. You'll receive the phone number to use when you get your startup kit.

Each of the three services works a little differently, so let's look at them separately.

## How Pay On-Line works

First, in Money, you prepare your payments to be made. Then you click the Call button and dial the On-Line Services computer. On-Line Services processes your request and sends a payment to the payee for you.

The payee receives your payment and deposits/cashes it. At that point, On-Line Services takes money from your checking account to reimburse itself, and the cleared electronic payment becomes part of your bank records.

## How Bank On-Line works

Although On-Line Services helps get you set up for online banking, this service is mostly between you and your bank. You set up your requests in Money—transfers to be made between accounts, statements to be requested, letters to be sent. Then you click the Call button, and Money sends all the information to the bank's computer. If you have requested anything to come back, such as a statement, Money retrieves it, then disconnects, and you can look at your statement offline at your leisure.

### How Quotes On-Line works

In Money, you make a list of the **ticker symbols** for all the stocks that you want to get current prices for. Then you click the Call button, and Money dials the On-Line Services computer, where a master list of the current prices is located.

 *Plain English, please!*

A **ticker symbol** is the same as a stock symbol—both refer to an abbreviation that's used on Wall Street as a shorthand for the company. For instance, Microsoft is MSFT and Apple is AAPL.

Money searches the master list and retrieves prices for the stocks you've requested, then disconnects, and your investment portfolio in Money is updated with the current prices.

# What equipment do I need?

To use Money's online features, you need Money (obviously!) and a modem. Almost any modem will do, although faster is better. You also need access to a telephone line.

I don't want to turn this into a book on selecting a modem, but here are some general tips, in case you haven't bought one yet:

- Make sure any modem you buy says "Hayes-Compatible" on the box. The Hayes command set is a language that your computer uses to talk to the modem.

- Modem speed is measured in bits per second, or bps. Buy at least a 14,400 bps modem. Get a 28,800 bps if you can afford it.

- Look for a modem that offers 32bis and MNP. These technical standards have to do with the way data is compressed to be sent over the phone lines.

# Does it work with my bank?

Two of the banking services, Pay On-Line, and Quotes On-Line, are bank-independent. That means it doesn't matter which financial institutions you use for your banking—the services don't need to work directly with your bank. They merely perform services for you, like pay your bills, and then pay themselves for the trouble while they're at it.

Bank On-Line is a different story. It requires a two-way communication with your bank, because you use it to retrieve bank statements. That's why it won't work with just any bank.

Which banks will it work with? Well, not very many, at least not at this writing. When I called On-Line Services to find out which banks were set up and ready to go, they listed only four in the whole country. However, they said that 16 more banks would be ready shortly, for a total of 20. By the time you read this, all 20 should be ready. (If your bank isn't listed, call (800) 200-7622 to see if it's been recently added.)

## Banks that work with On-Line Services:

| | | | |
|---|---|---|---|
| Bank of Boston | (800) 476-6262 | Home Savings of America | (800) 310-4932 |
| Centura Bank | (800) 721-0501 | M&T Bank | (800) 790-9130 |
| Chase Manhattan Bank | (800) 242-7324 | Marquette Banks | (800) 708-8870 |
| Chemical Bank | (800) 243-6226 | Michigan National Bank | (800) 225-5662 |
| Compass Bank | (800) 266-7277 | Sanwa Bank California | (800) 237-2692 |
| CoreStates | (800) 562-6382 | Smith Barney | (800) 930-0080 |
| Crestar Bank | (800) 273-7827 | Texas Commerce Bank in Houston | (800) 235-8522 (713) 216-7000 |
| E-Direct | (800) 708-8870 | Union Bank | (800) 796-5656 |
| First Chicago Bank | (800) 800-8435 | US Bank | (800) 422-8762 |
| First Interstate Bank | (800) 968-2634 | Wells Fargo | (800) 423-3362 |

If you find out that your bank isn't one of those that will work with Bank On-Line, you've got two choices. You can switch your checking account to one of the banks listed above. Just give one a call—believe me, they'll be thrilled to hear from you. They love new customers. Even if the bank is located in a different city, it shouldn't be a big deal, since you'll be using Bank On-Line rather than visiting the lobby physically.

Your other option, of course, is to forego the Bank On-Line feature, and stick to the other two online things you can do: Pay On-Line and Quotes On-Line.

**TIP** **Truth be told, Bank On-Line is not the strongest of the services** anyway—sure, you can make transfers and check your balance, but those are not the big time-eaters in your day. Bill paying, on the other hand, is probably the online service that will save you the most time and effort.

# How much does it cost?

Cost is important, of course—saving a couple of hours and some stamps every month is great, but you don't want it to take too large a bite out of your bank account.

The costs of each banking service are different and separate. Here's what the charges are as I'm writing this book (they may change by the time you read it):

- Pay On-Line: This is $5.95 a month, which includes 20 payments each month. Extra payments are $3.50 for each group of 10.

- Quotes On-Line are $2.95 a month, and you get six sessions. (You can get as many individual stock quotes during one session as you like.) Additional sessions are 50 cents each.

- Bank On-Line: The charges are determined by each individual bank. Some banks may let you do it for free—others may charge a fee (probably under $5 a month).

If you order both Pay On-Line and Quotes On-Line, you get a bit of a discount—the combined fee is $7.95.

# Okay, I'm convinced. How do I sign up?

The first step, no matter which of the online banking services you'll be using, is to register with On-Line Services. To do that, you'll need to fill out an application form.

If you bought a boxed version of Microsoft Money in a store, you may find an online banking application form in the box. If not, it's easy to print one out from Money. Follow these steps to get an application form:

1   From the Contents screen, click Pay On-Line. (Later, this button may change to Bank On-Line instead, but it's the same thing.)

2   The Online Services Signup wizard may appear automatically. If it doesn't, click the Signup button. Later you'll use this wizard "for real," but for now we're just going to get an application form from it.

3   Click Next, then Next again. Don't worry about filling in the information it asks for right now—we'll do this later.

4   When you see the Open Application Form button (see fig. 12.1), click on it. An application form opens (in either Microsoft Word, if you have it, or WordPad).

**Fig. 12.1**
Here's an easy way to open the application form.

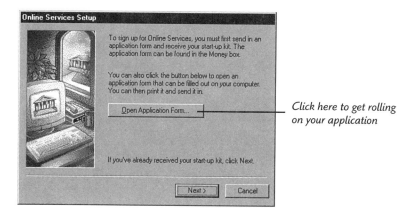

*Click here to get rolling on your application*

5   Open the File menu and select Print to print the application form, then fill it out on paper. Or, if you prefer, type in your answers on-screen, then print out the completed form.

**CAUTION** **It's important that you sign the form to make it legal. If you filled** it out on-screen, don't forget to sign it after you print it.

**6** If you're signing up for Pay On-Line, tear out a check from the checkbook of each bank account you'll be using with this service. Write VOID on each one. You'll include these with your application form.

**7** On the check for the account that should be used to pay the fees On-Line Services charges, write BILLING ACCOUNT.

**8** Put your signed form and your voided checks in an envelope and mail to:

On-Line Services
P.O. Box 3128
Lisle, IL 60532-3128

**9** Back in Money, click the Cancel button to cancel the wizard. We'll come back to it later, after the startup kit has arrived.

If you have any questions, you can contact a customer service representative for On-Line Services by calling 1-800-200-7622.

In a few weeks (it took about 2 weeks for me), you'll get your startup kit, containing a confirmation of everything you've agreed to, plus a 4-digit Personal Identification Number (PIN) that acts as your password. From here, you're ready to set up Money.

# Telling Money about your online plans

The next step is to set up Money to go along with your plans. To do this, we'll revisit that wizard that we so abruptly terminated when we were getting the application form. Follow these steps:

**1** From the Contents screen, click Pay On-Line (or Bank On-Line, whichever appears).

**2** The Online Services Signup wizard may appear automatically (see fig. 12.2). If it doesn't, click the Signup button.

**Fig. 12.2**
Start setting up Money
for online transactions
with this wizard.

**3** If you want to read what Money's Help system has to say about the online banking services, click the Learn About Online Services button. It'll tell you basically the same stuff that I've told you so far in this chapter. When you're done reading that, close the Help window to continue, then click Next to move to the next screen in the wizard.

**4** Enter the routing number for your bank in the Bank routing number text box. This is a 9-digit code that begins in the bottom left corner of your checks. You'll also find it listed on the confirmation sheet you got along with your PIN. Then click Next.

**5** Now you'll see that screen again where we opened the application form earlier (refer to fig. 12.1). Only this time, we have already received our startup kit, so we'll move on through by clicking Next.

**6** Next, you're asked for some personal information about yourself (see fig. 12.3). Fill it in, then click Next.

**Fig. 12.3**
Money needs to know
the same information
that you entered on
your application form,
so it can compare it
with On-Line Services'
records to make sure
you're who you say
you are.

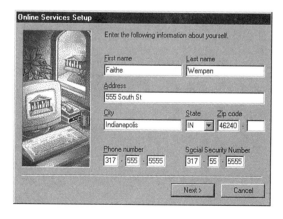

**7** In the Online Services phone number text box, fill in the phone number that was included in your start-up kit. It's on the same sheet of paper as your PIN number, which you'll use later. Then click Next.

**8** You'll set up each Money account one-at-a-time. From the Account list, select the first one you want to set up, then click Next.

**9** On the next screen, there are two check boxes: Online Banking, and Online Bill Payment. Select one or both, depending on what you signed up *for this account*, then click Next.

**10** Next, you're asked for Account Number and Account Type. Enter the account number from your start-up kit, and select the account type from the drop-down list. Then click Next.

**11** Next, you're shown that list of participating Bank On-Line banks that I showed you earlier in the chapter. (See fig. 12.4). Click on your bank if it appears—if it doesn't, click **(My bank isn't on this list)**.

**Fig. 12.4**
Choose your bank here, or tell Money that your bank isn't on the list. You'll also enter your bank routing number here.

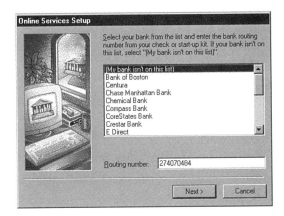

**12** Enter your bank's routing number in the Routing number text box. This is important! Even if you selected your bank from the list, you must also enter the routing number. You'll find it in your start-up kit. Then click Next.

66 *Plain English, please!*

Sometimes your bank may refer to the routing number as their ABA number. 99

**13** If you signed up to use more than one bank account, click Yes, I want to set up another account, then click Next and you're returned to step 8. If you're done setting up accounts, click No, I'm finished with Online Services setup, then click Next.

**14** Read the Congratulations screen, then click Finish. You're done!

From here, you can go straight into online banking, bill-paying, and stock quotes. I'll tell you more about each of these in the rest of this chapter.

# Save your stamp! Using online bill-paying

Okay, it's time to get down to business and pay some bills! Your first stop is your familiar old checking account register. Open it up, so you can enter the payments that need to be made.

## What should I put for the check number?

Go ahead and enter the transaction as if you were writing a check, but instead of entering a check number, open the drop-down list in the Number text box and select Electronic Payment (Epay), as shown in Figure 12.5. Epay appears in place of a number.

**Fig. 12.5**
Epay appears instead of a check number. An epay number will be assigned later.

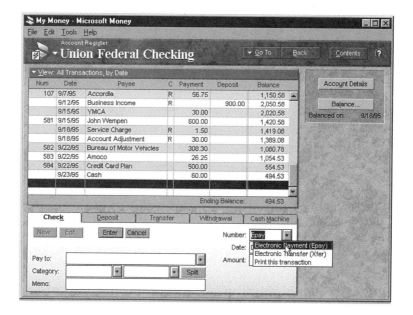

# What about the date?

In the Check tab, you'll notice that the words "Due Date" have been entered in the Date text box. Replace them with the date on which you want the payment made. Just select that text box, then type right over it.

You can schedule a payment as far in the future as you like, but no less than 5 days from now. That's because it takes 5 days for a payment to work its way through the epay system. For instance, if you wanted the bill paid on February 6, you would have to enter it on or before February 1. Of course, you can also enter payments that are due many months in advance, so you don't forget to make the payments. On-Line Services will not pay the bill until the date you have specified.

# And the rest of the stuff?

The rest of the transaction you should fill out normally. Make sure you enter a payee—that's important, of course, so that Pay On-Line will know who to send the payment to. You can use categories, classifications, memos, or whatever else you normally do. My completed transaction is shown in Figure 12.6.

**Fig. 12.6**
Except for the post-dated date and "Epay" instead of a check number, the transaction looks remarkably like any other.

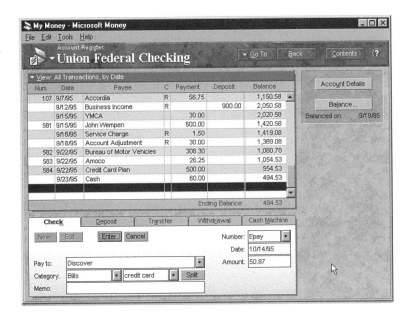

# Entering the Payee info

Everything looks normal—until you click Enter or press Enter to put the transaction into your register. Then (if it's the first time you've paid this payee with Pay On-Line), a box pops up asking for information about where to send the payment. Fill in all the information it asks for—you can see mine in Figure 12.7. Then click OK.

**Fig. 12.7**
You'll need to enter information about each new payee, so that Money will be able to tell On-Line Services where to send the payment.

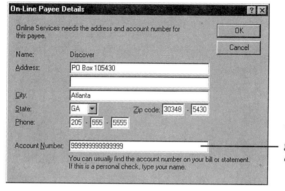

*You didn't really think I was going to give you my actual account number, did you?*

Enter as many payments as you want—we'll process them all in one batch when the time comes.

Once you've entered a payment, you'll see a reminder on the Account Register screen (see fig.12.8), along with a button that's a shortcut to the Pay On-Line (or Bank On-Line) screen. The reminder's a good thing, because until you actually tell Money to dial into On-Line Services and make the payment, nothing happens. You can enter all the payments you want, but they won't get paid until you tell Money to go online and make them.

**TIP**  **Remember the reminder you saw on the Contents screen when a** payment was due on your Payment Calendar? You'll see the same type of reminder on the Contents screen when you have online bills to pay.

**Q&A**  *Bank On-Line? Pay On-Line? Why are there two different names for the same screen?*

If you set up one or more accounts to use the Bank On-Line feature, all the references to online services in Money change to read "Bank On-Line." Otherwise, they stay with the original name, "Pay On-Line." The functionality of the screen doesn't change a bit with the name change.

**Fig. 12.8**
When you have online payments to make, this reminder appears, along with a shortcut button for your convenience.

*This symbol shows the payment will be made online.*

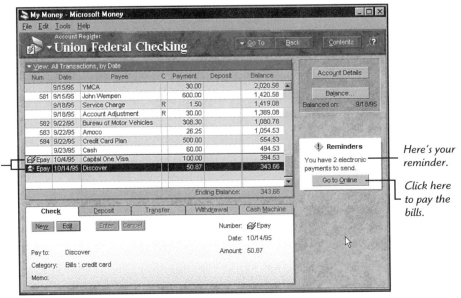

*Here's your reminder.*

*Click here to pay the bills.*

## Time to connect!

When you're ready to make the payments, click the Go to Online button in the account register, or click the Bank On-Line or (Pay On-Line) button on the Contents screen. All the activities that you've requested appear here. Notice that in Figure 12.9, the payments I set up in my account register appear in the step 1 list at the top of the window.

When you're ready, click the Call button.

If this is your first time, Money will immediately ask you to change the PIN number that came in your startup kit, for your own security. (See fig. 12.10.) Although these numbers are assigned by a computer, some human might have seen it, so it's safer to make up a new one. (You can change your PIN at any time later, as you'll learn later in this chapter). Type the PIN from your start-up kit in the Current PIN text box, and the new one you want to use in the New PIN text box. Repeat the new one in the Verify new PIN box, then click OK to continue.

**Fig. 12.9**
The Pay On-Line (or Bank On-Line) screen is where you execute your online activities. As you can see, I'm ready to pay these two bills.

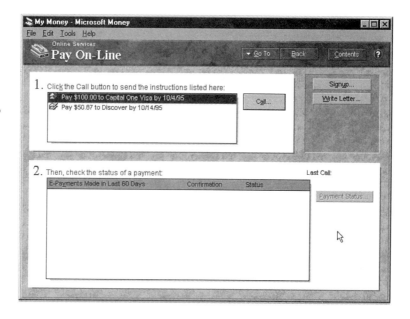

**Fig. 12.10**
The first time you use the service, you'll be asked to change your PIN.

Next, you'll be confronted with the Call Online Services dialog box, as shown in Figure 12.11. Verify that the settings are all correct (there's no reason why they shouldn't be), then click the Connect button to roll on through.

**TIP** **Dialing properties and Modem properties are both set by Windows** 95 itself, although you can modify them while using Money (see fig. 12.11). For more information about dialing and modem properties, refer to your Windows 95 documentation.

Money connects to On-Line Services and transmits your payments. You'll see an information dialog box telling you what's going on, but all you can do at this point is wait. When the transactions are complete, you'll see a Call Summary dialog box, like the one in figure 12.12, letting you know what happened. Click Close when you're finished reviewing the information.

**Fig. 12.11**
Ready to call? Then click the Connect button in this dialog box.

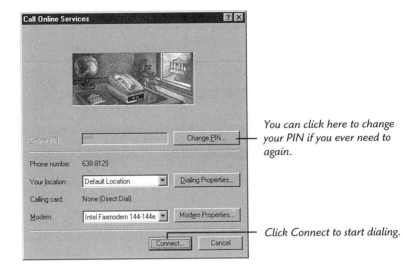

You can click here to change your PIN if you ever need to again.

Click Connect to start dialing.

**Fig. 12.12**
After Money disconnects, it tells you what happened.

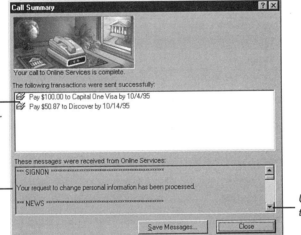

Here, I can see that my payments were successful. I would also be told here if a problem occurred.

Important! Review the messages here.

Use the scroll bar to see the rest of the messages.

**CAUTION**   **Make sure you read the messages in the bottom half of the dialog box!** They may contain important information you'll need to continue using the service successfully. You can save the messages to a text file by clicking the Save Messages button, then entering the name for the file and clicking OK. You can then review the messages later using Windows 95's Notepad or WordPad program.

Back at the Pay Online window, you'll see a summary of the completed activities in the step "2" area of the screen. Double-click on any of the listed items, or click on an item and then click the Payment Status button, to show the details about it (see fig. 12.13 for an example).

**Fig. 12.13**
You can double-click on any completed task to open a window containing details about it.

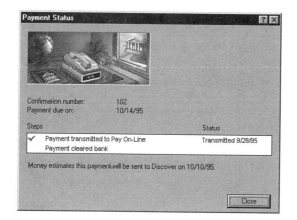

# Bank On-Line: Your online "line" to your bank

Bank On-Line is considered a separate component from the Pay On-Line feature. Unlike with Pay On-Line, which works through an independent "clearinghouse" to pay your bills, Bank On-Line works intimately with your own bank. Your modem dials the regular On-Line Services number, but the information it retrieves comes directly from your bank, not from On-Line Services.

Bank On-Line basically has two features:

- You can download a current bank statement at any time. This is better than your monthly paper statement you receive in the mail, because it is updated daily. If you have any questions about whether a transaction has cleared or not, you can check your statement and see.

- You can transfer funds between accounts (as long as they're both at the same bank). Most banks normally require a trip to the local bank branch office to do this, but with Bank On-Line you can do it from the privacy of your home.

**CAUTION** **On-Line Services' customer service representatives can't help you** with Bank On-Line questions that involve looking into your account (such as "did my transfer get made?"), because they don't have access to your account information. However, they do have access to your Pay On-Line information, and can confirm any payments you have made.

As I mentioned earlier, not all banks support Money's Bank On-Line feature. This feature is not the be-all and end-all—it's probably not worth it to switch banks just to be able to use this feature. Besides, over time, more banks may adopt it, so your current bank may offer the service next month or next year.

## Setting up Money to use Bank On-Line

When you completed the steps earlier in this chapter (under "Telling Money about your online plans"), you did most (maybe all) of the setup you need for Bank On-Line. If Bank On-Line is set up correctly, the Pay On-Line screen (and icon for it on the Contents screen) will be titled Bank On-Line instead. You may also see an action item in the "1" section that reads "Get statement and current balance for *xxxx*" along with the name of your account. Figure 12.14 shows what I mean.

*The title of the screen changes to Bank On-Line. (It was formerly "Pay On-Line.")*

**Fig. 12.14**
If one or more accounts is set up for Bank On-Line, the online screen will be labeled Bank On-Line.

*Money is ready to retrieve your statement and balance.*

*If you set up more than one account for Bank On-Line, each one has its own separate line here.*

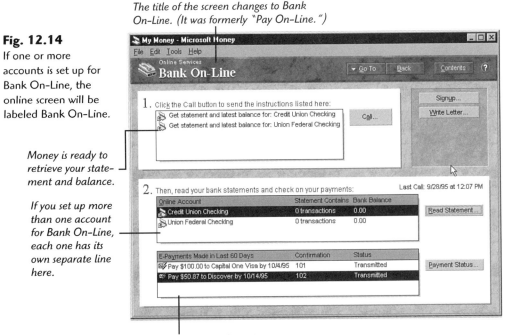

*The online payments I've made are separated from the statements.*

You can turn the Bank On-Line feature on or off with the Signup wizard that originally set it up. Click the Signup button, then keep clicking Next to move through the information you already entered. When you come to the dialog box shown in Figure 12.15, select or deselect the Online Banking check box to turn it on or off. Then continue clicking Next until you see the Finish button. Click Finish, and you're done.

**Q&A** **Why would I ever want to turn Bank On-Line off, once I've got it set up?**

You may not always want to retrieve a statement and balance every time you connect. Sometimes you might just want to pay your bills and not fuss with an incoming statement. When Bank On-Line is on, it always retrieves a statement, so you might want to turn it off temporarily while you do a Pay On-Line session.

# Retrieving a statement with Bank On-Line

Bank On-Line is extremely generous with bank statement information. When Bank On-Line is enabled (as explained in the preceding section), it always retrieves a statement whenever you call. You can call just for that, or you can call for another reason (for instance, to process a Pay On-Line payment or a Bank On-Line transfer). Either way, when Money disconnects, you'll find a statement in the "2" section, ready to read. Just double-click on it, or click it and then click the <u>R</u>ead Statement button.

**TIP** **Want a hard copy? You can print your statement while viewing** it by selecting <u>F</u>ile, <u>P</u>rint.

As you're reading the account statement, you can automatically balance your Money account register by telling Money to compare the statement to your register. Just click Add to Account Register. Money compares the transactions, and marks each one in your register with an "E."

# Making a transfer with Bank On-Line

Remember how, earlier in the chapter, we entered payments into the register that were to be paid with Pay On-Line? Well, you set up transfers in almost exactly the same way. To tell Bank On-Line to make a transfer between two accounts, your first stop is the Account Register for either of the accounts.

**CAUTION** **Don't forget, in order to make a transfer with Bank On-Line, both** accounts must be set up for online transactions (i.e. both their account numbers must appear in your startup kit you received), and they must both be at the same financial institution. You can add more accounts to your Bank On-Line or Pay On-Line service by calling the On-Line Services customer service department at (708) 852-7650.

Enter the transaction as if you have already transferred the money and are now recording it in your register, as shown in Figure 12.15. In the Number text box, open the drop-down list and select Electronic Transfer (Xfer). That tells Money you want the transaction to happen using Bank On-Line. Fill out the rest normally, then click Enter or press Enter.

**Fig. 12.15**

To transfer funds from one account to another, fill out the transfer normally, but set the Number to Electronic Transfer (Xfer).

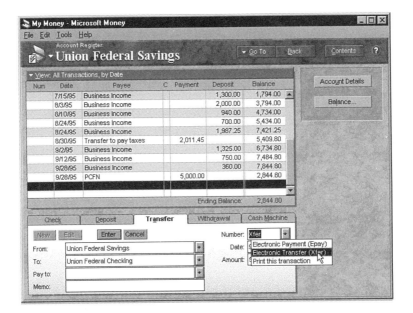

The reminder will appear in your register, just as it did with Pay On-Line. Click the Go to Online button to jump directly to the Bank On-Line screen. From there, you'll see that your transfer has been added to the list of things to do under "1" (see fig. 12.16). Click Call, and go through the connection process just as you did with bill-paying. You'll get confirmation of the transfer just as you got with your online payments.

**Fig. 12.16**
Your online transfers
are just like bill
payments to be made—
they appear on
Money's list of online
things to do.

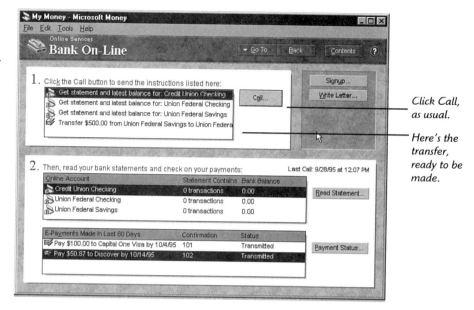

Click Call,
as usual.

Here's the
transfer,
ready to be
made.

# Have something to say? Write a letter!

If you need to talk to a customer service representative at On-Line Services,
the easiest way is to pick up the telephone and call them, Monday through
Friday from 8 am to 7 pm Central Time, at (708) 852-7650.

There are a couple of drawbacks to that, though. One is that those hours of
operation may not be convenient, and the other is that for most people, it's a
long-distance call. That's why On-Line Services offers an alternative—you
can send an electronic memo to them along with your payments and other
requests.

There are lots of reasons you might want to correspond with On-Line Services. If you use both Pay On-Line and Bank On-Line, you can:

- Write a general purpose letter regarding bill payment

- Inquire about a specific payment

- Write a general purpose letter to customer service

- Request a copy of a check

- Order new paper checks

Some of these messages, like the paper check orders, will get passed along to your bank. Others, like requests for bill payment information, stay with On-Line Services and are answered by their representatives.

**CAUTION** **If you use only Bank On-Line, or only Pay On-Line, you won't** have all the letter types shown here to choose from; you'll only have the ones that are possible with your setup. For instance, you can't order checks from your bank if you don't have Bank On-Line, and you can't inquire about payments if you don't have Pay On-Line. The dialog box shown in Figure 12.17 will have fewer choices.

No matter what you want to say to the bank or to On-Line Services, you start by clicking the Write Letter button on the Bank On-Line (or Pay On-Line) screen. You'll see a dialog box listing some of the prewritten letters you can use (see fig. 12.17). Click on one of them, then click Continue.

**Fig. 12.17**
Money helps you write several kinds of letters to On-Line Services. Just choose which kind you want.

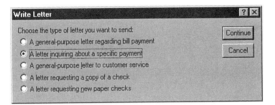

In most cases, you'll immediately see a window with a prewritten letter at this point. If you chose an inquiry about a specific payment, an extra dialog box appears asking which payment you're concerned about. Click on it, then click OK to catch up with the rest of us.

Figure 12.18 shows a letter that Money created for me to order new paper checks. It's ready for me to fill in a few details, like the starting number and the quantity. (I can also add more comments or information at the bottom if I want to.) Check out the letter to make sure it says what you want to say, and to make sure that you've filled in all the blanks. Then click OK, and the letter is added to the "1" area, ready to send when you place your next call.

**Fig. 12.18**
Here's a letter that Money prepared for me. Before I send this letter, I'll need to fill in the check quantity and starting number.

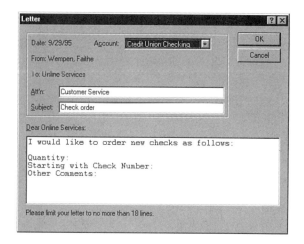

# High-tech investing: getting stock updates online

The stock market is one of those things I never really paid any attention to until recently, when I picked up a few dozen shares of Apple stock. (I'm a died-in-the-wool PC user, but the stock seemed like a good deal.) Suddenly I understand what all the fuss is about! Now, the first thing I do every morning is check the newspaper to see how my stock did.

If fumbling through the columns of tiny type in the newspaper isn't your idea of a good time, you'll be glad to discover Money's Quotes On-Line feature. Back in Chapter 10, you learned how to enter your stocks in a Money investment portfolio; now let's look at how to get updated prices for them without getting newsprint all over your hands.

We'll start from the account register of your investment account. (Mine is shown in Figure 12.19.) From there, click the Online Quotes button.

**Fig. 12.19**
Here's the account register for my investment account—it's the starting place for requesting an online quote.

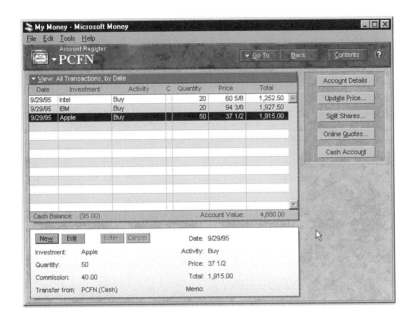

# Setting up Quotes On-Line (the first time you use it)

If this is the first time you've used Quotes On-Line, an Online Services Setup dialog box will open, just like when you set up Pay On-Line and Bank On-Line. Click Next to begin the setup.

The first thing you'll be asked to do is "Choose your online quotes provider from the list." This isn't a trick question—it's just a short list. There's Quotes On-Line, which is already selected, and then there's None. Just click Next to go on.

Next, you'll be told that you need your startup kit handy, and you'll have a chance to fill out the application form. But since you've already done that, just click Next again to go on.

Your name and address will appear, just as you typed them when setting up Pay On-Line and Bank On-Line (shown, back in figure 12.3). If you aren't using either of those services, you'll need to enter the information now. Then click Next to continue.

Next you'll be asked for the phone number to dial. Again, if you have already set up Bank On-Line or Pay On-Line, the number is already filled in. If not, enter it from your startup kit, then click Next. You'll be told that you're done (yeay!); click Finish to close it out.

# Let's get a quote or two!

After you've completed the setup procedure I just described, you're whisked into the Online Services dialog box shown in Figure 12.20. You'll see this dialog box immediately when you click the Online Quotes in the future, now that setup is complete.

**Fig. 12.20**
All the stocks you have set up in your investment profile appear on a list here. The checkboxes let you pick which ones you want to get prices for.

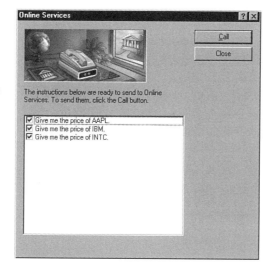

By default, all the checkboxes are marked for every stock you own. If for some reason you don't want to get the price of one or more of them, just deselect the check box.

 **TIP** **There's no reason NOT to get the price of every stock, since** you're charged by the call, not by the quote. The call may take slightly longer if you request dozens of quotes, but unless it's a long distance call for you, it shouldn't matter.

After you've chosen which quotes you want, click the Call button. The Call Online Services dialog box appears, the same as the one shown in Figure 12.11. You'll fill in your PIN (from your startup kit), then click the Connect button.

You'll have to wait a few minutes then, while Money connects to On-Line Services and retrieves your quotes. When it's done, you'll see a Call Summary screen showing the prices, like the one in Figure 12.21. Click Continue when you're done viewing it, and you're returned to your investment account register.

**TIP** **The stock prices that Quotes On-Line sent are automatically saved** in Money and your portfolio is updated. However, if you want to save the data in a separate file too, there are two ways to do it. From the Call Summary screen, you can click Copy to Clipboard to save the information to the Windows Clipboard (and then paste it in a text-editing program like WordPad or Notepad), or you can click Save As to save it as a text file for your records.

**Fig. 12.21**
Money shows me the stock prices it retrieved in the Call Summary window.

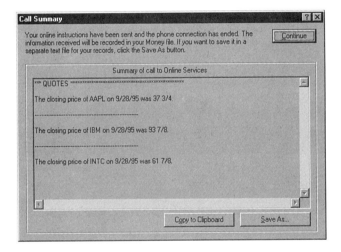

Now what? Well, now Money knows the current prices of your stock, so when you view your investment reports (see Chapter 11), you'll have an accurate picture of your portfolio value that day. You can also see the new prices and values at a glance when you view your portfolio from the Investment Portfolio screen, as shown in Figure 12.22. (There's a lot more information about this screen in Chapter 10.)

**Fig. 12.22**
The updated stock prices I just retrieved are reflected in my portfolio value, as you can see here.

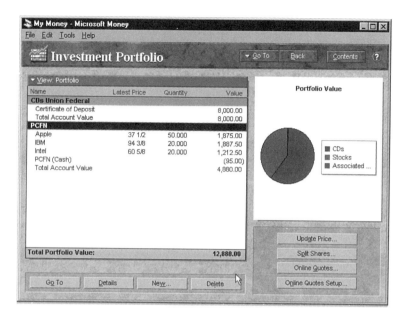

# And then there are the housekeeping details...

Well, you've learned the exciting stuff about online financial management in this chapter. I hate to end on an anticlimactic note, but there are a few housekeeping details you should know about too, just in case you ever need them.

## Changing your account information

If you move, change your name, or change your phone number, you'll need to let On-Line Services know. The best way is to call their Customer Service department at (708) 852-7650, or send them a letter online (as you learned to do earlier in this chapter).

You'll also need to change the name, address, and/or phone number stored in Money. To do that, click the Signup button on the Pay On-Line (or Bank On-Line) screen, then click Next until you come to the window where your name and address are listed. Make your changes, then continue clicking Next until you work your way through the wizard. Don't just click Cancel after you make your changes, because they won't be saved!

# Changing your PIN number

When you first used On-Line Services, you changed your PIN in the dialog box that popped up automatically (see fig. 12.10). You can make this dialog box come up again just before you dial by clicking the Change PIN button in the Call Online Services dialog box.

# Adding new accounts

If you get more bank accounts, you may want to add them to the list of accounts that On-Line Services can use. You can't do this by modem, however—you'll need to send an actual voided check from the account (or deposit slip if it's not a checking account) to On-Line Services at the same address you sent your original application form to:

> On-Line Services
> P.O. Box 3128
> Lisle, IL 60532-3128

You'll get a confirmation in the mail telling you that the account has been added.

# Canceling your online services

What if you decide that banking online isn't for you? Or that it isn't worth the fees? Just cancel your membership by calling the customer service department at (708) 852-7650. Your account will be terminated immediately and you won't be assessed any more fees or charges. (You will still be responsible for any fees you've racked up so far.)

# Part IV: Are You Ready for the Real World?

# 13

# Planning for the Future with the Planning Wizards

● In this chapter:

- Finally—a simple loan calculator!

- Figuring out your price range for buying a home

- How to plan ahead for big expenses, like college

- Am I saving enough to be able to retire when I want?

- Calculating how much money you'll make on an investment

*Whether it's a college fund or retirement security you're dreaming about, Money can help get you there with easy-to-use planning tools.* . . . . . . . . . . . . . . . . . . . . . . . ❯

I read an article the other day in an investment magazine that said nearly 50% of retired people live on incomes of less than $25,000 a year, even though many of them had sizable "nest eggs" that they thought would ensure their financial comfort in old age. (Well, $25,000 isn't exactly the poverty level, but it's probably less than those folks were accustomed to bringing in during their working years.)

The key to retirement security—and financial security in general—is to plan well in advance. Savings accounts don't just materialize out of nowhere. Smart people these days are beginning in their early 20s to sock away income in tax-deferred retirement accounts, and to establish goal-oriented savings plans to finance everything from their baby's college education to their next trip to Europe.

Even though almost everyone agrees that financial planning is important, very few people actually sit down and do the calculations. Why? Because up until recently, it's been a tedious chore, wrought with complicated math computations and scribbles on the backs of envelopes.

Fortunately, Microsoft Money changes that grim picture. Money provides five extremely easy and intuitive planning tools that anyone can use to plan for his or her financial future. You can calculate payments and interest on loans, plan a savings strategy for a special goal, figure out how much you can afford to spend on real estate, and much more. These are great features, worth the price of Money all by themselves! Check them out.

# What's up the Wizard's sleeve in the planning department?

Money's financial planning tools are called Wizards, because they're so easy to use—it's like a wizard waving his magic wand, compared to the old paper calculations that used to be required for these computations. To check them out, just click the Planning Wizards button on the Contents screen. You'll see the Planning Wizards screen, shown in Figure 13.1.

**Fig. 13.1**
The Planning Wizards
screen is your planning
"home base," from
which you select the
individual wizards you
want to use.

The Planning Wizards screen has a big collage of pictures of happy people, no doubt designed to make you feel good about saving money. More importantly, it's got five buttons down the right side of the screen. Click on the button to access the planning wizard that you want to use:

- **Loan Calculator**   Use this wizard to figure out a loan for money you're either borrowing or lending. You can figure out the loan amount, interest rate, or number of payments—whichever you don't already know.

- **Mortgage Planner**   This wizard helps you compare two mortgage deals to figure out which one is best for you. You input the price, down payment, interest rate, and other costs, and it tells you what your monthly payment will be.

- **Savings Calculator**   This simple wizard helps you calculate how much you'll save with regular contributions to a savings plan. You can factor in the interest you'll earn annually on the money, and the inflation rate.

- **Retirement Planner**   Use this wizard to estimate the amount of money you'll need to retire comfortably, and the amount you'll need to save each month (starting now) in order to achieve it.

- **Interest Estimator**   This wizard helps you determine how much interest you'll make from your interest-generating accounts (such as savings). The wizard looks at your account's balance over the specified time period and tells you how much interest that account has earned.

In the rest of this chapter, we'll look at each of these in detail. Forget everything you've ever heard about financial planning—these wizards make it easy and even fun!

## Some basic facts about loans

One of the terms you'll hear thrown around a lot in the lending business is **amortization**. Amortization simply means paying off a debt in installments. Each payment is a combination of principal (the original money borrowed) and interest (the fee for borrowing it). The interest portion of the monthly payment is based on the remaining amount yet to be repaid, so as the remaining amount decreases, a greater portion of each payment goes toward the principal. (This will become more clear later, as we examine loan planning.)

There are four factors whenever you borrow (or loan) money:

- *the amount of the loan.* A loan can be any amount, from a measly $100 or so to a multi-million dollar business loan or mortgage.

- *the annual interest rate.* All financial institutions charge interest. You can shop around to find out which institutions offer

the best rates—but rates are a constantly moving target. Depending on the individual institution and the national economy, you could pay anywhere from 6% to 25% a year.

- *the number of payments.* Almost all loans are paid at least monthly—some have weekly or biweekly payments due instead. Car loans are usually 60 months or so (i.e., 60 payments); home mortgages are usually 15 or 30 years.

- *the amount of each payment.* This is the amount you write the check for each month.

You can have a **simple** loan, in which each payment is equal, or you can choose a **balloon** loan, which requires a large lump-sum payment at the end of the loan period, called a Balloon Amount. For instance, with some car leases, you make fixed payments for 3 years, and then pay a fee (sometimes called a *residual*) when you bring the vehicle back.

# How much money can I afford to borrow?

Thinking about borrowing some money? The loan calculator can help you make your plans. Click the Loan Calculator button on the Planning Wizards screen to open the loan calculator (see fig. 13.2.).

If you know three of the four amounts (loan amount, loan term, monthly payment, and interest rate), you can calculate for the missing one. That's what Money's Loan Calculator helps you do. For instance, if you want to know how much your monthly payment will be when borrowing a certain sum of money, you can plug in the amount, interest rate, and term, and Money's Loan Calculator will tell you the payment amount. Or, if you know you can afford to spend a certain amount each month in payments, Money can calculate how much money you can borrow.

**Fig. 13.2**
The loan calculator can help you try out different loan scenarios to figure out the right combination for you.

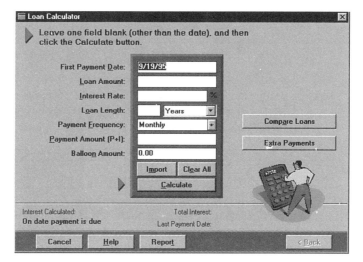

To use the loan calculator, just plug in the information about the loan you're considering. Leave the text box blank for the value you want Money to calculate. For instance, let's say I want to know how much my payment would be if I borrowed $10,000 and paid it back within 3 years, at an interest rate of 9%. I would plug the numbers in, as shown in Figure 13.3, and then click Calculate, and Money would fill in the payment amount in the Payment Amount (P+I) text box. The answer? $318.00. Ouch.

**Fig. 13.3**
What would my payment be if I borrowed $10,000 for 3 years at 9%? I'll click Calculate to find out.

*Money fills in this amount when I click the Calculate button.*

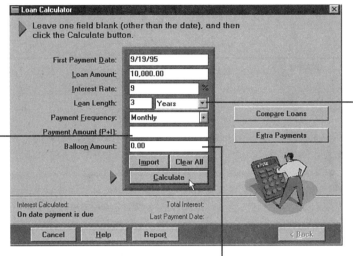

*You can choose between years or payments here, if the loan is not for an exact number of years.*

*If your loan involves a larger payment at the end, enter it here.*

Okay, let's say that $318.00 a month is a little steep for my budget. What are my options? I could change any of the other three factors to affect the payment amount. The interest rate is not very flexible—it's unlikely that I could find a better rate right now. So that leaves me with two choices, I could borrow less money, or I could take longer to pay it back.

Since I really need the whole $10,000 (I just *have* to have that new fishing boat!), let's recalculate the loan at 4 years. To do this, I'll replace 3 with 4 in the Loan Length text box, and delete the numbers in the Payment Amount text box. Then when I click Calculate again, the changed payment appears: $248.85. Now that's a figure that's closer to my budget.

What else can the loan calculator do? Lots of stuff. Here are some extra-value features that the loan calculator includes:

# Compare two loans to see which one's a better deal

You can calculate two loans side-by-side on the screen, to compare their merits, and make changes to each of them independently. Just click the Compare Loans button, and the wizard changes to show two identical boxes for plugging in numbers (see fig. 13.4). You can get back to the original view by clicking the Back button.

*Four years or three? I can see them both
at once here, for comparison.*

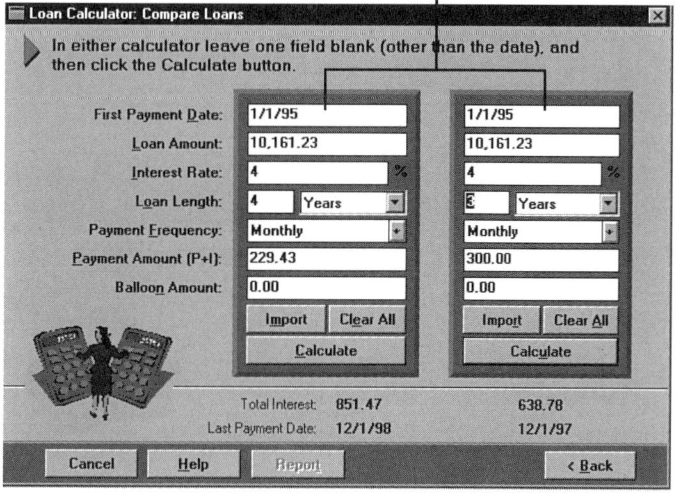

**Fig. 13.4**
Want to see two
different loan scenarios
side-by-side? Click the
Compare Loans button
to use this setup.

# Experiment with one of your existing loans

You may have several loans set up in Money already, from Chapter 3. (I do—there's my car, my home, and a small home improvement loan I took out to pay for the vinyl replacement windows that the salesman assured me would pay for themselves in energy savings.) If you're wondering if you could get a better deal on one of them, do some calculations with it with the loan calculator!

It's easy to import the current data from your loan directly into the loan calculator. Just click the Import button, and the Import a Loan dialog box appears (see fig. 13.5). Select the loan you want to import from the drop-down list. I'll choose my home mortgage. Then click OK, and that loan's information appears in the loan calculator.

Delete any factor that you want to recalculate, then change the other values and click Calculate to try out a different scenario. Any experimentation you do will not affect the actual loan, so don't worry about remembering the actual values. You can always re-import them if you need to start fresh.

**Fig. 13.5**
I can use any of my existing loans from Money in the loan calculator.

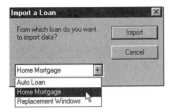

# Factor in the extra payments you'll make

Sometimes you may have a little bit of extra cash lying around (hey, it *could* happen!) and you'll want to apply it to one of your loans.

Paying more than the required amount is usually a great financial move, because the extra money reduces the principal directly—none of the extra money gets eaten up by interest. For instance, let's look at my mortgage that I just imported in the previous section. I make a $742.29 payment (not including taxes and insurance), but not much of that goes toward the principal—about $88, actually, which is pretty depressing. I'm going to be paying on this house forever!

But wait. What if I paid an additional $88 next month on my mortgage? That would be like paying the principal for another month in advance, without the interest payment to worry about. I've just knocked a month off the end of my loan!

Of course, the further into the loan I get, the greater the portion of my payment goes toward the principal, so an additional $88 a month wouldn't cut my number of payments in half. But it probably would shave several years off the loan. Let's use the loan calculator to see exactly how much I would save.

I've already imported my loan information into the loan calculator in the preceding section, so next I'll click the Extra Payments button. The Loan Calculator:Extra Payments dialog box appears.

I'll put my $88 in the Extra Amount text box, and select Monthly from the Frequency drop-down list. Then I'll click Calculate, and see the result (as shown in fig. 13.6). Wow! By paying $88 a month more, I can pay off my loan 7 years early (2015 versus 2022), and save $45,215 in interest. Why didn't someone tell me this sooner??

**Fig. 13.6**
Experiment with varying extra amounts to see how it will affect your loan payoff date and total interest paid.

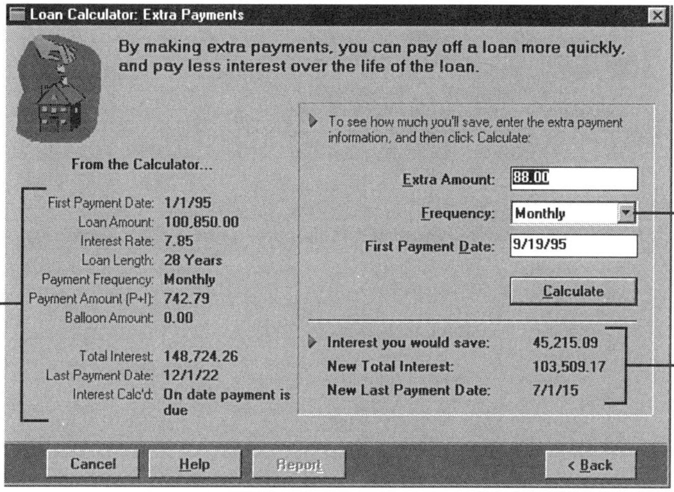

This information comes from the calculator, which got it from the loan account in Money.

*You can choose Only Once, Monthly, or Yearly.*

*Here's the calculated information.*

# Where does the payment go? Check out the amortization schedule

Several times so far in this chapter, I've mentioned that the portion of your payment that goes toward the principal changes as the unpaid balance (and therefore interest) decreases. But that's kind of hard to imagine without seeing it written out.

Fortunately, you can see a table that shows the amortization of the loan—that is, the amount of each payment that goes toward principal, and the amount that goes toward interest. To see it, just click the Report button from the Loan Calculator. You'll see a Loan Amortization Schedule (see fig. 13.7) that breaks it down for you. When you're done looking at it, click Back to return to the Planning Wizards screen.

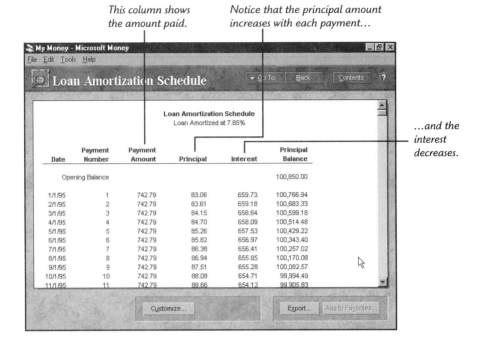

*This column shows the amount paid.*

*Notice that the principal amount increases with each payment...*

*...and the interest decreases.*

**Fig. 13.7**
Want to see the breakdown of each payment? Check out the Amortization Schedule by clicking the Report button.

**TIP**   **You can print the amortization schedule by selecting File, Print.** You can also customize it by clicking the Customize button. (You learned all about customizing reports in Chapter 11.)

# Which mortgage is a better deal?

There's a special calculator for planning real estate loans, called the Mortgage Planner. It's sort of like the Compare Loans portion of the Loan Calculator (refer to fig. 13.4)—its main purpose is to enable you to compare two mortgage plans to see which one is best for you.

## Firing up the Mortgage Planner

To start the Mortgage Planner, click the Mortgage Planner button on the Planning Wizards screen. You'll see an introductory dialog box that explains a bit about what the Mortgage Planner will do. Read it, then click Next to go on.

# Part I: How much will you be financing?

The first bit of information you're asked to enter is the purchase price of the property. You'll use the same purchase price for both of the loan deals you'll compare. (Otherwise it would be like comparing apples to oranges.) Enter it in the Purchase Price text box. For this example, I'll enter $100,000, an average price for real estate in Indianapolis, where I live. Then click Next to continue.

**CAUTION**  **Include your down payment in the purchase price you enter, but** do not include your closing costs or fees. You'll get a change to deduct the down payment from the total, and to factor in closing costs and fees, later in the process.

On the next screen (shown in fig. 13.8), you're asked to enter the down payment amount for each of the two mortgages you're comparing. For instance, I've entered $15,000 in one of them and $20,000 in the other in Figure 13.8. I entered dollar amounts, but you can choose a percentage if you prefer.

**Fig. 13.8**
The down payment affects the remaining amount of the loan, which in turn affects the payment you'll make.

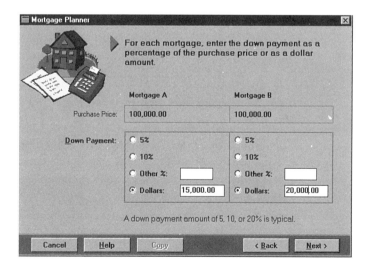

Click Next, and you'll be asked to confirm the information you've entered so far. If it's okay, click Next again to go on. If you have any changes to make, click Back until you've reached the screen where you want to make the correction. Then make it, and click Next until you've caught back up again.

# Part II: What kind of fees and special payments apply?

The next step is to enter any balloon amounts that may be due at the end of the mortgage. Some mortgages use the balloon payment as a way of helping you lower your payments. The balloon amount is due at the end of the mortgage term, which is bad, but the amount of money factored into your payments is lower, which is good. (See the Q&A below for some more stuff on balloon payments.) Enter the balloon amounts, if any, then click Next to go on.

The next screen asks for the term (length of time) and the interest rate for each loan. Enter them, then click Next.

**Q&A** *Are balloon mortgages a good deal?*

They can be if you're short on cash, because they can help you lower the payments you'll make. Instead of financing a $100,000 loan, for instance, let's say you choose a mortgage with a $20,000 balloon payment. That brings the amount included in your loan payments down to $80,000. Payment-wise, it means the difference between a $723 payment and a $709 one. Not a huge difference, but if every penny counts in your budget, it may enable you to buy a slightly nicer home.

**Q&A** *But what about that big pile of cash you're responsible for at the end of the mortgage?*

Well, in 15 or 30 years, you'll probably be more financially secure than you are now, so who's to say you won't have that cash lying around? But more likely, you'll move (and therefore sell your house and get a new mortgage) before the end of the mortgage term, so the balloon payment will never come due. If the payment comes due, and you don't have the cash, you can always borrow the money for the payment, and pay installments on that loan.

Next you're asked about **points**. If your lender is charging you any on either of the loans, enter them, then click Next.

*Plain English, please!*

**Points** is short for "percentage points", a.k.a. "loan origination fee." One point is 1% of the amount being borrowed—for instance, on a $100,000 loan, one point is $1,000. Most lenders charge you 1 point to set up the loan. You may also elect to "buy your rate down" with points. For instance, a lender might offer you 7.85% on your mortgage, but if you pay the lender 2 points, the rate would be 7.5% instead. If you're planning to keep your house for a long time, it may be advantageous to buy a better interest rate this way—if you are planning on moving in the next 3-5 years, you will probably not recoup the investment.

On the next screen, you're asked to enter any loan service fees. These are additional fees charged by the lender to set up the loan, besides points. Enter them in the Loan Service Fee text box.

 **TIP** **If you can't tell the difference between the points the lender is** charging and the service fees, don't sweat it. For the purpose of the planning we're doing here, it doesn't matter which of the two blanks you enter the number in.

Click Next, and you're asked about closing costs. (These are in addition to the fees you just entered.) For instance, when I bought my house, I had inspection fees, filing fees, Realtor fees, and several other fees I would never have imagined could be charged. You can find these out from the company that's issuing the mortgage. Add them all up, then enter the total in the Closing Costs text box.

Click Next, and you see a summary of the initial costs you've entered for each loan. You'll see your initial upfront costs, your monthly payments, and how much you'll pay in total if you keep the mortgage for the full term. As before, you can click Back to go back and correct anything, or click Next if you're satisfied. You'll see yet another summary screen that summarizes everything so far. Check it out, then click Next.

# Part III: Other factors to consider

The next few screens in the Mortgage Planner give you advice about various scenarios. The first one tells you about APR, or Annual Percentage Rate. Read the information, then click Next.

Then you'll come to the screen shown in Figure 13.9, where you indicate how long you're planning to own the property. If you plan to sell the property before the end of the loan, you'll want to consider different factors than if you plan to live in the property the rest of your life (or at least the next 15 or 30 years).

**Fig. 13.9**
The length of time you plan to own the property makes a difference in figuring up the best deal.

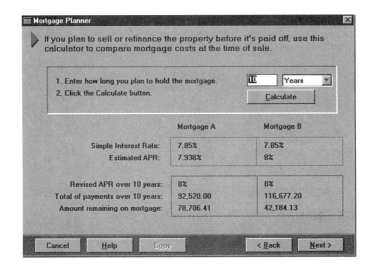

In Figure 13.9, there are two steps: first, enter the number of years you plan to hold the mortgage. Next, click the Calculate button, to see what shape your mortgage will be in after the specified time. For instance, in Figure 13.9 I've got a 30-year mortgage in Mortgage A, and a 15-year in Mortgage B. You can see that after 10 years, I'll still have $78,706 left on the 30-year mortgage, but only $42,184 left on the 15-year. When you're done working with this screen, click Next to go on to the big event: the Summary.

# The bottom line: understanding the Summary screen

Finally, the Summary appears on-screen. All the numbers you've entered in this Mortgage Planner wizard have been pointing toward one final summary, and this is it. Mine is shown in Figure 13.10.

**TIP** **Want a hard copy? At the Summary screen, click Copy to copy the** summary to the Windows Clipboard; you can then paste it into any Windows text editor or word processing program, like WordPad or Notepad, and print it from there.

**Fig. 13.10**
The Summary screen is your reward for entering all those numbers. It shows you line by line your mortgage options for each of the two loans.

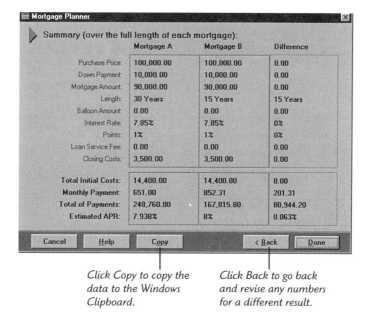

*Click Copy to copy the data to the Windows Clipboard.*

*Click Back to go back and revise any numbers for a different result.*

The information you get from the Summary screen depends largely on the differences between the two mortgages you entered. For instance, in Figure 13.10, you'll see that all the information I entered for the two mortgages was the same except for the term: one was 15 years and one was 30. Since I made them differ on only one point, I can clearly see the difference in Monthly Payment and Total of Payments between the two. The 30-year mortgage offers a lower payment rate, but I would end up spending a lot more money in total.

When you're done with the Summary screen, click Close, and you're whisked back to the Planning Wizards screen.

# Saving for little Jimmy's college fund (or a trip to Bermuda)

The Savings Calculator is like a loan calculator in reverse—you enter the amount you're saving, and the time it'll be saved for, and the calculator tells you how much interest you'll earn.

To open the Savings Calculator, click the Savings Calculator button on the Planning Wizards screen. From there, plug in the numbers in all the blanks except the one you want to calculate. For instance, in Figure 13.11, I want to save for a trip to Bermuda. I know that it'll cost $4,999 (at least that's what the brochure said), so I enter that number in the Savings Goal Amount text box. I want to go in 2 years, and I currently have $200. My savings account earns 3$^1/_2$% interest. With all these numbers in place, I simply click the Calculate button, and Money tells me (in the Regular Contribution Amount text box) that I need to save $192.86 a month to reach my goal in time to catch that flight to Bermuda.

**Fig. 13.11**
Use the Savings Calculator to figure out how much you have to save to reach a certain goal by a certain date.

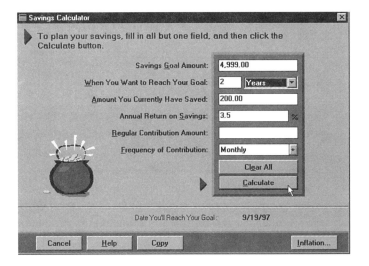

You can leave any one of the blanks empty, and have Money fill it in for you. For instance, if you regularly save $250 a month, you can have Money figure out how long it will take you to reach a certain Savings Goal Amount, or you can determine how much money you will have saved after 5 years. The choice is up to you.

**TIP** **You can copy the information on the Savings Calculator to the** Windows Clipboard, and then paste it into any text editor, the same way that you did with the Mortgage Planner. Just click the Copy button.

# What about inflation?

If you want to get really precise, you can have Money correct your totals for inflation. This is more useful for really long-term savings plans, like college funds, than for short-term goals like vacations.

To enter inflation corrections in your Savings Calculator, enter all the regular information about the savings plan (explained in the previous section), then click the Inflation button. You'll see the Effect of Inflation dialog box, which explains some basic facts about inflation (see fig. 13.12.) Enter the inflation rate that you expect in the Annual Inflation Rate text box, then click Calculate. You'll see a revised plan in the Revised Plan (For Inflation) area of the dialog box. Click Back to return to the Savings Calculator when you're finished.

**Fig. 13.12**
If your savings plan spans more than one year, you may want to have Money adjust the calculation to take inflation into account.

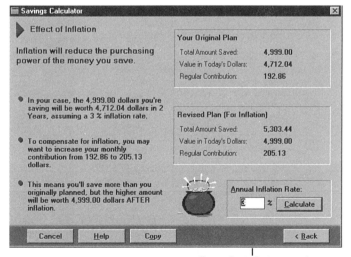

*Enter the inflation rate here*

# So you want to retire?

As I was saying earlier in the chapter, one of the biggest financial mistakes a lot of people make is to fail to provide a large enough retirement nest egg for themselves. The thought of socking away your hard-earned cash now for an event that's coming up 30 years or more in the future is not very appealing—especially when that money could be spent on an Alaskan cruise or new leather furniture. I guess that's why most people try not to think about retirement until it's too late.

Money's Retirement Planner may not be able to take the sting out of forgoing luxuries, but it can make thinking about your retirement a lot easier. Just click the Retirement Planner button on the Planning Wizards screen to view the Retirement Planner.

On the first screen of the Retirement Planner wizard (see fig. 13.13), fill in your current age in the Current Age text box. You should also verify Retirement Age (65 is the default) and the Life Expectancy (85 is the default). When you're happy with all three numbers, click Next.

**Fig. 13.13**
Start by filling in your age and telling Money when you're going to retire.

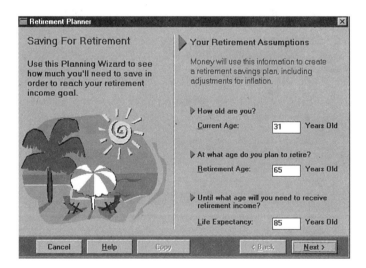

Next, you're asked to fill in your goal and your starting point (see fig. 13.14).

In the Retirement Income Goal text box, enter the amount of money you'll need to live comfortably. Think in terms of your current income—how much does it take today? Money will make the appropriate adjustments for inflation. In the Current Savings text box, enter how much you've currently got in savings and other secure investments (like CDs or retirement accounts). It's okay to estimate if you're not sure. Then click Next to continue.

 **TIP** **When figuring how much money you'll need to live on when you** retire, keep in mind that you may have your house paid off by then, so you won't be making a mortgage payment anymore. This can lower the amount of money you'll need by $12,000 or more a year.

**Fig. 13.14**
Next, decide how much money you'll need to live on when you retire, and enter the amount you've already got saved.

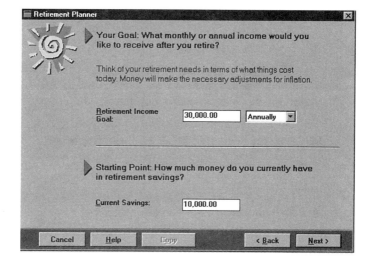

The next screen asks about the interest rate your savings or retirement accounts earn, on the average. There are two separate entries: Pre-Retirement Return and Post-Retirement Return. Again, it's okay to estimate the numbers you enter. If you're not sure, just leave the defaults in place: 9% for Pre-Retirement Return and 6% for Post-Retirement Return. Then click Next to continue.

Next, we'll adjust for inflation. Inflation is the real bite, as you see in Figure 13.15. If we don't take inflation into account, I'll only need $353,460 to retire, but with inflation at 3%, it raises my total needed to over $1.2 million. Geez. Thirty-five years from now, a dollar just won't buy what it used to! Enter the inflation rate you expect, or just leave the default 3% if you have no idea. Pause a moment to be depressed about inflation, then click Next.

**Fig. 13.15**

The Retirement
Planner adjusts your
goal for inflation. It's
a good thing, too—
because like it or not,
inflation is a reality.

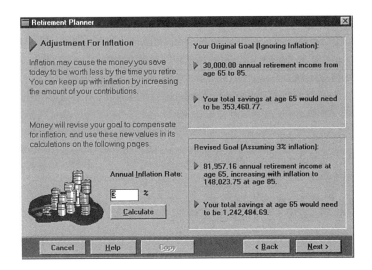

Next, you'll see a screen titled Two Ways to Reach Your Goal. It explains that
you can save a fixed amount each month until your retirement (Level Contributions), or save less now and more later, when presumably you'll have more
money (Growing Contributions). This screen (see fig. 13.16) has some critical
information on it: the amount you need to save monthly to reach your goal.
Read the info, check out the numbers, then click Next.

**Fig. 13.16**

Here's the bottom line:
how much is it going
to cost me per month
to retire in comfort?

*Here's the amount
I need to save each
month to reach my
goal. Ouch!*

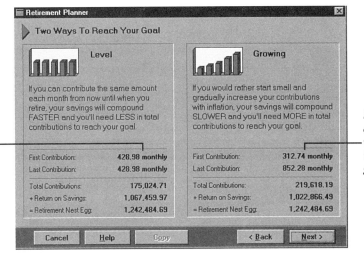

*Here's an alternate
amount I can start
with, and increase
the savings amount
gradually as I go.*

Finally, you'll see the summary screen, which shows a rather technical report and an amortization table for your retirement money. You can examine it on-screen (use the scroll bar to move through it), or copy it to the Windows Clipboard with the Copy button. When you're finished, click Done.

**TIP**    **By default, the summary is based on the Level Contributions** method. If you would rather see a report of the Growing Contributions method, click the Show Growing Contributions option button.

# How much interest can I make on this account?

If you're in good shape financially, you may be in the enviable position of having several interest-bearing accounts. When you're examining an account's performance, sometimes it's nice to be able to tally up how much cash it's actually made. The Interest Estimator can do just that. With the Interest Estimator, you can determine how much interest you've made on any of your accounts, during any time period you specify.

*CAUTION*    **The Interest Estimator is for past earnings only; it doesn't plan for** the future. For future planning, use the Savings Calculator.

To open the Interest Estimator, click the Interest Estimator button on the Planning Wizards screen. It'll look like the one shown in Figure 13.17.

Choose which account you want to check the interest for. For example, in Figure 13.17, I'm checking my IRA, which earns the highest interest of any of my accounts.

Enter the interest rate in the Interest Paid on a Positive Balance text box, and, if appropriate, enter an interest rate in the Interest Paid on a Negative Balance text box too.

**TIP**    **In most cases, you'll want to leave the Interest Charged on a** Negative Balance text box set to 0, since your account will always have a positive balance anyway. If, on the other hand, you have the option of carrying a negative balance in the account, and you're charged interest on it, enter the rate here.

Next, open the Dates drop-down list and select the date interval you want to check the interest for. For instance, in Figure 13.17, I selected Year to Date, and Money automatically filled in the numbers in the From and To text boxes. You can select Custom Dates and fill those numbers in manually if you prefer.

When you've entered all the facts, click the Calculate button, and your Estimated Interest Amount will appear above the button.

From here, click Cancel to return to the Planning Wizards screen, or Copy to copy the information to the Windows Clipboard, as with the other planning wizards.

**Fig. 13.17**
The Interest Estimator helps you figure out how much your interest-bearing account has earned so far.

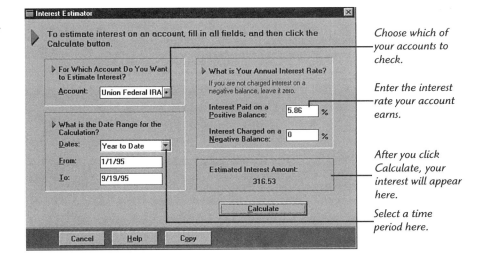

Choose which of your accounts to check.

Enter the interest rate your account earns.

After you click Calculate, your interest will appear here.

Select a time period here.

# 14

# Budgeting for Something Out of Nothing

● **In this chapter:**

- **What's the big deal about a budget?**

- **AutoBudget gets you started off right**

- **Making changes to individual budget amounts**

- **What if the amount changes from month to month?**

- **Taking a look at your budget performance**

*A budget can help you live better, both now and in the future, because it helps you decide what's important. . . .*

I don't know about you, but after that last chapter, I'm pretty depressed about my financial situation! It looks like I'm going to have to come up with over $400 a month for my retirement plan, or it's going to be generic macaroni and cheese 7 nights a week for me as a senior citizen! How in the world am I going to arrange my finances to handle the savings plan I need to follow?

Well, one great way to make your money go farther is to keep a close watch on it, with Microsoft Money's Budget feature. With a budget in place, you can get a realistic idea of how much you can save for the future without your standard of living suffering too much now. You can also find small ways to cut back on your expenses, to save for the things you want.

# What is a budget, anyway?

A *budget* is a detailed plan that lists where the income is going to come from, and what the money is going to be spent on. You've probably seen a budget before, if you've been a member of a club, church, or other organization that spent and received money.

For instance, a starving artist friend of mine, Lori, has a monthly income of $1,000. Her budget might look like this:

Income:

|  |  |  |
|---|---|---|
|  | Art lessons | $700 |
|  | Alimony | $300 |
|  | Total income: | $1,000 |
| Expense: | Rent | $400 |
|  | Utilities | $70 |
|  | Food | $200 |
|  | Art supplies | $50 |
|  | Entertainment | $50 |

| | |
|---|---|
| Clothes | $70 |
| Car | $100 |
| Gas | $40 |
| Total Expense: | $980 |

Hmm. Not a lot of room there for a retirement plan. Still, there is $20 extra each month (which Lori no doubt blows on a delivered pizza, instead of saving for old age). If she were serious about saving money, she might be able to trim a few bucks off of some of those expenses.

A budget is like a diet for your wallet. Instead of spending everything you want, and not worrying about the consequences on your bank account, you make a realistic plan well in advance. The plan outlines exactly what you'll spend, and for what. That way, you're less likely to spend unwisely.

Money's budgeting feature helps you plan your expenses by the month or the year, according to the categories you've set up. For instance, in my friend Lori's budget that I just showed you, she would have categories set up in Money that matched each of the lines on her budget: one for Art Lessons, one for Alimony, one for Rent, and so on.

 *CAUTION* **All along in this book, I've been telling you how important it is to** set up appropriate categories, and then use them in every transaction. Your budget is based on the categories you're using (and will use). If you haven't created appropriate categories yet, turn back to Chapter 5 and do so now. Budgeting won't be much good for you unless you have good categorization already in place.

# First, let's take a look at an example

Money comes with a sample file, called Sample.mny. This file contains two years' worth of financial data for an average family. (What is an "average family," you might ask? Not mine, that's for sure.) Anyway, they've already got a budget set up, so let's look at theirs before diving into the creation process.

To open another file in Money, as you learned in Chapter 9, Select File, Open or press Ctrl+O. In the Open dialog box, select Sample.mny, then click the Open button. Now we're working with the sample file—you can tell because the title bar now reads "Sample - Microsoft Money."

Now, select Tools, Budget, and the Budget dialog box opens, as shown in Figure 14.1.

*A complete list of the categories set up for this family's finances; yours will be different.*   *The amount shown next to each category is based on an entire year.*

**Fig. 14.1**
Here's a first look at the Budget dialog box, where you set amounts you'll spend on each category.

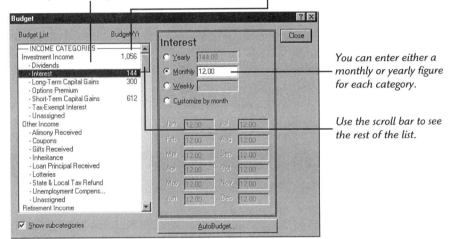

*You can enter either a monthly or yearly figure for each category.*

*Use the scroll bar to see the rest of the list.*

Let's check out a few things about this family's budget before we move on. For one thing, notice that there are a lot more categories and subcategories than the default ones—someone has obviously spent a lot of time setting up categories (which we covered in Chapter 5, if you'll remember). The INCOME CATEGORIES section alone takes up the first screenful. Scroll down and check out the EXPENSE CATEGORIES section, and you'll see that it's just as detailed. The default categories that didn't apply to this family have been deleted, and replaced with very specific, meaningful ones like "Piano Lessons," "Cosmetics," and "Ski Tickets."

 **TIP**   **I can't stress this enough: good categories are the key to a good** budget! Make sure you have the categories the way you want them before you start your own budget!

Next, click on one of the subcategories that has an amount next to it—for instance, Interest, as in Figure 14.1. You'll see the Monthly text box active, with the amount of money received (or spent) for this category each month. The Yearly and Weekly text boxes aren't available to change now, but you can see the numbers in them that Money has calculated. Now click the option button next to Yearly. The Yearly text box becomes active, and the other two are unavailable. Money lets you use any of the text boxes, but only one at a time.

Now click the Show subcategories check box to remove the check mark. Notice that just the main categories appear now, with subtotals (see fig. 14.2). This view is useful if you want to see the big picture, after you've completed your budget. Select the check box again when you're finished with this view.

**Fig. 14.2**
You can hide the subcategories for a birds-eye view of your budget situation.

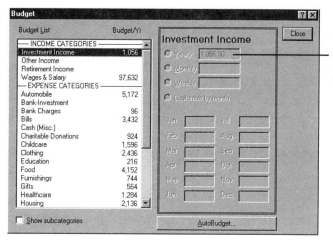

If a category has subcategories, you can't edit its amount with the subcategories hidden.

**Q&A** *What's that Unassigned subcategory under each category doing there?*

There is no such subcategory as "unassigned." This subcategory is for budgeting purposes only. When using Money's Budget feature, all amounts and transactions must fall into both a category and a subcategory. (The only exception is a category which has no subcategories at all.) Any transactions or amounts that use that category but no subcategory are stuck into this dummy "Unassigned" category to keep them out of the way.

# Enough samples, already! I want to do my own budget!

Had enough of looking at someone else's finances? Me too. (I'm especially jealous of that sample family's $97,632 entry under Wages & Salary. How do some people get these incredible jobs, anyway?) So let's get started on our own.

First, you'll need to reopen your own file, so select File, Open again, click on your file, then click OK. Now you're back where you belong—working with your own data. (It may be a bleak financial picture, but it's *mine*.)

Now, before diving into the budget process, take one final look at your categories and subcategories. Are you happy with them? Do you want to delete any that you don't ever use? Add some new ones? Now is the time to do it. Turn back to Chapter 5 if you need a refresher.

**TIP** **If you want to make regular contributions to a savings or retire-**ment account, set up an expense category for that fund, and include those contributions in your budget.

# AutoBudget: A great start

Ready to go? Then select Tools, Budget to see your own Budget dialog box.

The first thing you'll want to do is AutoBudget. AutoBudgeting asks Money to take a look at all the transactions in your accounts to date, and make ballpark estimates about your budget amounts. What a great time-saver! You don't have to go through your account register and average your electric bill payments for the last year, or figure out how much you spent on dentist appointments—Money does it all for you.

To use AutoBudget, follow these steps:

**1** Click the AutoBudget button to display the AutoBudget dialog box (fig. 14.3).

*Select from what dates AutoBudget should examine transactions.*

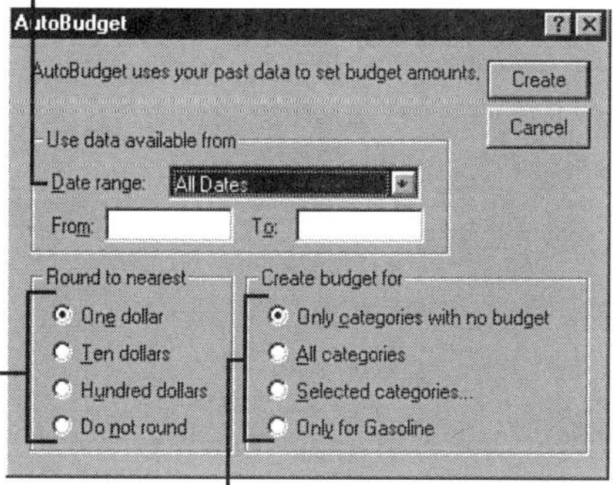

**Fig. 14.3**
Tell Money how you want the AutoBudget handled with this dialog box.

*Choose how precise the budget should be.*

*Specify which categories will be included.*

**2** Choose a date range in the Date range drop-down list, or enter a custom one in the From and To text boxes. In general, try to enter a range that matches how long you've been faithfully using Money for your finances. The longer the range, the more accurate your AutoBudget will be, unless a very untypical period in your financial life is included in the range.

**3** In the Round to nearest section, select how precise you want the budget to be. Personally, I think One dollar is precise enough.

**4** In the Create budget for section, choose which categories should be included in the budget:

- **Only categories with no budget**. If you have any budget amounts already entered that you want to keep, this option will leave them in place, and AutoBudget only for categories that have no budget amount already entered.

- **All categories.** This wipes away any previous budget amounts, and reevaluates all categories. (If you select this option, you'll get a warning message when you click Create in step 5—click OK to move past it.)

- **Selected categories.** Select this, and a dialog box opens enabling you to select each category and subcategory individually (see fig. 14.4). This option is for the truly picky at heart.

- **Only for_** You can select only the category that was highlighted when you clicked the AutoBudget button. In Figure 14.3, it's Gasoline, since that's the category that happened to be selected.

**Fig. 14.4**
You can select individual categories and subcategories to be AutoBudgeted if you like.

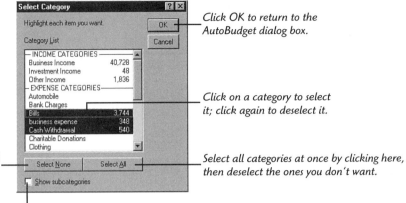

Click OK to return to the AutoBudget dialog box.

Click on a category to select it; click again to deselect it.

Deselect all categories and start over by clicking here.

Select all categories at once by clicking here, then deselect the ones you don't want.

Select this check box to see subcategories, too.

**CAUTION** **If you're planning to archive last year's financial records with** Money's Archive feature, do this after you're finished AutoBudgeting. That's because the archived information is needed to get the most accurate AutoBudget.

**5** Click the Create button.

**6** If you selected All Categories in step 4, you'll get a warning message. Click OK to move past it.

**7** You'll get a message saying that Money has created your budget. Click OK, and you're done!

AutoBudget creates your budget, and enters the appropriate numbers next to each category on your Budget screen. My budget, after using AutoBudget, is shown in Figure 14.5.

**CAUTION** **AutoBudget works best if you've been keeping your transactions** in Money for a long time—at least 6 months. Ideally, a whole year of transactions would give the best results. You may not get reliable figures if you have transactions of 30 days or less.

**Fig. 14.5**
Here's my budget after AutoBudget has been through it.

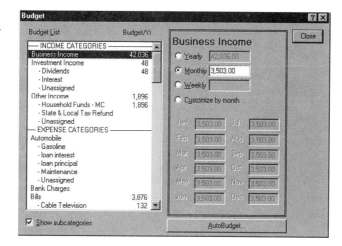

**TIP** **The AutoBudget feature can help you identify categorization** errors in your register. For instance, I usually pay for gasoline with cash or a credit card—never a check. And I notice that AutoBudget has not entered anything under Auto:Gasoline. That tells me I should start categorizing my gasoline credit card payments as Auto:Gasoline rather than Bills:Credit Card, so I'll be able to see more clearly how much I'm spending on gas.

# Fine-tuning your budget

AutoBudget can be an excellent start, especially if you've diligently categorized each transaction over several months, but it's not perfect. It can't know, for instance, that your natural gas bills in the last 3 months were very low because you don't run your furnace in the summer, so it probably estimated your natural gas budget too low. Similarly, if you just paid off your major credit cards in several large installments, AutoBudget might think that you need to make those huge payments on a regular basis. Wrong again.

Fortunately, it's easy to correct an AutoBudget figure. Just follow these steps:

**1** Click on the category for which you want to change the number. I'm going to change my natural gas payment, so I'll click Bills:Natural Gas.

**2** Click the Yearly, Monthly, or Weekly button, to choose how you'll enter the amount. I'm going to choose Yearly.

**3** Enter the budget amount in the text box for the option you chose in step 2. For instance, I know from looking at last years' receipts that I paid a total of $795 to my local natural gas company, so I'll enter that in the Yearly text box. Money immediately calculates the Monthly and Weekly values, so I can see that, on the average, I spend $66.25 a month for natural gas.

That's all there is to it! You can change any budget amount by just selecting it, selecting the interval, and typing a new number.

**TIP** **Yearly, Monthly, or Weekly? Choose whichever is most convenient** for you. In the end, your budget will be based on yearly figures, but if you don't know the yearly figure, choose Monthly, and the Budget will multiply your entry by 12, or choose Weekly, and it'll multiply by 52.

# What if I want different amounts each month?

Some categories of expense or income don't have equal activity throughout the year. For instance, I have to pay for my auto insurance twice a year, and it's $700 each time. (Okay, so I've had a few tickets!) I could enter an expense of $1,400 a year for that category, and Money would spread it out over all 12 months. That way, as I'm spending money, I'll know that I need to set aside $116.67 each month in preparation for the bill.

It's fine to spread out unequal payments over all months like that, but if you prefer, you can enter the expense in the month where it'll occur. Instead of shaving a little bit of money off of each month's budget to pay the bill, the full weight of the bill will fall in the month where it is due. This method probably reflects more accurately the way you actually spend money, although you might be more comfortable financially in the long run if you spread the amount out.

To include unequal monthly payments in your budget, instead of choosing Yearly, Monthly, or Weekly, choose Customize by month. Text boxes for each month will become available in the Budget dialog box, as shown in Figure 14.6. You can enter the exact amount you want for each month. For instance, in Figure 14.6, I've entered my auto insurance payments in the months where they actually belong.

**Fig. 14.6**

You can insert expenses or income where they really occur in your budget, rather than averaging them over the entire year.

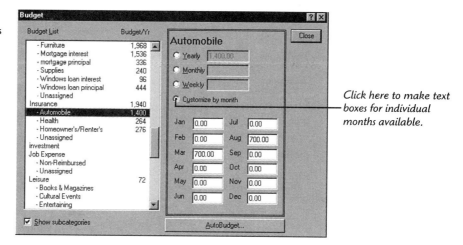

*Click here to make text boxes for individual months available.*

# Okay, I have a budget. How do I use it?

You'll notice that Money's Budget screen is serenely non-judgmental. It won't tell you if your expenses exceed your income, and it won't suggest ways to improve. In fact, as an analysis tool, it's not very helpful, standing alone.

Fortunately, though, you can create budget reports using Money's Report & Chart Gallery (which you learned all about in Chapter 11). There are two reports there designed specifically for use with your budget. They're called "My Budget" and "How I'm Doing on My Budget." You can view them by clicking the Report & Chart Gallery button on the Contents screen, then double-clicking the button for the report you want.

## Checking out the My Budget report

The My Budget report is a month-by-month list of each category's income and expense. It's a lot like the Budget screen itself, except that you can see all the info for every category and every month at once. Mine is shown in Figure 14.7.

From the My Budget report, you can double-click on any line to see a complete list of transactions that used that category. For instance, if I double-clicked on Business Income in Figure 14.7, I would get a window like the one shown in Figure 14.8, listing each transaction by date. Click Close when you're done looking at them.

**Fig. 14.7**
Get a good look
at your budgeted
amounts with the My
Budget report.

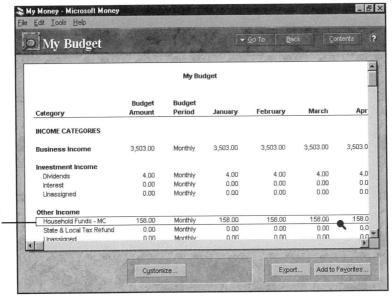

*Double-click on a
category to see its
transactions.*

**Fig. 14.8**
Want to see the
transactions you've
assigned to that
category? Just double-
click to bring up this
window.

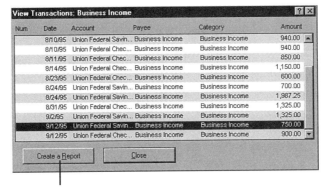

*Click here to create a separate report of only these transactions.*

 **TIP** **You'll get a better view of the My Budget report if you print it out**
rather than trying to see it on-screen. Just select File, Print, then click OK.
Mine took six pages.

# How am I doing, budget-wise?

The My Budget report is helpful, but it doesn't tell you if you're over budget, under budget, or on-target. That's where the second report comes in: How I'm Doing on My Budget. Double-click on that button on the Reports and Chart Gallery screen to see it.

By default, this report is a chart, as shown in Figure 14.9. I can see how my actual expenses compare to my budget in the most-used categories and subcategories. In Figure 14.9, it looks like I'm doing pretty well—my budgeted amounts are well above my actual amounts.

**Fig. 14.9**
The How I'm Doing on My Budget report is shown in chart form by default, so you can see graphically how you're doing.

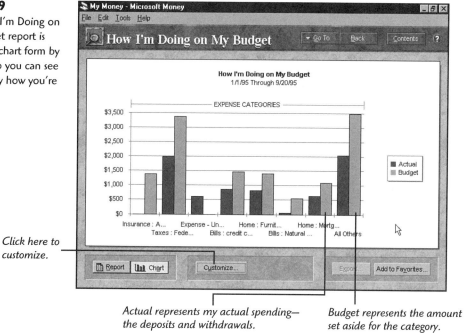

Click here to customize.

Actual represents my actual spending—the deposits and withdrawals.

Budget represents the amount set aside for the category.

An even better use of the How I'm Doing on My Budget report, though, is as an actual report. Click the Report button as you're viewing the chart to change to Report view. Here, you can see the difference between your actual and your budgeted amounts in individual categories, and most importantly, overall. Figure 14.10 shows my report (I've scrolled down to the bottom right corner so you can see the grand total).

**Fig. 14.10**
The How I'm Doing on My Budget information is even more helpful as a report. You can see exactly how much ahead (or behind) you are!

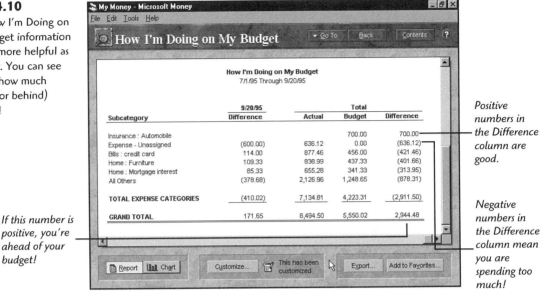

Positive numbers in the Difference column are good.

Negative numbers in the Difference column mean you are spending too much!

If this number is positive, you're ahead of your budget!

# I'm over budget—now what?

If you find that you are spending more than your budget allows, you're going to have to find ways of reining in your spending habits. Here are a few suggestions:

- Spend less on dining out. You can count on getting about twice the bang for your buck in groceries versus eating out. So if you're spending $200 a month on eating out and $300 on groceries, you could cut your Dining Out budget to $100 and increase your Groceries budget by $50, with a net savings of $50.

- Check your insurance policies to make sure you're not paying for duplicate coverage. For instance, if your health insurance pays all your medical bills, you don't need medical coverage for yourself in your auto insurance policy.

- Plan to shop at discount stores rather than more pricey department stores. You can create a report (see Chapter 11) that shows how much you spend at each store (by payee), then focus on decreasing your expenditures at high-priced stores in the future.

- If you're being eaten alive by high-interest credit card bills, consider consolidating all your credit card debt on one low-interest card, or get a debt-consolidation loan from your local bank. You'll save a few dollars on postage, paying only one bill, and hundreds more in interest savings.

Of course, these suggestions don't even scratch the surface—there are hundreds of books out there that list ways to save money without sacrificing your standard of living.

# 15

# Tax Time: Dealing with Old Uncle Sam

● **In this chapter:**

- **How do I keep tax records in Money?**

- **Making sure your categories are tax-aware**

- **Categorizing a paycheck with taxes in mind**

- **Tax day is here: printing out tax reports**

- **Can I import Money info directly to my tax software?**

*Money can't file your taxes for you, but it sure does help with the prep-work—which can make April 15th a bit easier to bear.* . . . . . . . . . . . . . . . . . . . . . . . . . . . . ➤

**P**aying taxes is a real bite in several ways. First, there's the depressing realization of how much of your hard-earned income is going toward taxes. Then there's the time and effort in filling out the income tax forms. (Eleven hours! Geez!) Finally, there's the panic in coming up with the money to pay, if you owe, and the frustration of waiting in line at the post office at 11:30 p.m. on April 15th in order to meet the midnight deadline

Well, Money isn't a magic pill that will make it all go away. But Money does shine in one area—it can help cut down the amount of time it takes you to fill out your tax forms, thanks to its most excellent way of keeping track of taxable income and tax deductions.

You can tell Money to keep track of a certain category or subcategory for tax purposes, and you can even tell it which tax form and line the category should be assigned to. Then, come tax time, all you do is print out one of Money's tax reports, and copy the information from your report to your tax form.

# Money: the perfect administrative assistant

Remember the character Radar O'Reilly on the '70s TV show M*A*S*H? Radar was the perfect administrative assistant. His primary duty was to take information, organize it, and give it back to his boss when needed. And he was uncannily good at it, too. Sometimes he provided the information before the Colonel even asked!

Microsoft Money, as you've seen so far in this book, is a pretty great administrative assistant too. Money doesn't try to tell you how to run your finances—it just provides information that helps you make the decisions, sometimes before you even ask for it. And like any good assistant,

Money doesn't desert you in your hour of need— or **hours** of need, when it comes to preparing your tax forms.

In its own typical style, Money's approach to your tax information is very non-judgmental. It won't give you advice about deducting certain expenses or let you know if you're categorizing something improperly. (You can buy special tax software for that, like TurboTax.) What Money *will* do, however, is total up every bit of expense or income in a category, and provide the total to you in a tax report that you can use to make filing your taxes a snap (well, snap-*like*, at least).

What could be easier? Glad you asked. If you're using tax preparation software, like TurboTax, you can export your Money tax report into a format that the tax program can understand, and then import the data directly in. So you don't even have to copy the information!

# First, make sure your categories are tax-aware

As you probably remember from Chapter 5, when you set up a new category, you have to specify whether or not it's tax-related. (There's a Tax-related checkbox you select or deselect.) On the Details screen for the category, you can even select a specific tax form and line.

 **Plain English, please!**

What exactly does "tax-related" mean? It just means that the category will be included on the tax reports that Money can generate (see Chapter 11). There's no big commitment in specifying a category "tax-related." You aren't forced to include it on your taxes—you're just giving yourself the option of viewing that category later, as you assemble your tax information.

Before we go any further in planning your tax preparation, you should go to your Categories list and make sure each category is appropriately marked as "Tax-related" or not (tax-related categories have an X in the Tax column of the Categories list). Now is also an excellent time to clarify exactly which tax form and line particular categories should use.

## Taking a look at your Categories list

From the Contents screen, click Payees & Categories, then click the Categories button to display your category list. (Mine is shown in fig. 15.1.) Some categories already have tax information assigned to them by default—for instance, Interest, as you can see in Figure 15.1, is already assigned to Schedule B, on the Interest Income line. (Money gives the name of the line rather than the number, because you probably don't know the number off the top of your head. This way you don't have to look it up!)

**Fig. 15.1**
Before you generate
any tax reports, you
should make sure that
your tax information
for each category is
complete and
accurate.

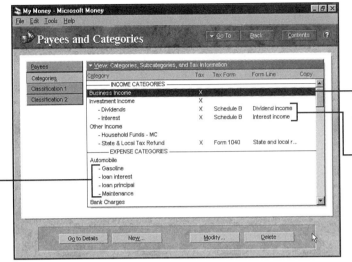

*This category is
already marked Tax-
related, but the form
and line haven't been
assigned yet.*

*Some of the
default categories
already contain
tax information.*

*Some categories are
not tax-related, nor
should they be.*

**CAUTION**  **Money's tax forms and lines that it lists for various categories are**
designed for use in the USA only. If you're filing taxes in another country,
you can still use the Tax-related check box to include the category on your
tax reports, but you won't be able to specify a specific form and line in this
software program.

**Q&A**  *How do I know which categories should be
tax-related?*

Well, the only way to know for sure is to check with a tax advisor, such as a
CPA, enrolled agent, or even a certified financial planner (CFP). He or she
can help you figure out exactly which of your categories should be included
on your taxes.

Generally speaking, all your Income categories should be tax-related,
because you have to pay taxes on all income that you receive. (There are
exceptions, of course, like certain tax-free investments or income and
capital gains you generate in tax-deferred accounts, but you'll have to ask
your tax advisor to tell you which ones fit this description.)

Some of your other expenses, on the other hand, may NOT be tax-related.
For example, medical bills can sometimes be deducted, as well as charitable
donations. You can deduct 100 percent of the interest you pay on your
mortgage too.

# Adding tax info to a category

If you know which tax form and line a particular category relates to, it will really help you in the long run if you assign it on your Categories list. For instance, in Figure 15.1, you can see that I have a category called Business Income. It's got an X in the Tax column, indicating that it's tax-related, but there's no tax form or form line.

**TIP** **It's difficult to know, unless you've used a certain form in the** past, which forms and schedules you'll be using. Check with your accountant, or better yet, call the IRS directly and ask! I called once, and a very helpful man figured out which forms I needed and sent them to me for free.

I happen to know, from doing my taxes last year, that business income is reported on Schedule C, on the Gross Receipts line, so I'm going to add that information to this category. Here's how to assign tax info to a category:

**1** Double-click the category, or click it once and then click the Go to Details button. The Category Details screen appears for that category. (The one for my Business Income category is shown in fig. 15.2.)

**Fig. 15.2**
Here's where you assign specific tax information to a category.

*Make sure this check box is marked.*

*If desired, select a form from this drop-down list.*

*If you select a tax form, you can also select a form line.*

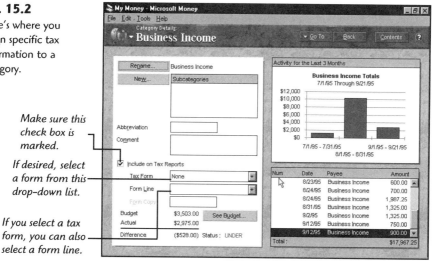

**2** If it's not already selected, select the Include on tax reports check box.

**3** To choose a tax form, open the Ta<u>x</u> Form drop-down list and select one. For instance, I'm going to select Schedule C.

**4** If you chose a tax form, you can also choose a form line. Open the Form <u>L</u>ine drop-down list and select one.

**5** Click <u>B</u>ack to return to the Categories list.

Repeat these steps for all the categories you want to set up until they're each fully described for tax purposes. Then you're ready to check out the tax reports!

# How to categorize your paycheck deposit

In Chapter 3, you learned about entering splits to divide the income or expense from a transaction across several categories. For tax purposes, it's important that you split your income from your paycheck, so you can keep track of how much money you're paying with each paycheck for various kinds of taxes: state, federal, local, FICA, and so on.

For instance, when you get a paycheck, it starts out with your Gross Pay (the real amount you earned) and then your taxes of various kinds are subtracted—such as Federal tax, Social Security, and in some cases, State tax—along with health insurance payments, retirement plan contributions, and maybe even more if you have other types of automatic deductions. (No wonder you have so little left to live on!)

As you're filling out your tax forms, you'll need to know exactly how much was deducted from your salary during the year for each type of deduction. Your employer will send you a W-2 form summarizing these deductions—by law you must receive it no later than January 31st following the specified tax year—but if you keep track of them yourself, you can see how you're doing tax-wise before you get the W-2 forms, and you can check the W-2 form's accuracy. (Mistakes happen!)

The trick to entering your paycheck into Money is to enter not the actual amount of the check you received, but the amount of your gross pay. Then categorize each of the deductions in the split as a separate category with a negative number. For instance, Figure 15.3 shows how a typical paycheck might break down:

The total left would be $876.78, which is the net amount that would show up in your checkbook after you entered this deposit with all those splits.

**Fig. 15.3**
I've created splits for the many categories that eat up my paycheck.

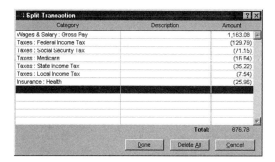

| Category | Description | Amount |
|---|---|---|
| Wages & Salary : Gross Pay | | 1,163.08 |
| Taxes : Federal Income Tax | | (129.79) |
| Taxes : Social Security Tax | | (71.15) |
| Taxes : Medicare | | (16.64) |
| Taxes : State Income Tax | | (35.22) |
| Taxes : Local Income Tax | | (7.54) |
| Insurance : Health | | (25.96) |
| | **Total:** | 876.78 |

Now, make all those deducted categories tax-related, if they're not already, and on your tax report, you'll get an itemized list of your year-to-date contributions in each of those areas.

# Let's take a look at the Tax reports

Money's tax reports can give you an easy worksheet that contains all the tax information you need. Just copy the numbers from the worksheet straight onto your tax forms. (If you need a refresher on viewing Money's reports, see chapter 11.)

From the Contents screen, just click the Report & Chart Gallery button, then click the Taxes button to see the list of tax reports (see fig. 15.4). You can click on any report on the list and see a brief explanation of it below. For instance, in Figure 15.4, we're seeing an explanation of the Tax-related Transactions report.

Let's look at each of these reports in detail, and see what we can use each one for at tax time.

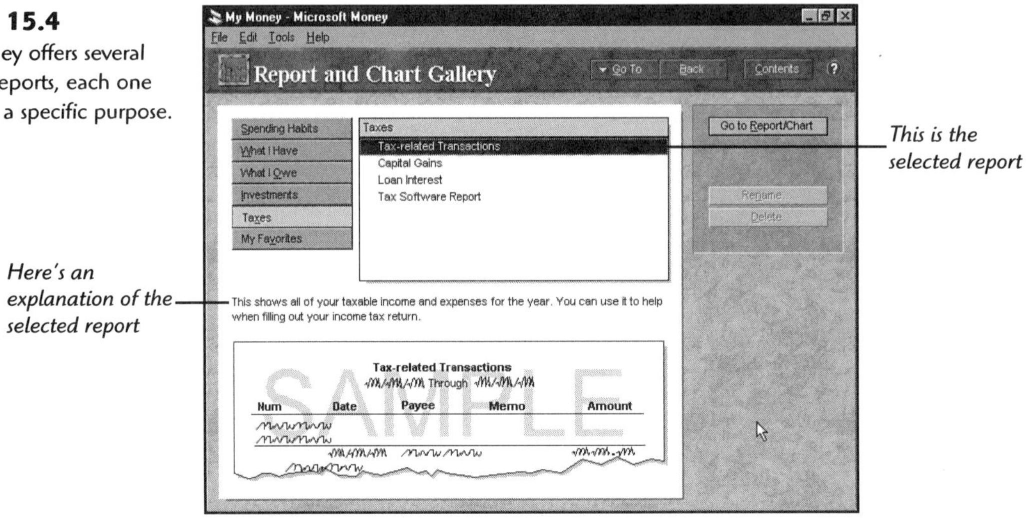

**Fig. 15.4**
Money offers several
tax reports, each one
with a specific purpose.

Here's an
explanation of the
selected report

This is the
selected report

# Tax-related Transactions: the complete list

The Tax-related Transactions report is exhaustive. It lists every tax-related category, and then lists every transaction under the category. As you can see in Figure 15.5, it totals each subcategory and category, so you can see exactly how much can be attributed to each category.

**TIP** **Don't forget, as with any report, you can double-click on any** individual transaction line to see the complete transaction in an Edit Transaction window.

## Isn't there any way to make this report less bulky?

Of course, you might not want this much detail. It may be that you'd like to skip the individual transactions and just see a summary of each category and subcategory total. No problem—you can customize the report to do just that.

While you're viewing the report, click the Customize button. The Customize Report dialog box appears (shown in fig. 15.6).

**Fig. 15.5**

Here's a master list, by category, of every single transaction that used a tax-related category.

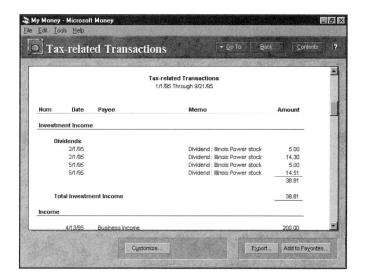

**Fig. 15.6**

Using the Customize Report dialog box, you can choose to eliminate some of the detail and just see summaries.

*Click here to change to a summary report.*

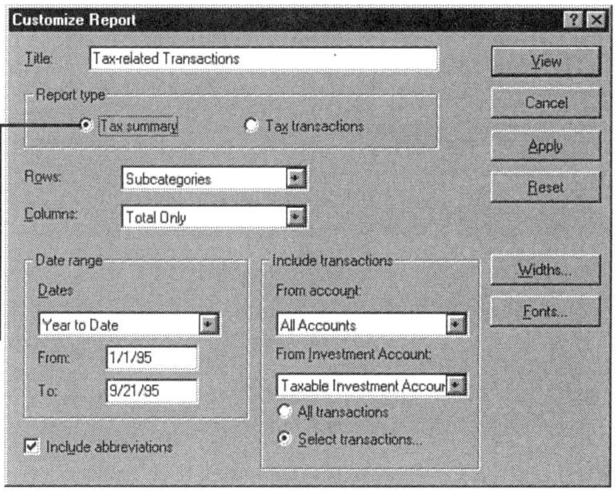

In the Report type section of the dialog box, click the Tax summary button. This turns off the detail of the individual transactions. Then click View to return to the report in a much more compact and manageable form (see fig. 15.7).

**Fig. 15.7**
When you select Tax summary in the Customize Report dialog box, the tax report shows only the totals for each category.

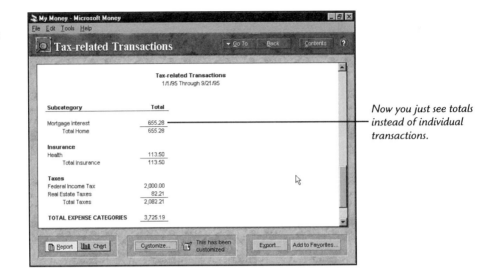

*Now you just see totals instead of individual transactions.*

## What else can I do with this report?

Of course, you can print the report (File, Print), export it (Export), and save it to your list of favorite reports (Add to Favorites), just as in any report.

If you're looking for slightly different information, you might want to revisit that Customize Report dialog box (fig. 15.6). If you choose Tax summary as the report type, you can choose to have additional columns on the report by selecting either Accounts or Payees from the Columns drop-down list. You may be interested in particular accounts (perhaps your accountant has advised you to exclude the interest earned from an account you hold jointly with a business partner, for example). In that case, choose Accounts from the Columns drop-down list to see columns for each of your accounts added to the report, as shown in Figure 15.8.

What else? Well, you can change the date range under Dates, although for tax purposes you will probably always want January 1st through today's date. (You might, however, generate a report for last year—in which case you would use January 1 of last year as the From date and December 31 of last year as the To date.)

You can also choose which accounts you want. Select a specific account from the From account drop-down list, or leave it set to All Accounts to see them all. You can include or exclude investment accounts with the Investment Account drop-down list. Again, though, for tax purposes, you should probably include all your accounts that you are the sole owner of, since they're all income and expense that you must report.

**Fig. 15.8**
You can divide the amount of each category into specific accounts or payees if you like. The one shown here is divided by accounts.

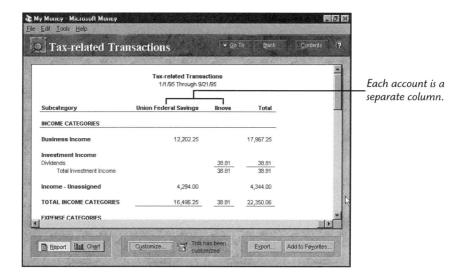

*Each account is a separate column.*

**CAUTION**

**Things get a little bit sticky if you are tracking an account in** Money for which you are are jointly responsible with anyone other than a spouse (if you and your spouse file joint taxes). For instance, if you jointly own real estate, who should deduct the mortgage interest? Who should claim the rental property income? Check with your accountant to find out the best way to handle your situation.

# Checking out your capital gains

If you're a heavy-duty stock trader, you'll really appreciate the Capital Gains report. Just double-click the Capital Gains button on the Report and Chart Gallery screen to see it. An example is shown in Figure 15.9. (No, this isn't from my own account—are you kidding? I'm no stock maven. This example is from the Sample.mny file that comes with Money.)

If you're interested in examining your stock sales in detail with this report, that's fine, but the main purpose of this report is the GRAND TOTAL. It tells you how much money you've made in profit (or lost) overall. Capital Gains are considered as profitable income on your taxes, so you'll need to report this money. For instance, in Figure 15.9, you can see that this person came out $844.48 ahead—that's the amount of income he'll report on his taxes on the Capital Gains line.

**Fig. 15.9**

The capital gains report shows how much profit (or loss) you've attained with your investment portfolio.

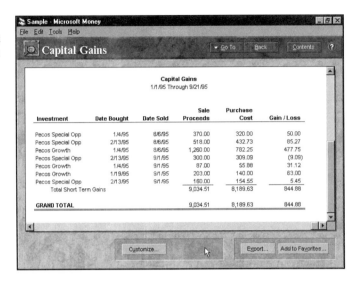

You can customize this report, too, just as you can other reports. The Customize Report dialog box for Capital Gains looks a little different, though (see fig. 15.10); open it, as usual, by clicking the Customize button.

**Fig. 15.10**

Here are some customization options for the Capital Gains report.

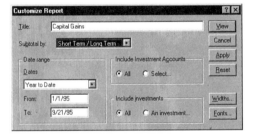

Some things you can do customization-wise include:

- You can subtotal by time period instead of by short term/long term (the default). Select a period from the Subtotal by drop-down list. For instance, in Figure 15.11, I've subtotaled by Quarter, which lets me see in which quarters the biggest gains or losses occurred. If you pay your taxes quarterly (as most businesses do), you may find this especially helpful.

**Fig. 15.11**
When you subtotal by a time period, such as Quarterly (shown here), you can see your investments over time.

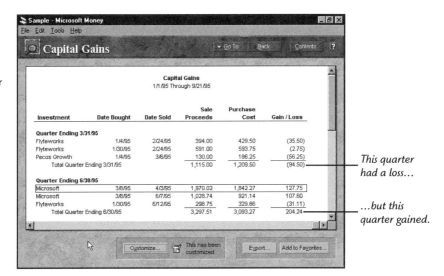

*This quarter had a loss...*

*...but this quarter gained.*

- You can change the date range, as with any other report, in the <u>D</u>ates section of the Customize Report dialog box. However, for tax purposes, make sure you are reporting on the same dates as those for which you're filling out the tax forms.

- In the Include Investment Ac<u>c</u>ounts section, you can choose Select to open a dialog box that lets you pick which investment accounts should be included. This is just like selecting regular accounts to include in a report, as you did when you customized reports in Chapter 11.

- You can base the report on only one particular investment by clicking the An investment button in the Include <u>i</u>nvestments section. A dialog box opens in which you can select one investment only (you can't make multiple selections here.)

**TIP** **Don't forget, you can also change the Fonts and Widths of any** report, as you learned in Chapter 11. You can also reset the report to its default settings by clicking the Reset button.

# Figuring out how much deductible interest you paid

One of the nicest tax breaks I receive as a homeowner is the deduction I take for my mortgage interest. Since I'm still in the first few years of my mortgage loan, a huge majority of each payment goes toward interest (something like $670 of a $750 payment, can you believe it?!). All the money I pay in interest is an itemized deduction.

The interest I pay is neatly summarized under the Interest:Mortgage category on the Tax-related Transactions report we looked at earlier in the chapter. To get a closer look at the interest I paid, I can use the Loan Interest report (shown in fig. 15.12). To see it, just click the Loan Interest button on the Report and Chart Gallery screen.

Though you can't see the whole thing in Figure 15.12, this report shows you how much interest you will have paid by the end of the current year—plus every year after that until the loan is paid off. For instance, if I wanted to see how much interest I would pay on my mortgage in 2010, I could scroll down in this report to the year 2010 and find the answer: $5,557.96.

**Fig. 15.12**
The Loan Interest report shows how much interest I'll pay with each payment.

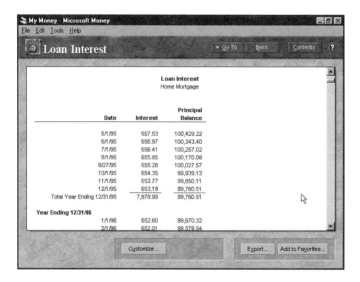

By default, this report shows the last loan you worked with in Money, not necessarily your home mortgage. Since it's your mortgage interest that's usually deductible (and other loans' interest usually isn't), you'll want to change the report to show your home mortgage if it's not displayed. You'll do this, and much more too, from the Customize Report dialog box.

Click Customize to customize this report. From the Customize Report dialog box (fig. 15.13), you can:

- Change the report title in the Title text box.

- Change which loan appears on the report by selecting it from the From loan drop-down list.

- Choose which fields to include from the account register in the Include fields area. The default is just Interest amount, since that's what you're concerned about when preparing your taxes.

- Choose how you want the report subtotaled. By default, it's subtotaled by year, since you pay your taxes yearly. But if you pay quarterly, you may want to change the Subtotal by setting to Quarter.

- The Show opening balance check box prints the opening balance at the top of the report. Deselect this to take it off.

- The Show splits check box includes the split categories of each payment on the report. This isn't necessary for tax purposes, but you may want to see it for your own edification.

- Choose a different date range from the Dates section, if you don't want to see the entire life of the loan. For instance, you could limit the report to only this current tax year.

**Fig. 15.13**
This dialog box shows the options you can set for the Loan Interest report. You can change dates, show a different loan, and more.

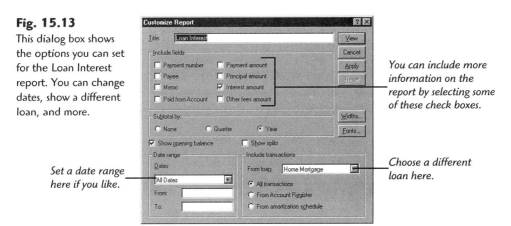

*You can include more information on the report by selecting some of these check boxes.*

*Choose a different loan here.*

*Set a date range here if you like.*

# Exporting data to your tax prep program

If you use tax-preparation software, and you've carefully entered the exact forms and form lines for each tax-related category, you're in luck now. You can export the information from Money, and then import it directly into your tax program, saving you the time of typing in all those figures!

For instance, I've been using the Business Income category for the money I make as a freelancer. I've got it set up as Tax-related, on Schedule C, on the Gross Receipts line. I've got several other categories set up too, with their appropriate forms and lines. Now, when I view the Tax Software Report from the Report and Chart Gallery, I see a compact list of every category for which I've assigned a form and line, along with the total amount that belongs there (see fig. 15.14).

**Fig. 15.14**
This report lists all the categories for which I've assigned tax form and form line designations.

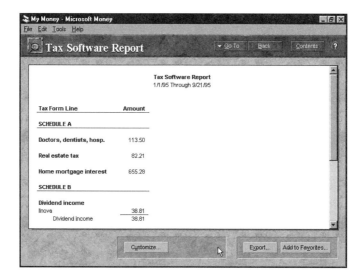

This report works great as-is; I can print it out and use it to fill out my taxes. But I can also export it for use with my tax program by following these steps:

**1** While viewing the report, click the Export button. The Export Tax dialog box appears (see fig. 15.15).

**2** Type a name for the exported file in the File name text box. For instance, I'm going to call mine **money94.txf**.

**TIP** **You don't have to type the extension .txf on the end of the name;** Money will add it for you automatically.

**3** Click OK. Money exports the data.

**4** Open your tax-preparation software and import the data. The exact procedure varies depending on the software you're using; check your tax prep software documentation for exact steps.

**Fig. 15.15**
Here's where you choose a filename to export your data to.

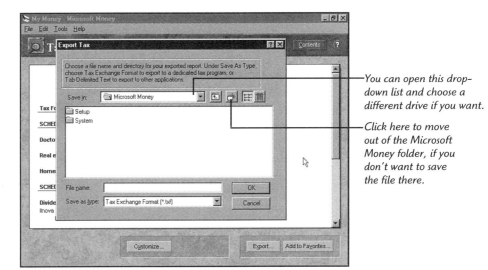

You can open this drop-down list and choose a different drive if you want.

Click here to move out of the Microsoft Money folder, if you don't want to save the file there.

# 16

# Be Your Own Accountant: Three Real-World Examples

● In this chapter:

- What if I'm just starting out financially?

- How Money helps growing families manage their money

- Money works great for retirees too!

*Starting a new family? Ready to retire? Money can lend a hand with your financial management, no matter what your age—or situation! . . . . . . . . . . . . . . . . . . . . . . . .* ❯

No matter what shape your finances are in, Money can help you become more organized and more efficient. It might even help you pay less on your taxes and find better investments! If your finances are too complicated for Money, that's probably a good clue that you need to hire a financial professional. The rest of us can save tons of money by being our own financial pros 99% of the time with Money, and calling in a professional in rare situations.

In this chapter, we'll look at three completely different households with very different financial scenarios, and talk a bit about how Money can help organize each family's finances. We'll talk about which categories are most helpful, which reports can provide useful data, and we'll even evaluate which of the Money "extras" might work well, such as online bill paying or banking.

# Example #1: No kids, no credit, no frills

For our first example, let's look at Jane, a single woman in her early 20s. She has a full-time job, which pays $20,000 a year—enough to live on but not much more. She lives in a small apartment, and drives a car that her father gave her as a graduation gift.

Jane has a checking account which usually has less than $100 in it, and a savings account containing $500 that she has been struggling to contribute to each month. Fortunately, Jane has stayed away from those tempting credit card offers that come in the mail, so she is currently debt-free.

Jane's main financial concern is savings. She can live on the income she currently makes, but she would like to begin growing her savings account, as a cushion against the uncertain future.

## A simple start in Money

Jane has only two bank accounts, so that's all she'll need to set up in Money—a checking account and a savings account (see fig. 16.1). Since she has no loans or investments, she can bypass those complicated setup procedures (which we covered in Chapter 2).

**Fig. 16.1**
A single person with no debts may need only one or two basic banking accounts.

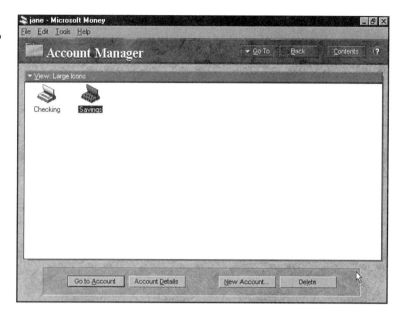

# Are categories even needed?

In an extremely simple financial situation like this, it's easy to decide not to even bother using categories for each transaction. But that's a mistake—categories are helpful for *everyone*. However, Jane might want to delete many of the pre-designed categories in her Money file that don't apply to her. (For instance, Child Care could go, as could Loans.) (Turn back to Chapter 5 if you need help with categories.)

The only income category Jane needs is the Wages & Salary one. However, she should keep the pre-designed subcategories underneath it including Bonus, Gross Pay, and Overtime, to categorize her paycheck (see fig. 16.2). That way, at the end of the year she can see how much of her income came from bonuses or overtime, as opposed to regular salary. (She can probably delete the Commission subcategory.)

**Fig. 16.2**
Everyone should use categories, but it's okay to delete the categories that you will never use, leaving a more streamlined list like this one.

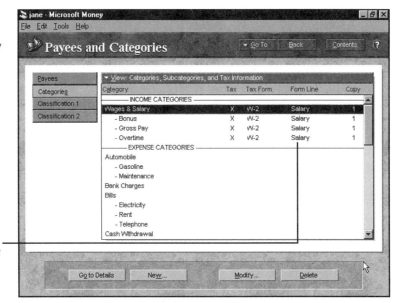

*Notice that Jane has deleted all the income categories except the ones that apply to her situation.*

To keep a tighter rein on her expenses, Jane might create extra Leisure categories to break down how she is spending her disposable income. For instance, if she's a pinball wizard, and spends $10 a week at the local video arcade, she should create a subcategory under Leisure for that expense.

Jane should also create a special category called "Planned Savings" and budget a certain amount each month to be transferred into her savings account using this category. (I'll talk about the budget feature in the following section.)

# Budgeting is important!

Since Jane has to watch her spending carefully if she expects her savings account to grow, Money's Budget feature can be her best friend. By carefully creating and adhering to a budget, Jane can make sure she is able to contribute to her savings account each month.

Budgets are explained in detail in Chapter 14, but here's a brief recap of what Jane should do:

**1** Select Tools, Budget.

**2** Enter budget amounts for each income and expense category and subcategory. Then click Close to return to the Contents screen.

**3** Click Report & Chart Gallery, then click Spending Habits. View the How I'm Doing on My Budget report.

**4** Click the Report button to change the chart into a report.

**5** Scroll down to the bottom right corner of the report, and look at the number in the Budget column on the GRAND TOTAL line. If it's in parentheses, as it is in Figure 16.3, Jane is over-budget by that amount.

**6** Go back to your budget by selecting Tools, Budget again, and adjust the budgeted amounts until the number in the GRAND TOTAL line of the report is positive.

**Fig. 16.3**
Oops! It looks like Jane has budgeted too generously for her expenses! She'll need to reduce the budgeted expenses so she's not spending more than she's earning.

*If the GRAND TOTAL for the Budget column is negative (in parentheses), you're over budget.*

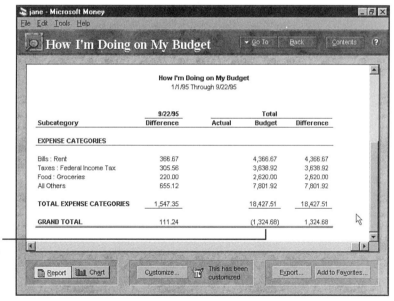

## Other ways to keep it simple with Money

After Jane has her budget and categories in place, she might want to:

- Investigate online bill-paying (see Chapter 12).

- Use the Payment Calendar (see Chapter 7) to make sure she pays her bills on time and keeps her credit rating good, so if she ever wants to make a major purchase, like a home, her loan approval will go smoothly.

- Use the Savings Calculator (Chapter 13) to figure out how much she should budget toward savings each month to meet her goals.

# Example #2: The typical growing family

Now let's look at another example—that last bastion of the traditional American social landscape—the nuclear family. Barbara and Chip Nelson are in their early 30s, and have two children: George, age 8, and Martha, age 6. (Did I mention that Chip is a history buff?) Last year they bought a new home, so now they have a $100,000 mortgage. They also have two late-model cars (and are making payments on both), and they're both employed full-time outside the home. Barbara is a bit of a shop-aholic, so they have about $5000 of credit card debt spread out over several credit cards.

The Nelsons have two main financial concerns. The first, most immediate one is their debt. They need a plan for getting out from under those bills. The second is that they would like to begin saving for George's and Martha's college education.

## Getting the family finances up and running in Money

Barbara and Chip have quite a few accounts to set up in Money because their finances are fairly complicated. Figure 16.4 shows their accounts in the Account Manager. Notice that there's a separate account for each credit card, each bank account, and each loan.

**Fig. 16.4**
Money really excels in keeping track of complicated family finances like these.

# More categories, please!

The Nelsons will probably use most of the pre-designed categories, and then some. Rather than deleting the ones they don't need, they will focus on adding new categories to pinpoint their expenditures accurately. (Chapter 5 discusses creating new categories.)

For instance, since they're carrying high balances on their credit cards, they might create Credit Card:Interest and Credit Card:Principal categories, to help them see how much of each credit card payment is going toward interest rather than decreasing the principal. Each credit card has a different interest rate, but each statement usually lists how much was assessed in finance charges that month. They might also want to create separate categories for the contributions they'll make to the children's savings plans—for instance, Savings:George and Savings:Martha. By creating these categories, they make those contributions show up in their budget and on reports.

Budgeting by category is just as important for the Nelsons as it was for Jane, in our previous example. (Turn back to the section "Budgeting is Important!" earlier in this chapter for a refresher.) The Nelsons might choose to budget a high percent of their income toward paying off those high-interest credit cards, rather than socking away great sums right now in the kids' savings accounts. Why? Because the interest rates charged by the credit card companies are much higher than the interest rates that the savings accounts are earning. By choosing to save rather than pay off the debt, the Nelsons are actually losing money.

## What about using classes?

To save for George's and Martha's education, the Nelsons have established separate savings accounts for each child: George's College Fund and Martha's College Fund, as you can see in Figure 16.4. However, they might earn a better yield if they pooled all the money from both funds together into a higher-interest long-term account such as a CD (certificate of deposit) or Money Market fund. They could then create separate classifications (see Chapter 5) to distinguish which money was George's and which was Martha's. Figure 16.5 shows a deposit being made into a joint "College Funds" savings account that's earmarked by classification for Martha, who is only six but says she wants to go to Harvard.

**Fig. 16.5**
You can create a classification like "Family Members" and then use it to earmark certain transactions for a particular person.

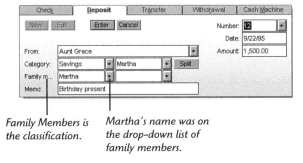

*Family Members is the classification.*

*Martha's name was on the drop-down list of family members.*

## Tips and tricks for keeping it all straight

Running a growing family's finances is no easy task! It's often difficult to balance keeping the entire family's money together for more earning power with splitting up the money for fair distribution. There's also that thorny problem of juggling the parents' short-term debts with the children's long-term needs.

Here are some things that the Nelsons could do with Money to make their road a little easier—many of them might apply to your situation also!

- Use electronic bill-paying (see Chapter 12) to save time each month paying all those loan payments and utility bills. If you look closely at

Figure 16.4, you'll see that a few of the accounts have little lightning bolts next to them—that means they're set up for electronic banking or payments.

- Use the Budget feature and the budgeting reports (see Chapter 14) to make sure they're not overspending.

- Save time each month by letting Money print the many checks they have to write (see Chapter 6).

- Secure their credit rating by never missing payments. The Payment Calendar (Chapter 7) can be set up to remind them in advance of each one.

- Place some of the kids' college money in investments such as CDs, stocks, or bonds. Chapter 10 covers how to enter investments into Money, and Chapter 11 explains how to check investment progress with reports and charts.

- Analyze their spending habits and their tax situation with the reports and charts (explained in Chapter 11).

- Take a realistic look at the kids' college savings plans with the Savings Calculator (covered in Chapter 15).

- Examine whether it might be a good deal to refinance some of their loans, or even their home mortgage, with the Loan Calculator and Mortgage Planner (Chapter 15).

 **TIP** **A family with complicated finances like the Nelsons' might do well** to hire a tax advisor at tax time rather than trying to do their own taxes. A tax advisor will help them find the greatest number of allowable deductions and help them plan a strategy to minimize their taxes in the upcoming years.

# Example #3: Retiring in security

Finally, let's look at a recently retired couple, Sherry and John Kemmerly. Forty years ago, John opened a small grocery store, and through his efficient management, it grew into a medium-sized business with about 25 employees. A few years ago, he sold it for about $400,000 and then retired.

John has invested most of the money (about $350,000) in moderate-risk investments that pay about 7% annually. He and Sherry live off the interest that comes in from this: $24,500. Since they don't have any debt, and their house is paid for, this is a comfortable income for them. With the rest of the money, John experiments with higher-risk ventures like stocks and mutual funds.

The Kemmerlys are comfortable—they don't have any immediate financial goals. However, John enjoys investing as a hobby, and wants to be able to keep a close watch on his more volatile investments. He checks the stock prices every day, and wants to create charts and reports to show Sherry (who is not really interested in investing, but tries to be polite about it because he's so enthusiastic).

## Setting up Money to track all the investments

John needs a separate investment account in Money for every brokerage and bank he works with. For instance, he needs an account for each bank at which he has purchased CDs (but not a separate account for each CD), and a separate account for each brokerage (but not for each company he owns stock in).

He also needs an Asset account for each major type of asset he owns—for instance, he collects antique tools, and Sherry has several thousand dollars worth of jewelry. And finally, he needs a loan account for each loan that he extends to his children. (He often loans his kids money. It's a great deal for everyone—he makes a higher interest rate than he can get at any bank, and they pay a lower interest rate than any bank would charge.) The Kemmerlys' accounts are shown in Figure 16.6.

**Fig. 16.6**
When you're retired, if you've saved and invested wisely through the years, most of your accounts will be assets rather than debts.

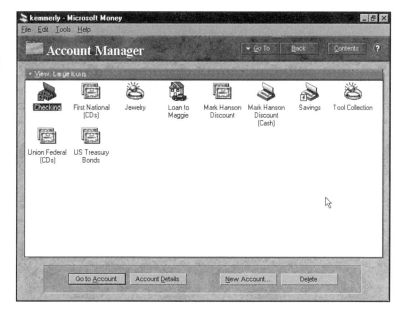

## What about categories or classifications?

The Kemmerlys will use all the normal categories that Money creates, plus any special ones they need for their lifestyle. For instance, since John and Sherry travel more now that they're retired, they might create special subcategories under the Travel category to keep track of travel expenses like camping fees for their motor home or guided bus tour vacations they take. They might also delete the Wages and Salary income category, since neither is employed, and add some more subcategories under Investment Income. The Kemmerlys probably don't need any classifications.

## Handling incoming interest

Since most of the Kemmerlys' income is in the form of interest and dividends, it's important that they use the right categories when entering transactions. For instance, Investment Income:Interest should be separate from Investment Income:Dividends, for tax purposes. Each of these should be set up for the appropriate tax form and form line.

John usually elects to roll over stock dividends into additional stock purchases ("dividend reinvestment," this is usually called). Money keeps track of reinvestment as an investment activity rather than a separate category. Let's say John's dividend for the past quarter on his Microsoft stock was $950. To reinvest it, John would choose Reinvest Dividend as the Activity, then choose Investment Income:Dividend as the category, as shown in Figure 16.7.

**TIP** **As you're entering an investment transaction, like in Figure 16.7,** there are three factors: quantity, price per share, and total. If you know two of these, you can let Money fill in the third one. For instance, in Figure 16.7, John entered the price per share and the total amount invested, and Money filled in the number of shares.

**Fig. 16.7**
When reinvesting dividends, enter Reinvest Dividend as the activity, and use the category that you would normally use for regular purchases ("Buy" activities).

## Online banking is great for seniors

Since John and Sherry no longer work outside the home, they find it a bit inconvenient to go out to the bank every few days. Money's online banking services are tailor-made for them! They've chosen a bank that uses Money's online banking capabilities as their primary checking and savings accounts. Even though it's located in a different town, it doesn't matter, since they never have to physically visit the bank. They handle all their transactions online. The Kemmerlys also save stamps—and trips to the post office—by paying their bills online. And John enjoys checking the prices of his stocks every day with Money's online stock price updates. (All the online banking services are covered in Chapter 12.)

# Other Money features that work for retirees

Money's time and effort-saving features are for everyone, but here are a few features that John and Sherry especially enjoy.

## Online banking

Since John and Sherry pay almost all their bills electronically, they don't write very many checks. However, the few checks that they do write are printed on their printer using Money's own checks (explained in Chapter 6). Although they're lucky that neither have arthritis or mobility problems, many of their friends do, and John has recommended Money's check printing features highly to those folks as a way of avoiding having to write out checks by hand.

## Payment reminders

Even though the Kemmerlys don't have any installment loans of their own, they do loan money to their kids. And sometimes the kids forget to pay! It's not that John and Sherry need the money, but it's the principle of the thing—the kids need to be taught some responsibility! So John has entered the dates on which each child's payment is due, so he can make a friendly phone call when payments are late, just to see if everything is okay.

## Home inventory

Awhile back, Sherry decided to make a detailed list of all their possessions and the current value of each, to include with her will. That way, she figured, it would be easy to divide their estate up equally among the children when the time comes. (The kids thought this was morbid, but couldn't talk her out of it.) So Sherry used an Asset account in Money to make a list of each valuable item and its current value. As it turned out, this was a great idea—John and Sherry realized that, based on the value of their assets, they didn't have enough home-owners insurance to cover replacement costs on everything, and they were able to bring their coverage up to date.

## Reports and charts

John has always been a bottom-line type of guy, and it didn't stop when he retired. That's what made his business so successful, after all! He loves creating and printing out reports showing his investment holdings. (This was covered in Chapter 11.) Based on his charts, he can see which stocks are performing well and which ones need to be dumped, and he can show Sherry how well her Wal-Mart stock that she picked is doing.

The Kemmerlys hire an accountant to do their taxes, but they save quite a bit of money by printing out tax report summaries at the end of the year to take to their accountant. The accountant appreciates having all the investment figures totaled neatly by tax form, and John appreciates being charged for fewer hours by his accountant!

# 17

# Money Strategies for Small Businesses

● **In this chapter:**

● **How do I decide whether Money can handle my business?**

● **Setting up your business accounts in Money**

● **What categories and classifications should I use?**

● **Working with payables and receivables**

● **What about paying employees?**

*Although Money isn't really a business management program, it can be an excellent tool if your business needs are simple . . . . . . . . . . . . . . . . . . . . . . . . . . . . .* ▶

**M**oney isn't naturally suited to running a business—it's more of a personal program. However, if your business needs are simple, you can get by with letting Money handle the financial end of the business, and supplementing it with a program like a word processor or spreadsheet that can create business documents and forms.

I'd like to leave it as-is here, because it flows nicely into the material that follows about what money CAN do. No matter what kind of business you run, you probably have some tasks that Money won't be able to help you with. Money won't print invoices, prepare bids, or keep a database of your customers, for example—all features that business accounting programs like QuickBooks and PeachTree Accounting will handle.

However, you probably have other programs on your computer already that can do the business tasks that Money can't. For instance, for typing up letters and invoices. Windows 95's WordPad program will work (although it's not fancy). You can also keep a list of your customers in WordPad, or in a spreadsheet or database program if you have one. It's a question of whether you're willing to pay extra for a single program that does everything your business needs, or whether you want to try to "make do" with what you have.

Now that the warning is out of the way, let's talk about what Money *can* do! If you run a small, simple business from your home, perhaps as a sideline to your regular employment, Money may be all you need. Combined with the simple word processor (WordPad) in Windows 95, you may be able to handle all your business needs without investing in extra software. Here are some business types that Money might be suited for:

- Handmade items (crafts, furniture)

- Freelance professional services (marketing, editing, consulting)

- Home-based purebred animal breeding (dogs, cats, horses)

- House cleaning/maid service

- Childcare/babysitting

- Newspaper delivery

- Lawn mowing/landscape care

When trying to decide if Money will work for your business, you might ask yourself these questions:

**Is your business incorporated?** Incorporated businesses tend to be more complex, and require more recordkeeping, than simple privately run ones. If you have business partners, they might want you to keep your records in a program designed specifically for business use.

**Are you the only person who gets paid to work for the business?** Businesses with employees must fill out lots of tax paperwork, and keep formal records. You need a business ID number, which is a Federal Tax ID number you request from the Internal Revenue Service, you need to fill out W-4 tax forms, and much more. Money is probably not your best choice if you have employees—go with software that includes a payroll module, such as QuickBooks with Payroll.

**Do you operate your business out of your home?** Most home-based businesses are closely tied to the owner's personal finances—for instance, some people can deduct a portion of their home expenses as a business expense if they meet certain criteria for a home business. That's a good reason to use Money. Many home businesses are casual, part-time endeavors for extra cash, and don't need all the features of special business software— Money will work just fine.

If you answered "Yes" to all three of the questions above, you might give Money a try before you spend the money on business software—Money may turn out to be all that you need!

# What parts of my business can Money handle?

What Money *can* do for your business is exactly what it does for your personal life: keep track of your bank accounts. And in the process of doing that, it can track certain aspects of your business. For instance, you can:

- Create an asset account that tracks the value of your inventory. For instance, if you sell homemade crafts, after you make an item, you can enter it into your asset account with its retail value. (Creating accounts is covered in Chapter 2).

- Create a cash account that monitors how much of your "out of pocket" money you are spending on the business. A cash account can also track your petty cash drawer, if you keep one of those.

- If you have an account set up at a certain store that your employees are authorized to charge to (for instance, at a lumber yard, if you're a building contractor), you can set up a Line of Credit account to track it.

- Create tax-related categories for each income and expense item, and then use Money's tax reports to help prepare your business's taxes at year-end. (You learned about reports in Chapter 11, and taxes in Chapter 15.)

# What accounts do I need?

One mistake that new entrepreneurs often make is to not keep the business finances separate from their own. You can separate them in either of two ways:

- If you have a single, separate bank account for the business, you can create a new account in your personal Money file (see Chapter 2).

- If you have several bank accounts for the business, create a whole new Money file for the business (Chapter 9).

Although I don't recommend it, you can also keep your business money in your personal checking and savings accounts, and create classifications (Business and Personal) to distinguish the transactions. (You learned about classifications in Chapter 5.) This would be appropriate only with the simplest of businesses—for instance, if you received money a few times a year for some small amount of freelance work. Otherwise, you'll want to formally separate the business money from the personal.

There are a couple of ways to keep business finances in Money. One is to construct an accounting system that is not necessarily based on your bank accounts. If you've ever taken an accounting class, you may be familiar with the concept of "double-entry accounting." That means that no number is entered only once—a loss from one account means a corresponding gain in another account. You can set up Money to work this way if you are familiar with this type of accounting—simply create pairs of Asset and Liability accounts that work together. I won't go much into this method in this book, since it's a more formal way of bookkeeping that probably isn't worth the hassle for most of the small, informal businesses that will be using Money.

**TIP** **If your business grows and you find you need a more formal** accounting system, it's a good investment to take a beginning accounting class from your local community college or continuing education division of a university. It's much cheaper to gain this knowledge yourself than it is to hire a full-time accountant!

The other way, which most small businesses using Money will prefer, is to create accounts in Money for the actual bank accounts you have. Then you track those accounts in exactly the same way that you track personal accounts.

You may also want to create an Asset account to keep track of your inventory or valuable assets, if your business has any. For instance, if you're running a dog kennel, and you own a dozen purebred Shetland Sheepdogs (each valued at anywhere from $300 to $1500, depending on the dog), an asset account can keep track of how much money you have tied up in livestock. (A farmer might do the same thing for cows, horses, pigs, or whatever.) Or, if you make handmade crafts, you could use an Asset account to keep track of how many of each item you have in stock, kind of like an inventory sheet.

## Why create a separate file?

One reason why you might want to create a whole separate file for your business income is that personal expenses are not usually tax-deductible, but business expenses may be depending on the circumstances. If your business finances are in a separate file, you can make certain categories tax-related that are only deductible in the business.

For instance, ink pens I buy for around the house are not deductible, but ink pens I buy for my business are. In my separate business file, I could make the Office Supplies category tax-related, but if the business account were in my personal Money file, and I made Office Supplies tax-related, my tax reports would show all the office supplies I bought, not just the tax-deductible ones.

# Setting up business categories and classes

As with personal accounts, it's absolutely crucial that you set up appropriate categories for your business. Only this way will you be able to track your business's performance with Money's reports and charts.

If you started a new file for your business, you can scrap all the categories that don't apply to your business (Delete them, as you learned in Chapter 5), and create new ones. Figure 17.1 shows the categories that were created for a dog kennel business. Notice that they're practically all new—most of the default categories have been deleted. Notice also that almost every category is tax-related and assigned to a specific tax form and form line (see Chapter 15). That's because unlike personal expenses, almost every business expense is tax-related.

**Fig. 17.1**
If you're using a separate file for your business, delete all the categories that don't apply to the business and create new ones!

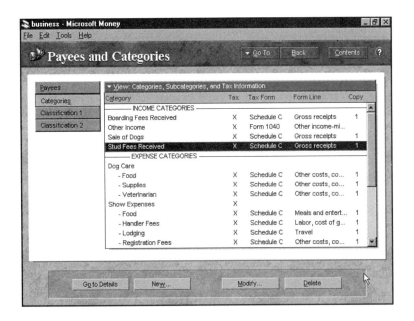

If you're using a single file for both business and personal, consider creating a whole new set of categories for the business. Create a Business Income and a Business Expense category, then make a series of subcategories beneath them for each business transaction. For instance, a freelance editor might have:

Business Income:Writing

Business Income:Editing

Business Income:Other

Business Expense:Office Supplies

Business Expense:Computer

Business Expense:Rent

Business Expense:Utilities

Business Expense:Postage

Business Expense:Online Services

 **CAUTION**  **The list of categories is shared among all accounts in the file.** If you're tracking your business in your personal Money file, don't delete any categories that you use for your personal accounts!

If you would like to break down your transactions by classification, you can do that too. This is especially helpful when you have more than one client that you work for, and you need to keep the expenses separate for each one. For instance, let's say you're a handyman who does work for three families, and each one gets charged for parts and labor. First, set up a classification called Customers (see Chapter 5) and create items in the classification for each family you work for. Then create categories for Repair:Parts and Repair:Labor. Then, when you receive a payment from a customer, you could enter it into your register like this:

Customer: Smith
Category (split):    Repair:Parts    $16.50
                     Repair:Labor    $25.00

Check back in Chapter 3 to refresh your memory about entering transactions into split categories.

# Receivables: what you earn

You'll need to use a separate program to create invoices and estimates for your customers. Any word processing program will do, like WordPad, Microsoft Word, or WordPerfect. On the invoice, include your name, address, and phone number, today's date, the services or goods being billed for, the invoice amount, and when the payment is due.

You won't enter the invoice information into Money until you receive the check from the customer. (It's important to keep track of which accounts are tardy, so you can send reminders, but Money can't help with creating reminder letters.) When you get the payment, enter it as a deposit in Money, and use the appropriate categories and classification to earmark it.

**TIP** **Actually, there is a way you can track payments that haven't been** received yet in Money. Create a separate Asset account called Accounts Receivable, and enter the payment into there, as if you had already received it. Then, when the payment comes, move the transaction into the account into which you deposit it. (You learned to move transactions in Chapter 4.)

# Payables: what you owe

As with receivables, you won't enter the information about the payment you make until you actually write the check or make the payment—if you are on a cash accounting system. However, you don't have to rely on sticky-notes to help you remember to make payments, because you can use Money's Payment Calendar. You learned all about the Payment Calendar in Chapter 7— you can enter upcoming bills, either recurring or one-time ones. Then Money will remind you to pay them five days in advance of their due date.

**TIP** **You can also create a Liability account called Accounts** Receivable, and pre-enter the bills into it. Then when it's time to pay the bill, you just move the transaction into your bank account register.

# Can I deduct it on my taxes?

The nice thing about business expensesis that they're mostly tax-deductible. Make their categories tax-related, and they'll appear on your tax reports you generate in Money (see Chapter 11).

I'm no accountant—check with a tax professional for details on any deduction. However, I do operate a small business out of my own home, and I've done a bit of research about tax deductions for my own situation. Here are some items that I have found to be deductible in most cases:

- Office consumables (paper, pens, staples)

- Office furniture and computer equipment

- Rent on office space, if you have a separate office from your home

- The materials you purchase to make the products you sell (for example, wood, nails, and glue if you make wooden crafts).

- Postage, or any costs of transporting business materials from one place to another. For instance, if I hired a courier to deliver my manuscript to my publisher, I could deduct that courier's fee.

- Professional subscriptions (for instance, computer magazines if you're a computer consultant)

- Online service memberships, if you use an online service for your business (for instance, editors who send files to their publisher through e-mail)

- Business insurance (for instance, liability or malpractice insurance, property insurance on the office building)

*CAUTION*  **Beginning in 1996, health insurance will become deductible for** self-employed people. Keep in mind if you do pay for health insurance for your employees, that cost is usually deductible, too.

- Gasoline and auto expense, when you use your vehicle for business. For instance, a Realtor who drives clients around to look at various houses can deduct that mileage. You can't normally deduct commuting expenses from your home to your office, however.

- A portion of home expenses (mortgage, utilities), if you have a home business. There are many restrictions, so check with a tax professional before you attempt this deduction.

# Keeping track of payroll

Most people who have employees (and hence, have to do payroll) will use a real business management computer program rather than relying on Money.

However, in a pinch, you can track payroll with Money using categories and classifications.

Turn back to Chapter 15, and find the sidebar titled "How to categorize your paycheck deposit." Use the advice there as a model for splitting each payment you make to an employee. You'll want to keep the amounts that you hold back for various taxes, insurance, and savings plans for each employee very separate, in its own category. You'll start by entering the gross amount of the pay in the split, then you'll enter negative amounts to indicate the amount you're holding back for each type of withholding: Federal Income Tax, State Income Tax, Local Income Tax, Insurance, Savings Plan, and so on.

**TIP** **Of course, if you have a savings plan set up for your employees** through automatic paycheck deduction, you won't keep the money in your own savings account—you'll deposit it in some interest-bearing investment, and you'll have a separate account set up in Money for it. You can enter a transfer to that account as part of the split you enter for the transaction.

# In summary...

Well, this concludes the main part of the book. Hope you had as much fun reading it as I did writing it! Throughout this book, Money continually surprised me with its intuitive interface and powerful features. When I first became acquainted with Money, I must admit, I was a die-hard, long-time Quicken user, and I thought that Money was too simple for my needs. But Money made a believer out of me, and I'm now using it for 100% of my personal finances.

The last few items in this book are appendixes, which cover extra topics that some people may be interested in. They cover installing Money, setting the many customization options Money provides, and protecting and securing your financial files. If you're interested in any of these topics, check them out!

# Part V: FYI

# Installing
# Microsoft Money

When you buy some new fixture for your home, like a ceiling fan or a dead-bolt lock, you don't just set it in the middle of your family room floor. You have to install the thing in the proper place before it becomes useful.

It's the same with MS Money. You have to install Money on your hard disk before it can be of any use to you. Installation **decompresses** and copies the files that Money needs to run from the floppy disks or CD to your hard drive on your computer.

 *Plain English, please!*

> Most programs that you buy are compressed so that they will fit on fewer diskettes. Compressed files take up less space, but are unusable until they are decompressed. The installation program decompresses the files and copies them to your hard disk.

Installation is a fairly simple and straightforward process that shouldn't give you any grief. In fact, if you're experienced with Windows, you don't really need to read this appendix at all. Just run the program SETUP.EXE on the first diskette (or CD, if you bought the CD version) and follow the instructions on-screen. There are no surprises.

For those who are a little less than comfortable with installing programs, the rest of this appendix walks through the steps involved. Just follow along.

# Starting the setup program

You have lots of choices about how to start the setup program. All work equally well, so it's just a question of preference.

If you're a rank beginner and you are not sure how to work with files, folders, and disks, it's best to use the Add/Remove Programs feature. Follow these steps:

1 Click the Start button, then click Settings, then Control Panel.

2 Double-click the Add/Remove Programs icon.

3 Click the Install button.

4 Insert the first diskette into your floppy drive.

5 Click the Next button.

6 Click the Finish button. The setup program starts.

Here are some other ways to start the setup program:

- In My Computer or Windows Explorer, display the contents of the first Money diskette by double-clicking on that drive's icon. Double-click on the file Setup (or Setup.exe).

- Click the Start button, then click Run. In the Open text box, type **A:\setup.exe** and click OK. (This assumes the Money diskette is in the A drive; if it's in another drive, start this command line with that drive's letter. For instance, if you're using the CD version, your CD drive might be D, E, or some other letter.)

# Okay, I've started Setup. Now what?

From here on out, it's just a question of following the directions that appear on the screen—you don't need to rely on the rest of this appendix. But just in case you'd like some company while you're going through the process, I'll be happy to walk you through the rest of the steps. Never let it be said that I abandoned you in your time of need.

**1** A warning appears. Read it, then click Continue.

**2** Your name appears, as you entered it when you installed Windows 95. If it's not correct, change the name in the Name box, then click OK.

**3** When asked to confirm, click OK. (They just want to make sure you've typed your name correctly.)

**4** Your serial number appears, along with some copyright information. Copy down your serial number, then click OK.

*CAUTION* **You'll need the serial number if you want to call Microsoft's** technical support phone number to get help. You can get the serial number at any time while using Money by selecting <u>H</u>elp, <u>A</u>bout Microsoft Money. But if you're having serious problems with the software, you might not be able to start the program to get the number. That's why it's important to write the number down in step 4.

**5** Click OK to accept the default folder and drive. Or click Change Folder, select new ones, then click OK to get caught up with the rest of us.

*TIP* **If you have more than one drive, you can choose whichever one** you want to install Money on. For instance, my C drive is rather full, but there's lots of space on my D drive, so I'm going to install it there.

**6** You'll see a big button next to the words "Continue— Install Microsoft Money 4.0." Click on that big button.

**7** Wait for the setup program to copy the files to your hard disk. When you're prompted, insert another disk and click OK.

**8** When you get a message that Money has been successfully installed, click OK.

That's it! You're ready to cruise. Now turn to Chapter 1 and get started.

# Customizing
# MS Money

Like almost anything you buy, whether it's a toaster, a stereo, or a computer program, Microsoft Money works pretty well right out of the box. Most people never even realize that they can adjust various settings in Money, and they get along just fine without ever doing it.

But for those of you with a particular idea in mind of how you want the program to work, Money offers lots of customization features. You can change everything from the currency being used (Dollars? Lira? Francs?) to the number of days in advance that you're reminded of a bill to pay.

No matter which settings you want to change, you always start with the Tools, Options command. That opens the Options dialog box, which has eight separate tabs. Each tab has a particular theme, so let's look at each one individually.

# General options control the big picture

**Fig. B.1**
On the General tab, you can turn the Sound on or off, control the backup reminder, and decide whether or not to use those tabbed forms in your register.

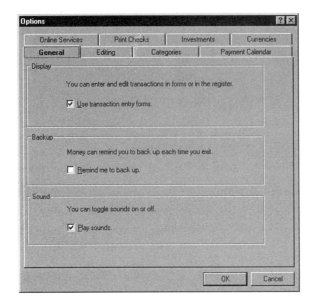

On the General tab, you'll find these settings (see Figure B.1):

**Display**. By default, tabbed forms appear at the bottom of your account register. (You used them in Chapter 3, among other places.) If you don't want the forms (that is, if you want to enter transactions directly into the register itself), deselect this check box.

**Backup**. By default, every time you leave Money, it reminds you to back up your file. If you find this annoying (I do!), turn it off by deselecting this check box.

**Sound**. Microsoft Money doesn't make a lot of loud and crazy sounds, but if you want to silence it completely, deselect this check box. (It's selected by default.)

# Editing: the way changes get made

**Fig. B.2**
Control data entry and confirmation settings from the Editing tab.

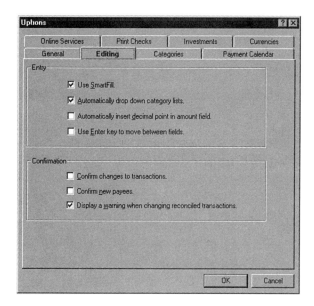

The Editing tab contains settings for when you're entering transactions into a register. They are:

**Entry**. This series of checkboxes controls the data entry portion of entering a transaction. You can choose:

> *Use SmartFill*. This feature (on by default) checks what you're typing, and if it seems to match anything else you've typed before in that blank, it fills it in for you. For instance, if you've entered Kroger before as a payee, and you begin typing K-r-o, SmartFill will complete it for you g-e-r. Handy feature, but some people find it irritating, in the same way that some people find a co-dependent spouse who is always anticipating your needs irritating.

*Automatically drop down category lists.* This feature (also on by default) enables those drop-down lists that appear in some blanks as you enter transactions. Turn them off by deselecting this check box if you like.

*Automatically insert decimal point in amount field.* This one is off by default. If you turn it on, Money will add a 2-place decimal to every number you enter. For instance, if you enter 1000, Money will change that to $10.00.

*Use Enter key to move between fields.* By default, pressing Enter completes a transaction and enters it in the register. If you find yourself accidentally pressing Enter before you're finished with a transaction, turn this checkbox on. To complete a transaction, you'll have to click the Enter button in the account register.

**Confirmation**. These settings affect what happens when you're finished acting on a transaction and you press the Enter key (or click the Enter button, if you've changed the meaning of the Enter key as described in the previous paragraph).

*Confirm changes to transactions.* This option is off by default. If you turn it on, you'll get a dialog box every time you change a transaction asking you if you meant to do that. I find such queries irritating, so I never turn this option on. But if you're worried about mistakes slipping through, this option supplies you with a great reminder to double-check your work.

*Confirm new payees.* You learned in Chapter 3 that you can enter a new payee as you enter a transaction. (Or you can set up a payee the more formal way, as you learned in Chapter 7.) If you want Money to query you with a "did you really mean to do that?" every time you enter a new payee, select this checkbox. It's off by default.

*Display a warning when changing reconciled transactions.* This one is on by default, and appropriately so. If you make a change to a reconciled transaction, it can make your Money register out-of-balance with your bank statement. Disable this warning at your own risk.

# How do you want your Categories?

**Fig. B.3**

Customize your categorization here.

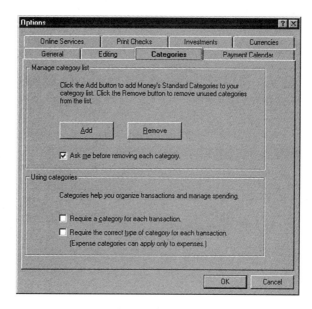

On this tab (Figure B.3), you'll find the settings that control your categories—those sublime little dividers that help you create more meaningful reports and charts. You learned to set them up in Chapter 5; now here's how to keep them in line:

**Manage category list.** Did you ever wonder how those prefab categories got there, the ones that were already in place when you created your account? They're on Money's standard Category List. You can add or remove categories on this list by clicking the Add or Remove button in this dialog box. If you choose Remove, you may want to check the Ask Me Before Removing Each Category check box. Money then gives you an opportunity to approve the removal of each category, individually.

**Using categories.** Here are a couple of checkboxes that control how you use categories in your register:

> *Require a category for each transaction.* By default, assigning a category to any given transaction is optional. You don't have to use categories at all! But if you select this checkbox, Money will require you to use categories.

*Require the correct type of category for each transaction.* Money lets you assign any category to any transaction by default, but if you select this check box, Money won't let you, for example, assign an Income category to an Expense transaction.

# Setting up how the Payment calendar will work

**Fig. B.4**
Change the way your payment calendar works with these options.

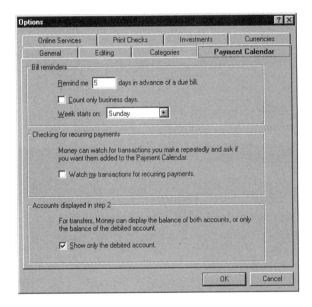

In Chapter 7, you learned all about setting up and making payments. But did you know that you can customize all that too? Click the Payment Calendar tab (Figure B.4), then use these options:

**Bill Reminders**. You can choose how many days in advance you want to be reminded of a bill, and you can even tell Money not to count weekends (with the Count only business days check box). You can also choose which day of the week your week begins with. (Some people like to start on Sunday, like a calendar, but others like to start with Monday, since it's the first workday.)

**Checking for recurring payments.** Not to be nosey, but Money notices a lot of things as you work. One thing you can ask Money to watch for (by selecting the checkbox in this section) is patterns in your bill-paying.

For instance, Money might notice that you make a mortgage payment of $721 every month, and ask you if you want to set it up as a recurring payment. Leave this checkbox unmarked, and Money will keep such advice to itself.

**Accounts displayed in step 2**. When you're transferring money from one account to another, you normally only see the balance of the account that the money is coming from. If you want to see both accounts' balances, deselect the Show only the debited account check box.

# What about Online services?

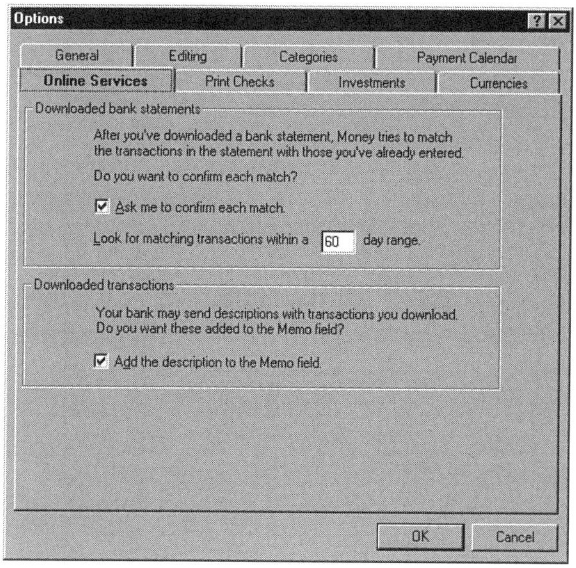

**Fig. B.5**
If you use online banking, set your options on this tab.

You can do several things online, like paying bills, getting stock prices, and getting your bank statement electronically (see Chapter 12). The options on this tab (Figure B.5) refer to the latter—they deal with electronic bank statement handling:

**Downloaded bank statements.** By default, when you download a bank statement, Money asks for confirmation before matching each line of the statement to a transaction in your register. For more automatic (and possibly error-prone) operation, deselect the Ask Me To Confirm Each Match check box. You can also choose how many days in the past Money will look for transactions to match with by changing the number in the text box. (The default is 60.)

**Downloaded transactions**. If you communicate online with your bank, you may receive transactions which get entered into your register. By default, Money enters the descriptions, if any, into the Memo field. If you use the Memo field for something else, and don't want this, deselect the A̲dd the description to the Memo field check box.

# Adjusting the way you print checks

**Fig. B.6**
You can make adjustments here to make your checks come out perfectly.

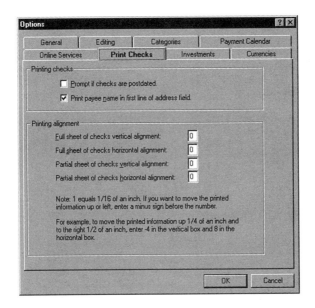

One of the really nice features about Money is its ability to print checks for you. No more writing them out by hand (well, except maybe at the grocery store, unless you want to lug your computer in there with you.) In Chapter 6 you learned all about it; now here are some check-printing options you can set (see Figure B.6):

**Printing checks**. There are two checkboxes here to help control how the print process runs.

*Prompt if checks are postdated.* If selected, this keeps you from accidentally entering future dates on the Date line. It's off by default.

*Print payee name in first line of address field.* By default, this happens, so there's a person or organization's name right above the address. If this isn't what you want, deselect the checkbox.

**Printing alignment.** Money's checks are set up to work on most printers perfectly, but sometimes a printer is a little bit out of alignment. You can adjust for slightly misplaced paper in your printer by changing the numbers in the text boxes of this section. A positive number moves down or to the right; negative numbers move up or to the left. Each whole number moves 1/16th of an inch. So, for example, if you want full sheets of checks moved up 1/2" and to the right 1/4", you would enter -8 in the Full sheet of checks vertical alignment blank, and 4 in the Full sheet of checks horizontal alignment blank.

# Recording investments the way you want them

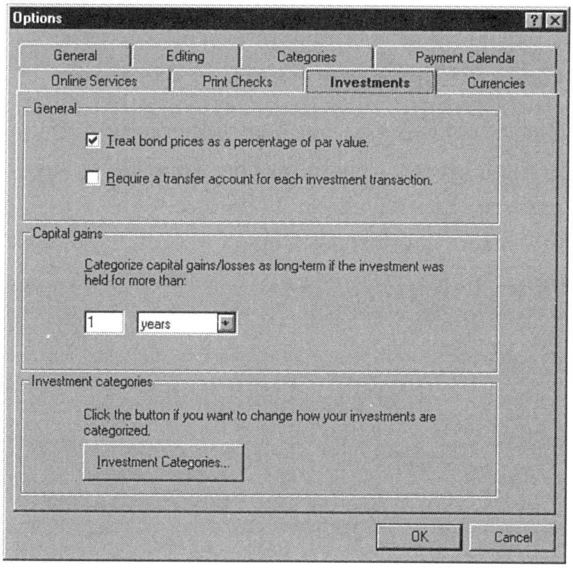

**Fig. B.7**
Want to change the way your investments are recorded? Make the changes here.

Investments (especially stocks and mutual funds) require a little bit of extra record-keeping. In Chapter 10 you learned the basics for an investment account; on this tab (Figure B.7), you see some special options that can make that record-keeping a little bit more convenient for you.

**General**. Two checkboxes here let you control the way investments are entered:

> *Treat bond prices as a percentage of par value.* This is selected by default. For example, if the bond was issued with a $1,000 par value, and you purchased it for $1,050, you will enter 105 in the Price field. Money will then use the percentage of par value to calculate the total in dollars. If you prefer, you can change the setting to display your bond prices as dollar amounts instead of percentage of par value by deselecting the check box.

> *Require a transfer account for each investment transaction.* By default, this isn't selected, because there may be times when you won't want to use a transfer account (see Chapter 10). However, if you want to always do so, select the checkbox.

**Capital gains**. Different people have different ideas of what a "long-term" investment is when dealing with capital gains (see Chapter 10). By default, Money sets it at one year, but you can change this by selecting a new number and period from the drop-down lists in this section.

**Investment categories**. Just like with regular transaction categories, Money creates a default set of them for you. To make changes to how your investments are categorized, click this button. A list of various investment types appears—select a different category and/or subcategory for any of them that you wish.

# Currencies

**Fig. B.8**

World currencies: it's a small world, after all.

This is the most fun setting (in my opinion) because you get to see what kind of currencies other countries use (see Figure B.8). I was amazed to find that the Irish currency is called a Punt, for instance. (Okay, I'm easily impressed.)

On this screen, you can set an exchange rate for each of the currencies listed. For instance, let's say I want to enter the rate for Canadian dollars versus USA dollars. I'd do the following:

**1** Select Canadian Dollar from the Currency list.

**2** Enter the exchange rate in the Exchange rate text box.

**3** Choose one of the option buttons under Display exchange rate as:

> Select *Local units for each foreign unit* if the rate is the number of U.S. dollars for every Canadian dollar
>
> Select *Foreign units for each local unit* if the rate is the number of Canadian dollars for every U.S. dollar.

# When it's all over...

After you've made a change on a particular tab, don't press Enter; that'll close the dialog box. Just click on a different tab to make more changes. Then, when you're finally finished with all the tabs, click OK or press Enter.

# Protecting and Securing Your Files

Hard disk crashes. File corruption. Toddlers spilling juice into the computer. Random attacks of stupidity that cause you to delete files you will later need.

None of us deserves these tragedies, but unfortunately, they happen all the time. My sister used to lose files all the time off her hard disk—they would just disappear into thin air overnight. It wasn't until the neighbor kid went off to college that she realized that he and her son had been systematically deleting files that they thought were "useless" to make room for the games they wanted to play.

If you consider your financial situation "sensitive information," there's another threat too—nosy people who have access to your computer can easily open your Money file and take a look at how much you're worth. If your finances are grim, this might cause laughter and ridicule behind your back. If you're old and extremely wealthy, a supermodel might decide to marry you. (Don't scoff—it happens.) You can prevent prying eyes from ogling your data by password protecting it.

In this appendix, you'll see how to protect your data with backups, and how to secure it with a password.

# Backing up for safety—it's the law
# (Well, it should be)

Since you can't really avoid the unexpected tragedies that might imperil your Money files, the best thing you can do is create backup copies regularly. Over the years of using Money, you'll invest hundreds of hours entering your financial information—that's thousands of dollars worth of time! (Figure that your time is worth at least $10 an hour, minimum!) If you had an object with that kind of value, wouldn't you insure it? Sure, you would. Well, creating a backup of your Money file is like buying insurance.

By default, every time you exit from Money, a dialog box pops up to remind you that you should back up to a floppy disk (see fig. C.1). If you're not asked this, the backup reminder must be turned off; see Appendix B to learn how to turn it back on again.

**Fig. C.1**
Before you exit,
Money asks if you want
to make a backup copy
of your work.

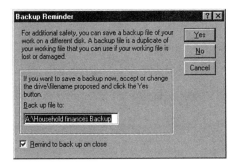

 *Plain English, please!*
Don't confuse backing up with saving. In Money, your file is saved automatically whenever you make a change to it. Backing up copies the saved file to a different disk, so if something happens to the original copy (on your hard disk), your data will be preserved. **"**

When you see this dialog box (refer to fig. C.1), take a look at the drive and file name in the text box. If it looks appropriate to you, insert a blank disk (or one that has some blank space on it) into the listed drive, and click Yes.

If you want to change the drive or the file name, just type them before you click Yes. There isn't much point in changing the file name, but if you have two floppy drives, and you want to use the other one, you might change A: to B:.

When you click Yes, Money springs into motion, saving a copy of your file onto the floppy disk. When it's done, the program closes. (Remember, that's what you were doing in the first place—exiting.) Now store that floppy in a safe place!

Each time you exit Money, you'll want to update your backup copy. Just place the same floppy disk into the drive each time, and the new copy will overwrite the old one. This is better than using a new disk every time, because you will never have to wonder which copy is the most current.

**TIP** **You can back up at any time, not just when exiting the program.** Just select File, Backup.

**Q&A** *What do you mean by "a safe place" for the disk?*

Disks like to be cool and dry, and away from magnets. You might buy one of those plastic boxes that are specially designed to safely store floppy disks, and keep it in a cool room. (Any room in your house where you feel comfortable, the disk will also feel comfortable. When you're too hot, the disk probably is too.)

Floppy disks (especially the 3½" ones) are pretty sturdy, but don't press your luck. Don't tack a disk up to your refrigerator with a magnet—magnets erase the data. Don't use a disk as a coaster for your drink. Don't leave a disk in your car in the hot sun, or in sub-zero temperatures. (Disks are less susceptible to cold than to heat, but it's best not to test cold resistance with a disk containing important data.)

Finally, resist the temptation to leave the disk in your floppy drive all the time. For one thing, your computer can't start with a disk in the A: drive (unless it's a special disk containing startup files). For another, you (or someone else using your computer) might accidentally write other data to the floppy, filling it up so it can't accept any more data, or you might even forget why it's there and erase or format it, thinking it's a worthless disk that can be reused.

# Passwords—they're not just for the paranoid

Remember the simple "good old days" when you could leave your door unlocked at night and your kids' bikes on the front lawn? Nowadays, it seems like there's a thief (or at least a voyeur) lurking around every bush.

With computing, it's the same thing. It used to be, you could leave your computer on all the time, with free access to all your programs, and nobody would touch it. Why? Probably because everyone else but you was computer-illiterate and didn't know how to operate it. Nowadays, though, any 4-year-old can browse through your files.

Passwords perform two useful functions. The most obvious is that they prevent unauthorized people from looking at your files, but they don't lock down the file so completely that the people you WANT to have access to it can't get in. Passwords are kind of like door keys that way. The second thing passwords do is prevent others from deleting or making changes to a file. Think about it—if someone can't access the file, then he or she can't change it either.

## Here's how to create a password

Here's how to create a password for a file:

**1** Select File, Password. The New Password dialog box appears (see fig. C.2).

**Fig. C.2**
Enter the password you want to use into the text box.

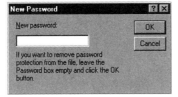

**2** Type a password into the text box, and press Enter or click OK.

**3** You're asked to reenter it; enter the same password again, and press Enter or click OK again. You're done!

# Time to use the password!

The next time you start Money, before the file opens, you'll be prompted to enter the password (see fig. C.3). Type it in, and click OK. You won't see the actual characters you type; you'll see asterisks instead. That's to prevent someone looking over your shoulder from learning your password.

**Fig. C.3**
Money politely asks you to enter the password before loading the file.

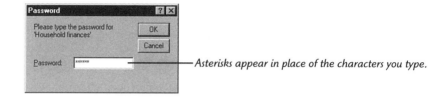

—Asterisks appear in place of the characters you type.

# Psst. The password is...

Remember that old game show, Password? It was my mom's favorite. Some second-rate celebrity gave you clues, and you tried to guess the word that was flashing on the screen for the home viewers, for valuable prizes.

To keep contestants from winning too much money and bankrupting the show, the writers and producers tried to pick words that were fairly difficult to guess. That same principle applies when selecting a password for your Money file. The less obvious the word you choose as a password, the less likely that someone will be able to "crack" your password-protection and access your file.

A password in Money can be anywhere from 1 to 16 characters, including letters, numbers, symbols, and spaces. Don't pick obvious words like your spouse or dog's name, your birthday, or your favorite TV show. The best passwords are jumbles of letters and numbers. For instance, if you have two children, Billy Rae Johnson and Norma Jean Johnson, and their ages are 8 and 4, respectively, a good password might be BRJ8NJJ4. It's easy for you to remember—it's their intials and ages—but difficult for someone else to guess.

# How do I change a password—or remove it completely?

To change the password, issue the File, Password command. Money will prompt you for the old password. (This is to keep others from changing the password without you knowing about it.) Enter it, click OK, and then:

1 Type a password into the text box, and press Enter or click OK.

2 You're asked to reenter it; enter the same password again, and press Enter or click OK again. You're done!

Removing a password is easy. Just follow the steps for changing a password—select File, Password, enter the old password, and click OK. Then for the new password, don't enter anything.

# Index